In my Sunday school days, we used to sing "This Little Light of Mine," motions and all. Erwin Lutzer reminds us in this important book that it's no longer just a Sunday school song but a call for Christians to engage the increasing darkness in our world with the penetrating and victorious light of Christ. And more importantly, he tells how this engagement is put into practice. I'm impressed with the wide berth of "darkness" issues that he addresses, leaving no stone unturned. And impressed as well with how he takes us from despair to a solid hope in the power of the light and the ultimate victory we have in Christ. This is a must-read book . . . take it to heart and then take the light into your world!

JOE STOWELL
President, Cornerstone University
Grand Rapids, Michigan

Erwin Lutzer reminds us how to live in a dark and dangerous world by shining the light of God's Word on our situation. Like one of the men of Issachar "who understood the times and knew what Israel should do," with clarity and relevance, insight and practicality, *The Church in Babylon* shows Jesus followers how to survive, and even thrive, in these troubling times.

MICHAEL RYDELNIK
Professor of Jewish Studies and Bible at Moody Bible Institute, Co-General Editor and Contributor, *The Moody Bible Commentary*, and Host/Bible Teacher on Moody Radio's *Open Line with Dr. Michael Rydelnik*

Erwin Lutzer is a senior leader in the Body and a watchman on the wall. In this, his latest book, he pulls no punches as he confronts a compromised American church and a lost American generation. Yet he does so with pastoral wisdom and with living faith. You will be convicted by his sober words, but you will also be moved to holy action. This is vintage Lutzer, delivering the burden of a lifetime. Read this book and be changed.

MICHAEL L. BROWN
Author, *Saving a Sick America*
Host, "The Line of Fire" broadcast

As usual, Erwin Lutzer can be relied upon to give Christians a laser-sharp analysis of the spiritual state of our culture, as well as the response required by the faithful, witnessing body of believers. In *The Church in Babylon*, he furnishes a devastating diagnosis of the spiritual maladies that afflict us, as well as a spot-on biblical and spiritual prescription for how we can inoculate ourselves and our neighbors against the deadly afflictions engulfing us, and emerge victorious.

RICHARD LAND
President, Southern Evangelical Seminary

Erwin Lutzer has just given a challenging wake up call to the twenty-first century church that finds itself in such a sad condition. May we heed his warning. Read and reread this book. It will encourage you to shine in a world that is dark and getting darker.

MICHAEL A. YOUSSEF
Author of the bestselling book *The Hidden Enemy*

The New Testament word for "church" is "ecclesia," which means "called out." That is fitting since Christians are "called out" to represent Jesus in this sinful world. Erwin Lutzer's new book, *The Church in Babylon*, is a much-needed resource for every who seeks to navigate the turbulent, secular times in which we live while seeking to maintain a biblical worldview and witness for Christ. Dr. Lutzer forthrightly and biblically addresses current controversial, societal topics without pulling punches, yet does so in a warm and kind manner. This is an excellent resource for any Christian seeking to live for Jesus in a society that looks more like ancient Babylon every day.

STEVE GAINES
Pastor, Bellevue Baptist Church, Memphis, TN
President of the Southern Baptist Convention

When God's people in the Old Testament found themselves in exile in Babylon, the memory of what they had lost caused them to lament and to cry out, "How shall we sing the LORD's song in a foreign land?" (Ps. 137:1–4). Today as followers of Christ, we often find ourselves asking the same question. Drawing on decades of faithful study of God's Word and pastoral ministry, Dr. Lutzer helps us grapple with what it means to love and honor Christ in a world that rejects Him, and calls us to return to our distinctive identity and calling.

NANCY DEMOSS WOLGEMUTH
Author, teacher & host of *Revive Our Hearts*

THE
CHURCH
IN
BABYLON

Heeding the Call to Be a
Light in the Darkness

ERWIN W. LUTZER

MOODY PUBLISHERS
CHICAGO

Unless otherwise indicated, Scripture quotations are from the ESV® Bible (The Holy Bible, English Standard Version®), copyright © 2001 by Crossway, a publishing ministry of Good News Publishers. Used by permission. All rights reserved.

Scripture quotations marked NLT are taken from the Holy Bible, New Living Translation, copyright © 1996, 2004, 2015 by Tyndale House Foundation. Used by permission of Tyndale House Publishers, Inc., Carol Stream, Illinois 60188. All rights reserved.

Scripture quotations marked KJV are taken from the King James Version, public domain.

Scripture quotations marked NIV are taken from the Holy Bible, New International Version®, NIV®. Copyright © 1973, 1978, 1984, 2011 by Biblica, Inc.™ Used by permission of Zondervan. All rights reserved worldwide. www.zondervan.com. The "NIV" and "New International Version" are trademarks registered in the United States Patent and Trademark Office by Biblica, Inc.™

Scripture quotations marked NASB are taken from the New American Standard Bible,® (NASB), Copyright © 1960, 1962, 1963, 1968, 1971, 1972, 1973, 1975, 1977, 1995 by The Lockman Foundation Used by permission. www.Lockman.org

Scripture quotations marked CSB have been taken from the Christian Standard Bible®. Copyright © 2017 by Holman Bible Publishers. Used by permission. Christian Standard Bible® and CSB® are federally registered trademarks of Holman Bible Publishers.

All emphasis in Scripture has been added.

Some details have been changed to protect the privacy of individuals.

Edited by Amanda Cleary Eastep
Interior design: Erik M. Peterson
Cover design: Faceout Studio
Cover photo of city and sun copyright (c) 2014 by Vera Lair/Stocksy (473394). All rights reserved.

ISBN-13: 978-0-8024-1308-6

Library of Congress Cataloging-in-Publication Data

Names: Lutzer, Erwin W., author.
Title: The church in Babylon : heeding the call to be a light in the darkness / Dr. Erwin W. Lutzer.
Description: Chicago : Moody Publishers, 2018. | Includes bibliographical references.
Identifiers: LCCN 2018013316 (print) | LCCN 2018026397 (ebook) | ISBN 9780802492432 (ebook) | ISBN 9780802413086
Subjects: LCSH: Christianity--United States. | Christianity and culture--United States. | Babylon (Extinct city)--In the Bible.
Classification: LCC BR517 (ebook) | LCC BR517 .L88 2018 (print) | DDC 261.0973--dc23
LC record available at https://lccn.loc.gov/2018013316

We hope you enjoy this book from Moody Publishers. Our goal is to provide high-quality, thought-provoking books and products that connect truth to your real needs and challenges. For more information on other books and products written and produced from a biblical perspective, go to www.moodypublishers.com or write to:

Moody Publishers
820 N. LaSalle Boulevard
Chicago, IL 60610

5 7 9 10 8 6

Printed in the United States of America

To him who loves us and has freed us from our sins
by his blood and made us a kingdom,
priests to his God and Father,
to him be glory and dominion forever and ever.
Amen.
(Revelation 1:5b–6)

CONTENTS

Every book Erwin Lutzer writes, I read. He's never disappointed me. This timely book is no exception. He has his finger on the pulse of the culture and the church, providing sage insight in a balanced, biblical manner. Every page of this book will engage your mind and stir your heart. It will enlighten you, warn you, and equip you to discern and withstand the siren song of Babylon that surrounds us. I'm glad I read this book. Read it, and you will be too.

MARK HITCHCOCK
Senior Pastor of Faith Bible Church, Edmond, OK
Associate Professor of Bible Exposition, Dallas Theological Seminary

Erwin Lutzer has been my pastor for over thirty-five years, and my walk with Christ has been challenged and changed by his ministry time and again. But his words in this book have powerfully confronted me even more and to a deeper degree than the hundreds of sermons I have heard him preach. This is not a comfortable book to read, because it simply doesn't "let you off the hook" and allow you to shift the blame for the condition of the church today to anyone or anything else than yourself. And, for that reason, every Christian—and especially all of us in church leadership—need to open our minds and hearts to the urgency of its message and the personal transformation needed for us to stand true to Jesus in our ever-deteriorating culture. Yes, it is convicting, but Pastor brings great hope and encouragement to see how we can be the people we should be in our Babylon.

MARY WHELCHEL LOWMAN
Founder and Speaker of The Christian Working Woman radio ministry and Director of Women's Ministries at The Moody Church

Defining moments call for biblical insight, societal understanding, and prophetic boldness. One must be willing to emphatically declare truth with extraordinary power. In *The Church in Babylon*, Erwin Lutzer delivers a deeply relevant message that has the force to turn the pages of history and spawn a great spiritual awakening. This is a cry of both desperation and hope and an invitation to join in the battle for the soul of our nation.

BYRON PAULUS
President, Life Action Ministries

Praise for *The Church in Babylon*

Few pastors combine prophetic boldness, biblical fidelity, and cultural insight as well as Erwin Lutzer. As with his other books, not only did I read and enjoy it, I filed it at arm's length for frequent use as a teaching resource.

J. D. GREEAR
The Summit Church

This book sheds a hopeful light on the cultural battles we must encounter today. Pastor Lutzer has been able to combine fidelity to the Scriptures along with compassion as he speaks about issues such as sexuality, the pressure the church faces in a pagan culture, and the danger of losing the gospel. He ends by showing that the ancient church of Laodicea has a message for us and that we must invite Jesus back into our churches. This book is clear, convicting, and points the way by which the witness of our churches can be revitalized.

TONY EVANS
Senior Pastor, Oak Cliff Bible Fellowship
President, The Urban Alternative

The church was founded by Jesus in the contrary culture of the first century. In *The Church in Babylon*, Erwin Lutzer provides a clarion call for the church to make a midcourse correction in the contrary culture of the twenty-first century. This book astutely exposes the dangerous winds blowing against the Christian faith, and effectively resets the sails toward a godly and biblically informed conviction for the individual Christian and the church alike to survive and thrive in an ungodly world.

MARK L. BAILEY
President and Sr. Professor of Bible Exposition
Dallas Theological Seminary

Before I even had time to put up my bookish, evangelical defenses, I could feel the conviction of the Holy Spirit in the pages of *The Church in Babylon*. I truly wish that every Christian I know could read this book. Why? Because it gives us an unclouded view of where we find ourselves in today's culture. Moreover, it shows a clear path as we navigate issues that are manifestly new to the Christian church. Erwin Lutzer brilliantly isolates the key concerns that confront us and gives us the right balance for maintaining a tightrope walker's stability in a lopsided society.

SKIP HEITZIG
Senior Pastor of Calvary Church, Albuquerque, NM
Author of *The Bible from 30,000 Feet*

FOREWORD

As Aladdin and Jasmine once sang, soaring on a magic carpet ride in the Disney classic, it's "a whole new world." But instead of a love story filled with wonder and excitement, Christians find themselves in a whole new world that is vastly different than the one in which many grew up.

America is losing much of the general religious ethos that was our cultural norm for hundreds of years. The culture is becoming increasingly polarized as the world around us becomes more comfortable admitting that the secularization, which had been an undercurrent, is now mainstream. The question we come to is this: How should Christians relate to this new world where they have lost a home-field advantage and are increasingly marginalized in popular culture?

In one sense, nothing is new under the sun. We have always lived in tension with the world around us. Paul writes two long books to the Corinthians to help them navigate the cost and nuances of syncretism with the culture around them. The prophets experienced extreme persecution from God's chosen people, and even Jesus was rejected in the public and religious sphere. There has always been opposition to God's missionary movement in the world, and America has not been insulated from this despite the false narrative that some may espouse.

In this book, Erwin Lutzer points out that we are now faced with new challenges and cultural changes that will test the resolve, dedication, and conviction of true Christians living in America. It is true that American culture is becoming increasingly dissimilar to biblical values and that followers of Jesus have become increasingly marginalized, in some cases despised, for their beliefs, values, and attitudes. People in America, according to Pew Research data, are less likely to identify with any particular religion, believe in God, pray daily, and attend church services. These numbers have dropped since the early 2000s.

We have to take an honest, hard look at why we are seeing this trajectory now. Many have noted that the decline of Christian values can be attributed to a reactive, angry, disengaged, and politically motivated Christian culture that has sought to assert itself in order to win a culture war that was destined to be lost. We have the best news in the world, but often we have communicated it as the right news instead of the good news. Many times, we have preferred to be right instead of loving, and lost our reputation in the process.

Christians today are faced with at least three ways to respond: (1) assimilate the secular culture, (2) isolate from the secular culture, or (3) engage the secular culture. In light of the gospel, the only choice for the Christ follower is to engage.

When I think of a guide for this time, I think of leaders who have been faithful to the gospel for decades. And one of them is my friend Erwin Lutzer. As I write this foreword, I am the interim teaching pastor of the church he served for decades, The Moody Church. And every time I preach there, I am reminded that he loved these people, taught them the Bible, and helped them navigate not just any culture, but the culture of a rapidly changing urban environment in cosmopolitan downtown Chicago.

In others words, this was not Kansas anymore.

As such, Lutzer's book will be a great blessing as he maps out a path for how the church should respond and engage in meaningful ways that are linked to biblical truth and values, while at the same time winsomely impacting the world. You don't have to agree with everything he says to benefit from the advice of a man who's been in the heart of culture's shift for decades—while consistently preaching the gospel.

He deals with highly important, sometimes divisive, issues that will hit home to many readers. Lutzer addresses topics ranging from the impact of the sexual revolution to the technological quantum leap that has massive implications for families and culture.

We've got to stop the Israel thinking, which is, "this is our place, our home." Instead, we must remember that we are foreigners and strangers in exile. It's someone else's home. We're not Israel in the Promised Land. If anything, we're Israel in exile. Jeremiah 29:5 speaks to those like us; we are called to plant gardens and grow, flourish, seek the good of the city, and more. But we must always remember we're in Babylon.

Erwin Lutzer did that at Moody Church for decades. Now he shares with you how to do the same.

Christians living in America need to realize that the world's hostility should strengthen our resolve to bring hope to the hurting and restoration to the broken, and that now, more than ever, the church needs to be bold in its proclamation and humble in its presence. We cannot wholesale embrace wickedness in the world, but we cannot isolate from it either. We must engage the world with purpose and meaning. We might not be on a magic carpet ride in the night sky, but in this whole new world, the words of the psalmist ring truer every day:

The earth is the LORD's and the fullness thereof,
the world and those who dwell therein.

(PS. 24:1)

ED STETZER
Billy Graham Distinguished Chair, Wheaton College

HEEDING THE CALL

From My Heart to Yours

W here is your God?

That's a question the world is asking Christians. It's a question that should haunt us since, according to a Pew Research Center survey, more and more people are abandoning religion and giving up on God. The religious "nones" (those who self-identify as atheists or agnostics or who say their religion is "nothing in particular") make up about 23 percent of the US adult population. And one-in-five Americans (18 percent) who were raised as Christians or members of another faith now claim no religious affiliation.[1]

Many who have left the church perceive Christians as finger-pointing, self-righteous people who are quick to judge others but not themselves. In the church, they experienced backbiting, envy, and materialism, but none of these sins were addressed. Their congregations highlighted moral and social issues and were quick to criticize those who disagreed with them politically. In walking away from the church, they also walked away from God.

One thirty-five-year-old from California explained his aversion to the faith in a way that is, sadly, becoming more representative for his generation. "Christians have become political, judgmental, intolerant, weak, religious, angry, and without balance. Christianity has become a nice Sunday drive. Where is the living God, the Holy Spirit, an amazing Jesus, the love, the compassion the holiness? This type of life, how I yearn for that."[2] We are perceived as being blind to our own hypocrisy.

Many within the younger generation simply do not feel at home in our churches. They long to have honest sharing within a community of authentic believers who are realistic about their walk with God. They see many of our churches as being too formal, too rigid, and prepackaged. Recently, a friend of mine visited a well-attended suburban church and found it to be unfriendly, joyless, buttoned up, and "cliquish." He said he'd never return.

Many of our churches pretend that all is well among the congregation, but beneath the surface the story is quite different. In his book *The Christian Conscience*, Ron Sider writes, "Scandalous behavior is rapidly destroying American Christianity. By their daily activity, most 'Christians' regularly commit treason. With their mouths they claim that Jesus is Lord, but with their actions they demonstrate allegiance to money, sex, and self-fulfillment."[3]

But if Christians are to be light in a dark culture, we need to ensure we are not adding to the darkness.

A church that has assimilated the world cannot be a vibrant witness to that world. To adopt prevailing cultural values hardly gives the world a reason to believe that we are a viable alternative to lives of brokenness, greed, and addiction. To quote Sider once more, "We divorce, though doing so is contrary to his commands. We are the richest people in human history and know that tens of millions of brothers and sisters in Christ live in grinding poverty, and we give only a pittance, and almost all of that goes to our local congregation. Only a tiny fraction of what we do give ever reaches poor Christians in other places. Christ died to create one new multicultural body of believers, yet we display more racism than liberal Christians who doubt his deity."[4]

I'm writing at a time when America is polarized politically, racially, morally, and religiously. Common ground with the wider culture seems to have vanished. Meanwhile, as I watch some of the angry and often violent demonstrations on television and read the vitriol on social media, I think it is not an exaggeration to say that we are in danger of mob rule. Someone has said, we are a nation addicted to rage.

Yet, it is into this atmosphere of shrill voices and disdain for genuine tolerance that we have been called to represent Christ. The message we have and the lives we lead ought to permeate society and be a beacon of light in the approaching darkness. The church of Jesus Christ is still the best hope for the world.

I love the church. For thirty-six years it was my privilege to serve as the senior pastor of The Moody Church in Chicago—a church that has had a continuous ministry in the city for more than 150 years. I have witnessed many changes since the days when I was installed as the senior pastor back in 1980. At that time, the worship wars had hardly begun.

There was general agreement on what form a worship service should take. Most churches had a piano, and possibly an organ, and the phrase "seeker sensitive" was just coming into its own. The "Emerging Church" did not as yet have a name. In the past four decades, several great cultural changes fed off of each other to transform our society and contribute to the moral and spiritual disarray we see today.

Where we are today?

The Bitter Fruit of the Sexual Revolution

It is easy for the older generation to forget that "the good old days" of the 1950s and early 1960s were not good for everybody. In particular, racism ran unchecked and Martin Luther King Jr. was just beginning his much needed crusade for equal rights. But some "revolutions" have a dark side—such as the sexual revolution—that were detrimental to our families, our churches, and mainstream culture and continue to have consequences.

Back when I began as a pastor, no one could have predicted that in thirty years our White House would be arrayed in rainbow colors to celebrate the Supreme Court's ruling allowing same-sex couples to marry or that many in our society would support what the Bible so strongly condemns. Fed by the media, the floodgates have opened, and society, and even our churches, are being called upon to accept, if not condone, people's decisions to determine their gender and even their age.[5] Who would have ever dreamed that a pregnant woman, for example, would insist that a nurse use the pronoun "he" to refer to her and was finally satisfied when the nurse relented and stated, "*His* cervix and bloodwork look healthy"?[6] As we shall discover later in this book, all of these issues and more like them do not just exist "out there" but within our churches and families.

We have the privilege—and I call it such—of giving hope and healing to a generation emotionally scarred in the wake of uninhibited sexual expression and nearly unlimited access to the "dark web" that reaches through computers and phones and into hearts and minds. We have more broken families and more neglected and abused children accompanied by sexual confusion of every sort. While a highly sexualized society is not new for the church (witness early Rome), a transformation of another sort has given us even greater challenges.

The sins of Rome are now at our fingertips.

The Technological Revolution

I've lived long enough to witness how technology has changed our culture. Back on the farm in Canada where I grew up, we had a phone that came in a box mounted on a wall in our house, but it was on a "party line." As children, we quickly learned that if we quietly picked up the receiver we could listen in on a conversation even if the phone had rung for a neighbor and not for us. And, of course, we assumed that our neighbors probably played the same game and returned the favor.

We've come a long way—from wall phones to smartphones, from clunky typewriters to laptops. When we were told in the early '90s that someday we would have access to an information highway called the internet, I was skeptical. But today, thanks to this technology, we enjoy instant communication with people around the world. We can share news and learn new ideas. Amazingly, formerly "closed countries" now find it difficult to keep their people isolated from the rest of the world and the message of the gospel. The internet has given ordinary people a voice and an ear.

But there is a downside. Many people are addicted to electronic devices. We now carry an information highway in our pockets. Teenagers (and adults too!) are reading less and watching videos more. Few families share a meal together. Children have their own schedules, their own peers (who "friend" or "unfriend" them at will on social media), and their own private entertainment. We sit at the table waiting to hear that "ding" from our phones that tells us that some new bit of information has come our way. With all this information and "entertainment" so handily available, it's no wonder we find it more difficult to focus on what is truly important. Some parishioners surf the internet while in church. And we are flooded with a tsunami of pornography.

We have, of course, lived with television for many decades; this medium has consistently promoted the sexual revolution in its extensive programming. In countless shows, fidelity is ridiculed, immoral relationships are regular fare, and same-sex marriage and broken relationships are the norm. We should not be surprised that there is a national current of support for marriage relationships of every sort and for every one of the many perceived genders. Many talk shows effectively try to normalize the bizarre while any objective story about the negative impact of illicit sexual relationships of various kinds is vilified and silenced. The demise of natural marriage is celebrated as light, not the darkness that it is.

We dare not ignore the negative fallout from the technological revolution. Technology provides us with great blessings along with great dangers and risks. (More about this later.)

The Anti-Christian Revolution

Meanwhile, there has been a change in the attitude of Americans toward the church, specifically toward Christians. There was a time when freedom of religion was simply assumed; today freedom of religion is being restricted, redefined, and otherwise compromised in deference to secular agendas. During my years as senior pastor of The Moody Church, we had a lawsuit filed against us that bounced in and out of the court for several years. We were sued because the church leadership withdrew an ordination it had bestowed many years earlier. Although we withdrew the ordination based on biblical reasons, after a ten-year court battle, we lost. That would have been unheard of decades ago when the separation of church and state meant that the courts had no right to interfere with the deliberations of a church body.

This hostility to Christianity in the United States was largely unknown thirty or forty years ago. Today, we are accused of bigotry, hate, and intolerance for exposing the agenda of radical Islam or opposing various aspects of a sexualized society. In a bizarre twist, freedom of speech for Christians is openly condemned by those who see themselves as the bastions of tolerance, freedom, and love. It's difficult to even have a conversation with those who believe that to question their viewpoint on social issues is hateful, bigoted, and without merit. If we want to be known as good citizens, such people feel we should at least keep our "antiquated" views to ourselves.

Meanwhile, parents have to combat the LGBTQ agenda

21

taught to their grade school children. A parent of a child in our Chicago public school told me that a teacher asked those who were in favor of same-sex marriage to line up on one side of the room, and those who were opposed were to line up on the other side of the room. The few who had the courage to line up in opposition to same-sex marriage were, in effect, shamed for their convictions.

Students aren't the only ones singled out. A teacher in our school system told me he was warned that it was not enough for him to tolerate same-sex relationships—he had to celebrate such a union or he might be fired. Many Christians feel embarrassed to defend traditional marriage and a reasonable understanding of gender. Like a deer caught in the headlights, we don't quite know what to do and whether we are willing to pay the price of our fidelity to Scripture. We are shamed into silence.

We need to be a courageous church at the time of weak knees and carnal living.

To summarize the late Haddon Robinson: In the past we, as American Christians, always had home-field advantage. We knew that in the crowd, there were those from the other team who were opposed to us, but the larger stadium crowd was either on our side or indifferent to our witness as Christians. All that has changed. Now we play all of our games on enemy turf. A minority is on our side, but the wider culture sits in the stands shouting hateful epithets at us, rejoicing at our losses.[7]

Today, I see the church as having to fight on multiple fronts while at the same time trying to maintain a positive ministry of bringing hope to the world. I see a church that desperately needs to learn the lessons that the people of God have to relearn in each generation: *We have to be a church that is, in some ways, repulsive to the world because of our authentic holiness and yet very attractive to the world because of our love and care.* We need to be a courageous church at the time of weak knees and carnal living. In short, we have to live lives that are a credit to the gospel we preach and the Savior we worship. God has humbled us, and we must enter into our cultural decline not with a swagger but with humility and brokenness. And transparency.

Let those of us in our churches not sit in judgment of the world, however, for all too often, *we are the world*, sharing in our culture's sins and failures. Remember, it was because of Jonah and not the pagan sailors that the storm blew on the sea! Too often we are blind to our own darkness. We criticize the world for calling darkness light, but perhaps we do the same.

Alasdair MacIntyre, an influential Catholic moral philosopher, said that Western civilization has lost its moorings and that "the time was coming when men and women of virtue would understand that continued full participation in mainstream society was not possible for those who want to live a life of traditional virtue . . . [and that] these people would find new ways of living in community just as St. Benedict . . . responded to the fall of Roman civilization by founding a monastic order."[8]

What do we do when our light is perceived by the world as darkness?

Some have suggested that the only way to preserve a dis-

If we are not distinct from the world, we will have nothing to say to the world.

tinctly Christian lifestyle is to isolate ourselves from the world. I am not suggesting that the church isolate itself as St. Benedict proposed. I am saying that if we are not distinct from the world, we will have nothing to say to the world. As you read this book, you will discover that there is much good that is taking place in our churches, but too often our light flickers and our witness goes silent.

We don't have to agree with Spanish conquistador Hernando Cortes's motives in order to appreciate how he convinced his men to help him conquer Veracruz, known today as Mexico. In 1519, he took about seven hundred men and eleven ships and after they disembarked, a clarion call went out to destroy the ships. The men watched as their only means of returning home disappeared into the ocean.[9] The point was very simple: There was a call, and the call was conquest. *And there was no turning back.*

Join me on this journey that seeks to help us refocus the light that a stumbling world desperately needs. We have the privilege of heeding the call to be a light that shines in the darkness. Like the men on the Mexican shore, *there is no turning back.*

Jesus said to him, "No one who puts his hand to the plow and looks back is fit for the kingdom of God" (Luke 9:62).

ERWIN W. LUTZER
Pastor Emeritus
The Moody Church, Chicago

CHAPTER 1

WELCOME TO BABYLON

We Have Arrived, and We Are Here to Stay

The church in Babylon!
Those four words plunge us into the heart of our present cultural context here in the West. We are called to be the church in the midst of rampant idolatry, violence, false religions, and willful spiritual blindness. We live in a sexualized culture bent on defiance of biblical authority.

Why another book about the church?

Many excellent books have been written about the church, about its ministries, methodologies, and challenges of the future. You, as a reader, might well ask: Why should another book be written on the topic? What will be said here that has not been said by others, perhaps more eloquently?

This is not a book about methods or better ways to spread

the gospel. This book does not address the question of how to plan more effective worship services or to streamline the leadership of a church staff. My heart lies elsewhere.

Let me explain.

JESUS AND HIS CHURCH

Whenever I think of the church, my mind gravitates to the introduction John gave to the seven churches of Revelation. Jesus is seen walking among the seven lampstands, and He is

> *clothed with a long robe and with a golden sash around his chest. The hairs of his head were white, like white wool, like snow. His eyes were like a flame of fire.... In his right hand he held seven stars, from his mouth came a sharp two-edged sword, and his face was like the sun shining in full strength.... As for the mystery of the seven stars that you saw in my right hand, and the seven golden lampstands, the seven stars are the angels of the seven churches, and the seven lampstands are the seven churches.*
>
> (REV. 1:13–16, 20)

Visualize it. First, John says Jesus was walking among the seven lampstands (the seven churches), and then John says Jesus was *holding* seven stars in His right hand (the angels or "messengers" of the seven churches). Jesus both *observes* the churches as He walks among them and also *holds* the leadership of the churches in His right hand. He loves His people whom He died to redeem. He observes us, and like these seven churches, He commends us for our faithfulness. I agree with John Stott, who said that the church needs to have its blinders taken off to see Jesus as He is! If only!

Jesus loves His people whom He died to redeem. He observes us, and like the seven churches of Revelation, He commends us for what pleases Him and rebukes us for our failures, but always with a marvelous promise of reward given to the overcomers. And thus seven times He admonishes, "he who has an ear, let him hear what the Spirit says to the churches" (Rev. 2:7, 11, 17, 29; 3:6, 13, 22).

Here's my premise. Jesus loves His people and carries them in His right hand. *He who has been given all authority in heaven and earth has made available to us all that we need, not merely to survive but to thrive in this hour of growing darkness.*

We will not go into the future unprepared—*if* we are willing to hear "what the Spirit says to the churches." Salvation is free, but as the seven churches of Revelation discovered, there is a cost to living authentic lives of holiness in a godless culture. We cannot take the resources Christ offers for granted but must diligently seek Him and His Word with prayerful wisdom.

The Faithful Remnant

We can be grateful that there are still many pastors who faithfully teach the Scriptures and have not compromised their convictions. Ministries such as The Gospel Coalition draw thousands of pastors to their conferences; I'm sure that the majority of these pastors are being true to the faith and are preaching the gospel and its implications. Much more could be said about the many who are faithful, in both big churches and small ones. As Francis Schaeffer used to say,

"There are no little people and no big people in the true spiritual sense, but only consecrated and unconsecrated people."[1]

It is fashionable today to condemn the church for its many failings. Some will disagree with me, but I don't believe that the disintegration of the United States is entirely the fault of the church. Certainly, the church has not done all that it should; certainly, we have contributed to the moral and spiritual bankruptcy we see around us. But there are many streams that have contributed to the climate of anti-Christian bigotry and the conscious rejection of our Judeo-Christian heritage.

Assuredly, I will be critical of the church's lack of faithfulness, but I believe there are certain inevitabilities in history and in the purposes of God that even a vibrant church cannot change. That is why Jesus used the little word *must* so often! To give but one example, "And when you hear of wars and tumults, do not be terrified, for these things *must* first take place, but the end will not be at once" (Luke 21:9; see also passages such as Matt. 16:21; 24:6; 26:54). Certain things *must* come to pass.

Sometimes God's light is most clearly seen in times of darkness.

But—and this is critical—Jesus and His followers believed that spiritual and moral darkness was no obstacle to God; His will would be achieved not just in good times, but also in bad times when the church was most sorely oppressed.

So, the inevitability of certain events should never make us collapse into fatalism, but rather give us the comfort of knowing that history is, after all, in the hands of God. God has a purpose for the church that will come to pass; He loves His people and wants us to be a light no matter the cultural currents, no matter the opposition, and no matter the consequences. Sometimes God's light is most clearly seen in times of darkness. *In every era, that light is the gift of His presence in and among His people.*

In these pages, we will be surprised at God's patience, but also His willingness to judge a nation that turns away from the truth it was given. We will also rediscover the lengths God is willing to go to remain faithful to His people, whether to ancient Israel or the bride of Christ so beautifully described in the New Testament.

OLD TESTAMENT BABYLON/NEW TESTAMENT CHURCH

We must be careful when we turn to the Old Testament for instructions for the New Testament church. I wince when I hear someone applying God's dealings with Israel to the New Testament church without giving thought to the fact that we are in a radically different era, when many of the Old Testament practices simply do not apply. For example, when Elijah won the contest with the prophets of Baal on the top of Mount Carmel, he summarily took 450 false prophets and had them killed at the river Kishon. As we shall see later in this book, the New Testament warns against false prophets and teachers, but we certainly are not expected to have them slaughtered! They are free to buy time on television, build their churches, and promote their heresies. The best we can do is expose them and help our flocks realize their danger. We no longer stone people for adultery, homosexuality, or disobeying one's parents. We are in a different age with different relationships and expectations.

However, we do have a convincing Old Testament parallel for what we face today, and that is Israel's experience of being refugees in Babylon (strictly speaking, it was *Judah* in Babylon). Here God's people had to live as a minority in the midst of a majority pagan culture. The Jewish consensus with its laws and temple worship was gone. Tragically, Solomon's beautiful temple was totally destroyed, left in a heap of ruins.

The Jews had to survive among pagan idolaters who had no regard for the God of Abraham, Isaac, and Jacob. Ten thousand Jews trekked about eight hundred miles over a period of weeks and months to arrive at a strange country with a strange language. All the social, religious, and cultural supports they'd been accustomed to were gone. Their tears of regret could not restore their previous privileges, which now were only a memory.

BABYLON IS NOW

Mention the name *Babylon* and many images come to mind. We might think of occultism, immorality, and violence—an apt description of our own culture. But more often, what comes to mind is the word *idolatry*. The Tower of Babel was built to oppose God's explicit command to populate the whole earth. Instead, the people settled down in one place and chose to build a tower to reach heaven. Their intention was to worship the stars rather than God and serve their own lusts rather than obey God's instructions.

The name *Babylon* occurs about two hundred times in Scripture. Mostly, we read about the Babylon of the past, but in the book of Revelation, we have both a description and a prediction of the fall of a future Babylon (see Rev. 18). When Jeremiah the prophet was preaching and writing, ancient Babylon had long since passed off the scene as a world power, but now a new Babylonian Empire had emerged. This revived neo-Babylonian Empire had recently overtaken Assyria and was at its peak as a world power. And Jeremiah, God bless him, would actually live to see these Babylonians destroy the city of Jerusalem, enslave the citizens of Judah, and leave Solomon's temple in ruins. He would weep until he could weep no more.

The rebellion of Babylon has carried on throughout history. The people of those days sacrificed their children to pagan gods; we sacrifice our unborn children on the altar of convenience. We do not bow down before stone idols; we give wholehearted allegiance to the gods of money, power, and sex. Too often our devotion to God is an "add on," something done in church once a week.

Christians are a minority in an increasingly hostile culture. We are exiles, not geographically, but morally and spiritually. "Beloved, I urge you as sojourners and exiles to abstain from the passions of the flesh, which wage war against your soul. Keep your conduct among the Gentiles honorable, so that when they speak against you as evildoers, they may see your good deeds and glorify God on the day of visitation" (1 Peter 2:11–12).

Exiles face opposition; they are misunderstood and are tempted to lose their distinctiveness. And, as those who belong to Christ, we are called to spread the good news and yet avoid being ensnared by the passions of the flesh and the many seductions of the world. Thankfully Jesus, at the right hand of God, prays for us that we might be in the world but not of it (see John 17:14–16).

Jeremiah, under the inspiration of the Holy Spirit, not only helps us analyze our own cultural context but also gives us fresh insight into the nature of God—His meticulous justice and His mercy along with His intense hatred for sin. In the book of Jeremiah, we are also led into the mysteries of God and His sovereignty even over the hearts of those who hate Him.

Best of all, we see God's faithfulness to His people while they are living in the midst of a pagan nation that worshiped the gods of their culture, the gods of their own making, and the gods of their sexual preference. If the book of Jeremiah is a book of *judgment*, it is also a book of *hope*—the kind of hope we need when we are confronted with the complexities and hostilities of our culture today.

Jeremiah's Difficult Assignment

Jeremiah prophesied at a time when the Word of God was neglected and even ridiculed. A few decades earlier, under the reign of Josiah, the Book of the Law was found; it was buried beneath the clutter of trash within the temple. There were so many other gods in the sanctuary that only as the rubble was being cleared away, God's Book was found.

When the leaders read it, a revival broke out, but it was too little too late. Some repented, but the nation as a whole was unmoved. The hopes of the godly were short-lived. There was some light, but not enough to overtake the darkness.

Jeremiah lived in a day of deaf ears. He was the weeping prophet, but the people around him remained dry eyed. He always told the truth but no one believed him. His ministry was so hated that he was thrown into a pit. In his discouragement he lamented:

> O LORD, *you have deceived me,*
>   *and I was deceived;*
> *you are stronger than I,*
>   *and you have prevailed.*
> *I have become a laughingstock all the day;*
>   *everyone mocks me.*
> *For whenever I speak, I cry out,*
>   *I shout, "Violence and destruction!"*
> *For the word of the LORD has become for me*
>   *a reproach and derision all day long.*

(JER. 20:7–8)

God, you have deceived me! Jeremiah expected that God would give him a word of peace, but he only received a word of judgment. As Jeremiah spilled out his heart to the people, he was rewarded with slander, mockery, and condemnation by false prophets. As the nation began to crumble, the king called for him but had no intention of listening to what this prophet had to say. *The nation was deaf to God's warnings.*

Our nation will be more stringently judged than Judah. The people of Jeremiah's day had only a few copies of the law, and only a few people could read while others relied on what they were told. Contrast that with us. We have more translations of the Bible than we can count; we have the Bible on our iPads and smartphones. We are almost universally literate; and if we don't care to read, we can have the Bible read to us by accessing any number of electronic devices and programs.

The nation had drifted so far from God that He told Jeremiah to stop praying for the nation (Jer. 7:16). Judah had crossed the point of no return. Whether the United States is at that point, we cannot be sure. But our slide toward moral and spiritual rebellion is accelerating with each passing day. What a wonderful opportunity for the church to display both the power of God to keep us and the love of God to authenticate us.

A Sexualized Culture

Later in this book we will discuss more specifically the idolatry of sexuality in our culture, but for now we answer a question: Why were pagan idols so attractive to the people of Israel and Judah? Why did the people constantly flirt with other gods?

Study history and you will discover that idolatry justified and encouraged sexual permissiveness of every sort. Shrines were built on every high hill, and God said, "Under every green tree you bowed down like a whore" (Jer. 2:20). Prostitution, homosexuality, and every form of perversion was practiced, and the people loved it. Orgies were common, and the false gods stood by in silent approval.

God was displeased. "Be appalled, O heavens, at this; be shocked, be utterly desolate, declares the LORD, for my people have committed two evils: they have forsaken me, the fountain of living waters, and hewed out cisterns for themselves, broken cisterns that can hold no water" (Jer. 2:12–13). The water they thirsted for proved to be bitter, guilt-inducing, and destructively addictive. It promised freedom but brought bondage, broken relationships, and endless pain.

People were gagging on the guilt, shame, and brokenness that their idols brought. But they refused to turn away from what was destroying them. The nature of evil is to plunge ahead, deliberately closing one's eyes to the consequences. Or even worse, seeing the consequences but being so addicted to behavioral patterns that change seems impossible.

Think America. Our nation is drinking from similar poisoned wells. Like salt water that promises to satisfy but only increases a deadly thirst, so our nation plunges into a sexual wasteland that drives people to emptiness and despair. All of this has to be mentally justified no matter what our consciences tell us. The bumper stickers used to say, "If it feels good, do it." Now the bumper sticker should say, "If it feels good, *believe* it."

The people had their own home remedies for their emptiness and guilt. "Though you wash yourself with lye and use much soap, the stain of your guilt is still before me, declares the Lord GOD" (Jer. 2:22). Using rationalizations as detergent, they were trying in vain to cleanse their consciences. But their self-made attempts to manage their emptiness only enflamed their desires. They looked everywhere for a remedy. Everywhere except to God.

The people didn't wait for sin to come to them, they went looking for it. "How can you say, 'I am not unclean, I have not gone after the Baals'? Look at your way in the valley; know what you have done—a restless young camel running here and there, a wild donkey used to the wilderness, in her heat sniffing the wind! Who can restrain her lust?" (Jer. 2:23–24).

God said that the day was coming when the people would feel shame, but for now, they could not blush. "As a thief is shamed when caught, so the house of Israel shall be shamed:

they, their kings" (Jer. 2:26). There was a time was when unmarried couples living together would try to hide that fact,
but not anymore. They openly say that they are living together
and have no sense of shame. Times are changing.

It has been said, once we open the door to sin, it takes us
further than we intended to go, keeps us longer than we intended to stay, and costs us more than we intended to pay.

With their conscience deadened by unrestrained sexuality,
the people of Judah ended up sacrificing their children to the
god Molech. In the United States, we are sacrificing our unborn on the altar of sexual freedom, and now with one-third
of America's children born out of wedlock, they are thrown
into a world of insecurity, anger, and too often, abuse. Sadly,
this vicious cycle is often repeated in the next generation.

Every god demands increasing allegiance. Whether it's
money or fame or sex, our god of choice is not easily satisfied.
John Calvin, the great theologian, said that the human mind
is an idol factory. The human heart keeps generating one idol
after another.

What a marvelous opportunity for God to show up
through His church!

False Prophets Aplenty

Jeremiah found himself at sharp odds with the false
prophets of his day who had a more welcome message for
the people. The populace knew that they didn't like Jeremiah
or his message and longed for something more acceptable.

The false prophets said, in effect, "We have a better message; we don't like the negativity of Jeremiah; we are pre-
senting a positive message that people will accept." They

knew that as long as Jeremiah spoke about judgment, his crowds would be small. The wider populace was eager for a different message, a more hopeful word. That's why Jeremiah was thrown into a pit.

> They had a theology of success, but not a theology of suffering.

The false prophets did what false prophets almost always do: *they appealed to the ego of their listeners by telling them that God owes them special blessings because they are the people of God.* They preached blessings without repentance, prosperity without piety. They had a theology of success, but not a theology of suffering. They preached about the good life in this present world and gave no thought to the world to come.

This was their argument: "Sure we serve other gods, but we also continue to worship Jehovah, and so we are sons and daughters of the Most High God. There is no way that He would let us be humiliated at the hands of the Babylonians, a people far more wicked than we." Their message was one of peace and continued prosperity, but it was like putting a bandage over a cancerous tumor. In short, their message was: we must learn to live like a King's kid.

God was not pleased. "They have healed the wound of my people lightly, saying, 'Peace, peace,' when there is no peace. Were they ashamed when they committed abomination? No, they were not at all ashamed; they did not know how to blush. Therefore they shall fall among those who fall; at the time that I punish them, they shall be overthrown" (Jer. 6:14–15). Yes, these false prophets healed the wounds of the people far too lightly! It was all about *how to live your best life right then!*

Jeremiah wept, but they didn't. They were prophets of hope, a false hope to be sure, but it was hope. God said, "They [the false prophets] have spoken falsely of the LORD and have said, 'He will do nothing; no disaster will come upon us, nor shall we see sword or famine'" (Jer. 5:12). Just blessing upon blessing!

Jeremiah rejected the false prophets' one-sided emphasis that God had chosen the nation and therefore they could presume on His unending favor despite their lifestyle. "An appalling and horrible thing has happened in the land: the prophets prophesy falsely, and the priests rule at their direction; my people love to have it so, but what will you do when the end comes?" (Jer. 5:30–31).

In our day, too many are preaching a gospel that does not humble anyone. Instead, it's presented as a means of self-exaltation and fulfillment. We are awash with so-called "evangelists" who tell us that if we send them "seed money," this act will break curses, we will inherit wealth, and we will be healed from all of our physical ailments. Just send them money, and God will open the windows of heaven and give a bountiful harvest of financial and physical blessing.

These same false prophets claim to have special revelations from God. This is exactly what the false prophets were doing in Jeremiah's day. "The prophets are prophesying lies in my name. I have not sent them or appointed them or spoken to them. They are prophesying to you false visions, divinations, idolatries and the delusions of their own minds" (Jer. 14:14 NIV).

Delusions of their own minds!

The people loved what they were hearing. They were assured that there would be neither war nor famine, only prosperity. We can almost hear them say, "Let's not let the devil rob us of what is rightfully ours. We belong to Jehovah, the God of the universe, let us live accordingly!"

God says, "I have heard what the prophets say who prophesy lies in my name. They say, 'I had a dream! I had a dream!' How long will this continue in the hearts of these lying prophets, who prophesy the delusions of their own minds?" (Jer. 23:25–26 NIV). No wonder the Lord says, "Do not listen to what the prophets are prophesying to you; they fill you with false hopes" (Jer. 23:16).

False hopes!

Let us hear Jeremiah speak on behalf of God: "They have spoken falsely of the Lord and have said, 'He will do nothing; no disaster will come upon us, nor shall we see sword or famine. *The prophets will become wind; the word is not in them. Thus shall it be done to them!*'" (Jer. 5:12–13).

The prophets will become wind!

Paul knew that we in our day would encounter the same deceivers. "For such men are false apostles, deceitful workmen, disguising themselves as apostles of Christ. And no wonder, for even Satan disguises himself as an angel of light. So it is no surprise if his servants, also, disguise themselves as servants of righteousness. Their end will correspond to their deeds" (2 Cor. 11:13–15).

My heart breaks for people who are deceived by false prophets. Often the poor are susceptible because they are saying to themselves, "If I just had enough faith, if I had the same faith as this guru or this prophet, then I would be able to drive the same car that he drives and wear the clothes that he wears." These dear people send in their meager funds and never see the windfall they have been promised.

Jeremiah teaches us that false prophets must be exposed for what they are.

CALLED TO OBEDIENCE, NOT SUCCESS

God was pleased with Jeremiah, not because he was successful but because he was faithful. And as God prepared Jeremiah for his role, so God has also prepared us. "Now the word of the Lord came to me, saying, 'Before I formed you in the womb I knew you, and before you were born I consecrated you; I appointed you a prophet to the nations'" (Jer. 1:4–5). Please notice that Jeremiah was not called *while* in his mother's womb, but *before* he was formed in his mother's womb. The timing of his birth and calling were in God's heart long before the prophet arrived on the scene. In fact, God had planned both Jeremiah's birth and mission in eternity past.

The clearer we hear our call from God, the more courage we will have to face spiritual battles.

And He has the same plans for us. We might not have exactly the same calling as Jeremiah, but God did know us before we were born. We are also called to be alive and represent Him at this hour of our history. We could have been born in a previous era, a future era, or not born at all. God has a reason for us living *now*. Jesus said to His disciples, and thus to us, "You did not choose me, but I chose you and appointed you that you should go and bear fruit" (John

15:16). *The clearer we hear our call from God, the more courage we will have to face uphill spiritual battles.*

Jeremiah did not see the revival for which he had prayed and worked. His urgent call to return back to God was received by a few, not the masses. In our day, there are thousands of us who pray for a nationwide revival. We have not yet seen it, but perhaps we shall yet see the fulfillment of our prayers. Perhaps not. Either way, we are called to faithfulness. This book is about what we should be doing even as we wait and pray for a revival. Faithfulness to our calling should be our overriding passion.

The God who calls is the God who provides. God gave Jeremiah all the gifts and strength he needed to face the opposition of his culture, and our heavenly Father does the same for us. Young or old, married, single, or widowed, God has equipped us to live for Him in this hour. As we shall see, we are to live without fear and with joy at the privilege of representing Christ even at great personal cost.

Read about how God prequalified Jeremiah for his role.

> *"But you, dress yourself for work; arise, and say to them everything that I command you. Do not be dismayed by them, lest I dismay you before them. And I, behold, I make you this day a fortified city, an iron pillar, and bronze walls, against the whole land, against the kings of Judah, its officials, its priests, and the people of the land. They will fight against you, but they shall not prevail against you, for I am with you, declares the LORD."*
>
> (JER. 1:17–19)

When did God make Jeremiah a fortified city, an iron pillar, and bronze walls? This was not a prediction; it was a present reality. Jeremiah was prequalified to walk in victory, to withstand the opposition, and to fulfill his assignment. Like Isaiah, he could not point to a list of successes, but nonetheless, he died faithful to his calling.

Jeremiah's God will walk with us and will be faithful to His promises; He will stand with us during dark times. We are not expected to generate our own light and shine it into the darkness; the moon does not need to generate its own light but only reflect it.

THE PURPOSE OF THIS BOOK

The title of this book is *The Church in Babylon*, but the subtitle is *Heeding the Call to Be a Light in the Darkness*. We want to be strong, courageous, and gracious, but also uncompromising as witnesses to the gospel of Jesus Christ in a culture that is becoming increasingly hostile to the Christian faith. Like Israel in Babylon, *our challenge is to impact the culture without being spiritually destroyed by it.*

In brief, the purpose of this book is to answer three questions:

First, what does faithfulness look like in a nation that has lost its way, a nation that appears to be under the judgment of God?

Second, what are those issues that we, as a church, must confront in order to represent the God we worship? Or to put it differently, what instructions might Christ give us as we prepare ourselves for the darkness that is closing around us and the deeper darkness that's on its way?

Finally, Jesus told five of the seven churches of Revelation to repent. Might that not be His message to us? What might He be asking us to repent of? Where might we have lost our way?

We have to know how to engage the culture without becoming contaminated by it.

I believe that the time is coming, and is already here, when the church will not be able to depend on the media, the courts, our universities, or even some so-called evangelical churches to stand with us as the onslaught against Christianity comes to us from every direction. We have to learn how to conduct ourselves as a minority in a majority post-Christian world. We have to know how to engage the culture without becoming contaminated by it.

God's passionate invitation to Judah is given to us today.

> *"Return, faithless Israel,*
> *declares the LORD.*
> *I will not look on you in anger,*
> *for I am merciful,*
> *declares the LORD;*
> *I will not be angry forever.*
> *Only acknowledge your guilt,*
> *that you rebelled against the LORD your God*

and scattered your favors among foreigners under every
green tree,
  and that you have not obeyed my voice,
declares the LORD.
Return, O faithless children,
declares the LORD;
  for I am your master."

(J E R . 3 : 1 2 – 1 4)

To the church in Ephesus that had lost its first love, He warned, "Remember therefore from where you have fallen; repent, and do the works you did at first. If not, I will come to you and remove your lampstand from its place, unless you repent" (Rev. 2:5). Visit Ephesus today and you will discover that its lampstand was removed many centuries ago.

As Leonard Ravenhill once said, "The church is waiting for the world to become regenerate, while the world is waiting for the church to become repentant."[2]

A repentant and humble church need not fear the future. Jesus, who walks among us and holds us in His right hand, can empower us to "be blameless and innocent, children of God without blemish in the midst of a crooked and twisted generation, among whom you shine as lights in the world" (Phil. 2:15). Only pride and self-righteousness will prevent us from fulfilling our calling.

As mentioned, our light is as borrowed as is the light of the moon. Only the Light of the World is able to keep our own lights burning in an age that tells us we must snuff them out.

I have read that when Augustine was told about the fall of Rome to the Vandals, he felt deep sadness because he loved that city. He also believed its demise was a judgment for its sins, lamenting, "Whatever men build, men will destroy. Let's get on with building the kingdom of God."

Yes, whatever men build, men will destroy, so let us get on with building the church that is highly prized by God and empowered by the Savior who gave His life for it.

> *". . . on this rock I will build my church, and the gates of hell shall not prevail against it."*
>
> (MATT. 16:18)

What seems impossible with men is possible with God.

CHAPTER 2

A LIGHT TO THE CITY, A HEART FOR GOD

Finding God in Enemy Territory

The church is to be in the world like a ship is in the ocean. But when the ocean begins to seep into the ship, the vessel is in trouble. John Newton, writer of "Amazing Grace," knew something about a ship that was about to go under in a storm. He was converted after being overwhelmed with fear when a ship he was on encountered a terrifying storm in 1748. Later in life, after being ordained as an Anglican clergyman, Newton saw dissension within the church and commented, "When a ship is leaky, and a mutinous spirit divides the company on board, a wise man would say, 'My good friends, while we are debating, the water is gaining on us—we had better leave the debate, and go to the pumps.'"[1]

I believe it is time for Christians to rally, leave aside trivia, and meet at the pumps! We have plenty of water from Babylon that has seeped into our ship! There are risks involved when Christians live in a pagan culture without proper safeguards. The culture can devour us. And yet, I believe that the mandate found in Jesus' prayer, "I do not ask that you take them out of the world, but that you keep them from the evil one" (John 17:15) is still applicable today.

We are asked to be a holy witness within the world rather than to isolate ourselves from the world despite the risks. Pastor Ed Stetzer put it this way: "Doing the King's work requires us to live *within* the world in some ways and to rebel *against* it in others. God calls us to both."[2] Living within the world involves us in a war, and in a war there are casualties.

The Jews, in losing their land and temple, lost the battle for their religion, land, and culture. And they lost much more besides. Marduk, the patron god of the Babylonians, triumphed. Yet these chastised Jews, pained and humbled by their losses, were called to represent God in Babylon! We will be surprised as to what God expected of them.

The Jews left one important city, namely Jerusalem, to live in another influential city, namely Babylon. They had no choice in the matter. In 605 BC, the armies of Babylon swept down, captured thousands of people, and carted them off to Babylon. In this first deportation, they chose Judah's brightest and best and put them to work to advance the Babylonian agenda. Among them were Daniel and some of his friends.

Then about eight years later, the Babylonians returned to

Israel, this time capturing almost all of the remaining people and deporting them. The beautiful and costly temple that Solomon had built was totally demolished, and Jeremiah was there to witness it all. He had good reason to weep.

Some Jews were killed when Jerusalem was under siege, others died of starvation. Children were malnourished; babies starved for lack of milk. Those who survived and trekked to Babylon had relatives who died during the treacherous journey. Finally, those who survived settled in the city of Babylon, eight hundred miles from Jerusalem and about sixty miles from the modern city of Baghdad.

Jeremiah records his personal description of the suffering: "My eyes are spent with weeping; my stomach churns; my bile is poured out to the ground because of the destruction of the daughter of my people, because infants and babies faint in the streets of the city" (Lam. 2:11).

HEARTS, NOT BUILDINGS

Wouldn't it be wonderful if we could visit Israel today and tour Solomon's temple? This mighty structure would probably still be standing if the Babylonians, or some other army, had not destroyed it. Although it housed God's glory, He was willing to allow this gigantic temple to be laid bare by cruel, pagan soldiers. If that's what was needed to humble His people and lead them to repentance, it was worth it.

Centuries later, a second massive stone temple complex would be built under the direction of King Herod. This temple, begun around 20 BC and completed in AD 64, was the one visited by Jesus. But Jesus, sitting on the Mount of

Olives, predicted that it too would be destroyed and "there will not be left here one stone upon another that will not be thrown down" (Matt. 24: 2). In AD 70, just six years after the temple was completed, the Romans came and took the temple apart, stone by stone. It too would be standing today if an army had not destroyed it. God again says, in effect, "Your beautiful houses of worship mean nothing to me if I don't have your hearts!"

Think of Washington, D.C. Almost every government building has a verse of Scripture engraved on it because America was founded by those who had great respect for the Bible and the Judeo-Christian worldview. Today, of course, these scriptural references are an embarrassment to secularists who wish to scrub our country clean of its religious roots.

More importantly, our church buildings, though dedicated to God and useful as meeting places, matter little to God. He looks elsewhere. "For the eyes of the LORD run to and fro throughout the whole earth, to give strong support to those whose heart is blameless toward him" (2 Chron. 16:9).

The church is not the building, as Stetzer explains: "Many Christians, if they believe anything about the kingdom at all, think of it as the *church itself*, with its spires and steeples on top that make it almost look like a castle. But while the church is definitely inseparably involved in the work of the kingdom, the kingdom itself is not visible in the same way a church building is. You can't see it with ordinary sight."[3]

Thank God for our church buildings, but let us never forget that our heart is Christ's true residence. God dwells among His people, not in temples made with hands. Yes, the temple was very important in Jewish life, but in Babylon,

God said that His presence would always be the true temple. *God would meet them on enemy territory.*

ARRIVING IN BABYLON

Visualize the Jews arriving in Babylon. Those with family members back in Jerusalem knew they'd never see those relatives again. Their houses and belongings were lost forever. In Babylon, they probably met together in homes or makeshift facilities. Religiously, economically, and emotionally destitute, the Jews entered their strange new surroundings.

In summary, in Babylon, the Jews lost three symbols of their identity: their *land,* their *king,* and their *temple.*[4] The moment they arrived, they were surrounded by Babylonian gods. There was Ishtar, the goddess of fertility, sacred prostitutes, and sexual freedom. Then there was Baal (or Bel), the god of the sun, agriculture, and thunder. These foreign gods knew nothing of the Ten Commandments. These impersonal gods were tolerant of every form of sexual perversion and thus condoned the lifestyle of the Babylonians.

The Jews were now to serve these Babylonians. They had to learn a new language, earn a living, buy food, and as much as possible, get along peacefully with their neighbors. And God expected them to do it while maintaining a God-honoring lifestyle and personal holiness.

Same Country, Different Culture

Unlike the Jews, we haven't changed countries. But, in the eyes of Christians, the core values of our culture seem to have changed drastically, especially in the past couple of decades.

In general, America was founded by Europeans, who, for the most part, identified as Christians. In his book *The End of White Christian America,* Robert P. Jones explains that our forefathers wrote our laws, built our political structures, and established the core values that helped shape our nation. Frances Schaeffer spoke of this as the "Judeo-Christian Consensus." Jones explains that although this "prominent cultural force" in American history originally provided "a shared aesthetic, a historical framework, and a moral vocabulary," the WCA [White Christian America] has died.[5]

Today, for many Christians, the country looks different than it did just a few generations ago. We applaud the progress made regarding integration and racial equality, but other changes are troublesome. Jones begins his book with "An Obituary for White Christian America," explaining the cause of "death" of this group "was determined to be a combination of environmental and internal factors—complications stemming from major demographic changes in the country, along with religious disaffiliation as many of its younger members began to doubt WCA's continued relevance in a shifting cultural environment."[6] This group's credibility was also damaged when it became mired in partisan politics in the closing decades of the twentieth century. He explains that "late in its life, WCA also struggled to adequately address issues such as lesbian, gay, bisexual, and transgender (LGBT) rights, which were of

What concerns me is the death of Christian America.

particular importance to its younger members, as well as to younger Americans overall."[7]

But I am not concerned about the death of *white* America. Our racial diversity is a strength, and it gives churches the opportunity to display the diversity of heaven (Rev. 5:9–10). Although we still have far to go, churches are increasingly more intentional about multiculturalism, racial reconciliation, and reaching out to the refugees among us.

What concerns me is the death of *Christian* America. Many of the biblical values upon which America was founded are no longer being allowed to shape our laws or our lives. In some lesser ways, Christians can identify with the Jews in Babylon. Our culture is instead being shaped by religious fragmentation, widespread disaffection with the church, changing sexual attitudes, and moral and spiritual relativism. Add to that "political correctness" and the "religion" of our political parties run amok, and it's no wonder America—in the eyes of Christians—looks different each day.

Yet, we are called to witness within this larger culture that adheres to the values of trash television, hedonism, ever expanding homosexual power and influence, religious antagonism, racial hatred, political wrangling, and the exaltation of individual rights. The words I saw emblazoned on a man's T-shirt as I walked near The Moody Church captured those values perfectly: "Just worship me and we'll get along fine!"

Too often, we as evangelicals find ourselves as a minority, out of step with the cultural currents that have been widely accepted by an ever-changing America. The future is easy to predict because many of the children raised in evangelical homes and churches are opting for a more inclusive

How do we share our faith in a culture that often despises our Christian values?

theology along with more liberal political agendas. Some will disagree, but I believe researcher John Dickerson is right when he says the church is declining in members, in dollars, and in influence.[8]

So the question before us is this: How do we share our faith in a culture that often despises our values and Christian commitment? How did the Jews, who were at the mercy of the Babylonians, maintain their identity and continue to worship Jehovah? The Jews knew they had little chance of impacting the Babylonian culture, but feared that there was a much greater chance that the Babylonians would influence them.

The Jews survived, and so can we, but it won't be easy, and the risks will be great. As Russell Moore put it, "Our call is to an *engaged alienation*, a Christianity that preserves the distinctiveness of our gospel while not retreating from our callings as neighbors, and friends, and citizens."[9]

As far as their captors were concerned, the Jews were trusting in a weak god who proved unable to defend his followers. In the minds of the Babylonians, Jehovah lost to their chief god, Marduk. How would you feel if your God was deemed a loser?

The Babylonians believed that Jehovah's light was darkness.

THE OPTIONS THE JEWS FACED

According to Jeremiah, the Jews were subject to "affliction and hard servitude" (Lam. 1:3). Discouragement, despondency, and depression were common. How would they react?

The Option of Isolation

The first option for the Jews was to angrily isolate themselves from the Babylonian culture and condemn their captors—who could blame them? Their anger would be justified because of the harsh treatment they and their families had received at the hands of these ruthless murderers.

The Babylonian soldiers took delight in throwing Jewish babies against rocks, raping women, and putting others in chains. To top it off, the displaced Jews were being taunted by these captors who wanted to be entertained by hearing them sing songs of Zion.

Read how the Jews felt about this offensive request:

By the waters of Babylon,
there we sat down and wept,
when we remembered Zion.
On the willows there
we hung up our lyres.
For there our captors
required of us songs,
and our tormentors, mirth, saying,
"Sing us one of the songs of Zion!"

How shall we sing the LORD's song
in a foreign land?

If I forget you, O Jerusalem,
  let my right hand forget its skill!
Let my tongue stick to the roof of my mouth,
  if I do not remember you,
  if I do not set Jerusalem
    above my highest joy!

(PS. 137:1-6)

This psalmist, echoing the despair and anger of the refugees, doesn't end there. He prays that he could repay his captors for their wanton evil:

O daughter of Babylon, doomed to be destroyed,
  blessed shall he be who repays you
  with what you have done to us!
Blessed shall he be who takes your little ones
  and dashes them against the rock!

(PS. 137:8-9)

You can just hear it: "You dashed our children against a rock, and we long for the day when we will repay you!"

With that attitude, no doubt some Jews withdrew from all social involvement, except what was strictly necessary in order to live. They exercised their faith privately, in their homes and in their minds. They said nothing about the Babylonian gods; they were silent about their own faith. They were too embarrassed and angry to share their devotion to their "defeated God" Jehovah. They could remain silent about how God brought their forefathers out of Egypt and gave them the land of Canaan. If they did speak, they would preach judgment without mercy.

Some Christians in our culture wag their finger, pronouncing doom on offending sinners. They are angry at those who "stole their country"—the liberalism taught in the schools, the media, which too often is rife with violence and sexual depravity, and the politicians who constantly push for legislation that undermines our faith tradition and values.

Yes, we might have "righteous anger" as we see our culture destroyed, but if our anger spills over into our Christian witness, it only fuels the stereotype that the world already has of us. Yes, we are called to expose the sins of the world, but to do so with redemption, in humility and compassion. And, yes, with courage. And tears.

Anger and rebuke change nothing. In fact, they cause our leftist friends to entrench themselves ever deeper into their hatred of Christians. Moreover, these actions don't represent our Master who "when he was reviled, he did not revile in return; when he suffered, he did not threaten, but continued entrusting himself to him who judges justly" (1 Peter 2:23).

Anger, vengeance, and a spirit of retaliation are not the ways of the Master. But as we shall see later in this book, neither is silence nor cowardice.

The Option of Assimilation

If the first option was *isolation*, a second extreme was *assimilation*. In other words, some of the Jews just drifted with the cultural flow, not making waves but living lives that were indistinguishable from the people around them.

Spritual assimilation is always the path of least resistance; it is the most natural and cowardly way to live. It allows the culture to exploit our natural tendency to get all the world has to offer with only a nod in the direction of the God we say we love.

A WORD FROM GOD

God gives a third option; we could call it *infiltration without contamination*.

Jeremiah stayed in Jerusalem, but his revelations from God did not cease. When he received a word as to how the exiles were to conduct themselves in Babylon, he sent the refugees a letter with God's instructions. They would discover that *God does not bring us into a future He has not already prepared for us.*

Though outnumbered and marginalized, the church is still *sent* into the world.

God says He *sent* the Jews to Babylon (Jer. 29:7, 20). Think about this: The Jews were in Babylon as a judgment for their own depravity, but now that they were there, they were to take advantage of their plight and be witnesses of God's grace to the evil people of Babylon! They were to see themselves as *sent* there as God's ambassadors.

Take heart. Though outnumbered and experiencing the humiliation of being marginalized in our culture, the church is still *sent* into the world to represent Christ. We are still the best witnesses of hope this hapless planet has! We, as the church, will never be effective unless we see ourselves as *sent* by Christ into the world. He prayed, "As you [the Father] sent me into the world, so I have sent them into the world" (John 17:18). We are pilgrims, out of step with the ever-changing culture—yet we are *sent* by Christ, the Head of the church. The church is the last barrier between the present moral breakdown and total chaos.

What do we do when we are in a strange country? God gives five instructions for people who are outnumbered and struggling to know how to live in a pagan culture:

> *"Thus says the LORD of hosts, the God of Israel, to all the exiles whom I have sent into exile from Jerusalem to Babylon: Build houses and live in them; plant gardens and eat their produce. Take wives and have sons and daughters; take wives for your sons, and give your daughters in marriage, that they may bear sons and daughters; multiply there, and do not decrease. But seek the welfare of the city where I have sent you into exile, and pray to the LORD on its behalf, for in its welfare you will find your welfare."*
>
> (JER. 29:4-7)

When in Babylon, Settle Down

Build a house. Connect with your neighbors. Don't live in your tents, because you are going to be in the land for seventy long years! Implied in these instructions is "learn the language of your captors"!

Predictably, the false prophets showed up—they survived the trek of nearly eight hundred miles—and they had a different message, assuring the people their stay would be very brief. In summary they said, "God will deliver us out of here quickly. He won't allow us to be with these pagans for any length of time." (See Jer. 28:12–17; 29:29–32.)

Once again, the false teachers were healing the wound of

the people too lightly. God says you are not getting out of this as easily as you think. "Don't accept cheap promises. It is going to be difficult; I want you to plant crops and build houses because there will be no quick fix."

I was asked to speak at a conference on the topic, "How to Reclaim America." In other words, how do we roll back same-sex marriage, abortion rights, and the indoctrination of children in our public schools, and install judges who respect the Constitution? I began by saying that there is no quick fix; we might never be able to return to our original values and what is nostalgically referred to as "the good old days." Our task is to be faithful even if we can't restore the erosion of the Judeo-Christian consensus. We must adjust to a long fight for the gospel and its implications. Change happens one person, one family, and one community at a time. And it's not easy.

Jesus came to live in a dangerous world, and we must follow His example.

God tells us to take the long point of view. Our task today is uncompromising integration with the people of this nation, establishing and maintaining safeguards so that we might not be absorbed by the world. We are not called to settle on a hill in North Dakota surrounded by a fence so that we can be far away from grinding human need and the danger of living in a chaotic and intoxicated world. Jesus came to live in a dangerous world, and we must follow His example.

Remember, God calls us to obedience, not success.

When in Babylon, Build Strong Families

Only strong families can weather the cultural storms of Babylon. "Take wives and have sons and daughters; take wives for your sons, and give your daughters in marriage, that they may bear sons and daughters; multiply there, and do not decrease" (Jer. 29:6). One preacher put it this way: "God says, have some singles parties so that young women can meet young men, and you will have marriages and families."

That comes as a surprise, doesn't it? How can you raise children in a pagan environment? In Judaism, there were strong fathers who took responsibility for the home. The father led his family in the Passover rituals; fathers were charged with teaching children the Word of God. And God knew that with strong fathers, grounded in the Word of God, these families could survive paganism.

With strong families, God would have future seed, and the message of His gospel (as understood in Old Testament times) would flourish. God needed children so that a future generation would be able to return to the land and continue His work. So God said, "Have families in the midst of this pagan culture." Thankfully, their children probably did not have to attend Babylonian schools. I can imagine, however, that what the children heard on the streets made up for it.

In the United States, many of our public schools indoctrinate children with the values of Babylon and can succeed in confusing them and casting doubt on the morals and beliefs parents and churches have instilled. I agree with theologian Al Mohler Jr. that parents of today need an exit strategy from those public schools that increasingly impose godless views of sexuality even in the early grades.[10]

Education alternatives, such as homeschooling or faith-based private school, are not viable options for some families. But regardless of where their children go to school, parents (particularly the father) are held accountable by God for the education of their children. If the children are being, in effect, brainwashed by secular teachers, the parents must intervene. At all costs, parents should not allow a school to sexualize their children.

One option for parents whose children attend traditional public school is to be proactive, said Education Analyst Candi Cushman of Focus on the Family. For example, parents can request to see the school's curriculum and lesson plans. In addition, a "Bill of Rights" for parents provides a valuable resource to help moms and dads be "effective advocates" for their children.[11]

I recall my friend Tony Evans, pastor of Oak Cliff Bible Fellowship in Dallas, saying that when his children came home from school, he and his wife, Lois, would spend some time "deprogramming" them, asking them what happened in school, what they were taught, and what values were communicated. Then they would correct inaccuracies and clarify teachings in the light of their family's Christian worldview.

I can imagine the same in Babylon. When their children came home from playing in the streets or returning from the market, the fathers might ask them what they had heard and seen during their day and then give them instruction on how to recognize the lies of a pagan culture—and emphasize why their allegiance must always be to Jehovah.

God basically said to the fathers, "I'm going to entrust large families to you, and my presence will be with you in your homes. You no longer have a temple and sacrifices, but I will be among you. And if you adhere to me and seek my face, I'll give you the wisdom that you need to rear your children for the glory of God." Seeking God for wisdom in parenting is always the key to raising families in a confused world.

Churches that don't help families grow and thrive despite the culture are failing in their God-given responsibility of strengthening the most important of all social institutions. We must help families of all kinds: the divorced, the single parents, the pregnant teenager, and the homeless. The disintegration of our families means the disintegration of society as a whole. We are called to walk alongside others with sacrificial instruction and compassion.

There's no quick fix to win the culture back. It's one home at a time.

When in Babylon, Get Involved in City Life

Be good neighbors. "But seek the welfare of the city where I have sent you into exile, and pray to the LORD on its behalf, for in its welfare you will find your welfare" (Jer. 29:7). The Hebrew word for welfare is *shalom*. So what God is saying is, "Seek the *shalom* of the city."

That word *shalom* is often translated as "welfare" or "peace," but it actually means something more; it is a holistic view of what peace is all about. It can refer to prosperity, wholeness, blessing, or favor. God would say to us today in Chicago, "Become a servant. Shovel the snow off of your sidewalk and perhaps the sidewalk of your neighbor too! Show hospitality. Build relationships. Pay your taxes." For some citizens of Chicago, God might say, "Seek to become an alderman or establish a food pantry for the poor."

We should invest in our cities because, "In its *shalom*, you will find *shalom*." When the tide comes in, all boats float. So as you permeate the city with righteousness, with a sense of determination to bless the city, blessing will come back upon you. Your own welfare will be connected to the city's welfare.

When in Babylon, Pray!

Pray for your neighbors who worship false gods. "Seek the welfare of the city where I have sent you into exile, and *pray to the LORD on its behalf*" (Jer. 29:7).

This must have shocked the Israelites. Is God serious? Are they really supposed to pray for Babylon—this nation whose cruel soldiers destroyed their families and perhaps killed their parents and relatives? Pray for the people who stole your country? Pray for their blessing. Pray for their *shalom*?

Self-righteousness was wrung out of the hearts of these Jews, and thanks to their suffering, they were prepared to even pray that God would bless their cruel enemies. Desperation would do what success and prosperity could never accomplish.

Chicago is known as a city of violence, a city whose murder rate simply will not subside. What we hear on the news is really the tip of an iceberg that doesn't even take into account all the abuse, addiction, and the alcoholism that goes on in our city's homes and apartments.

Many churches participate in an organization called "Pray Chicago." Scores of members from diverse congregations gather at least three times a year to seek God on our behalf and on behalf of Chicago and its great needs. We often pray over the seventy-seven neighborhoods of the city. We pray for the city economically and racially, but we primarily pray for its great spiritual needs. We pray for the *shalom* of the city.

Some skeptics point out that God does not seem to be answering our prayers. We continue to pray for Chicago's *shalom* not knowing how much worse it would be if we had not prayed at all. Steps are being taken to unite the city's gospel-believing churches in community work and outreach.

We should pray for kings and for those who have authority over us. We are to pray for the mayor, the aldermen, and of course, our national leaders. But we know that the real *shalom* is found only through the gospel of Christ.

God told the Jews: Pray for Babylon. Pray for its leaders, and even pray for your enemies.

When in Babylon, Remember God's Promises!

Be optimistic.

> *"For thus says the LORD: When seventy years are completed for Babylon, I will visit you, and I will fulfill to you my promise and bring you back to this place. For I know the plans I have for you, declares the LORD, plans for welfare and not for evil, to give you a future and a hope. Then you will call upon me and come and pray to me, and I will hear you. You will seek me and find me, when you seek me with all your heart."*
>
> (JER. 29:10-13)

This is not a promise to be hung as a plaque in your home. In context, it's a specific reference to Israel's future. God is saying, "After seventy years, I am going to come to you and you will be going back to Jerusalem, and I promise you a future and a hope."

Think for a moment. Let's suppose that you were forty years old in Babylon. You survived the difficult eight-hundred-mile journey and have tried your best to adapt to Babylonian culture without losing your faith. Now you hear that in seventy years the nation will be allowed to return to Jerusalem. You'd be thinking, "I'm thankful for the promise, but I'm going to die here." And yes, of course, you will die in Babylon and so will most of your family and relatives.

Let's skip ahead.

The children of that first generation, whose parents died in Babylon, did return, but in the meantime, they had lost their ability to speak Hebrew; they now spoke Akkadian, the language of Babylon. This is why, when they returned seven decades later, the Book of the Law had to be interpreted for them (Neh. 8:1–8).

But what about those who died in Babylon? They could die in faith knowing that although they would not see Jerusalem in this life, they would inherit promised blessings in the life to come. Abraham, for example, died in faith, not having received what was promised, but some day he will see God's promise completely fulfilled (Heb. 11:39–40).

We might not see the return of Jesus in our lifetime, but we also die in faith, "waiting for our blessed hope, the appearing of the glory of our great God and Savior Jesus Christ" (Titus 2:13).

Let's never lose sight of God's end game.

LESSONS FOR US

What lessons are there for us in Israel's history?

The Blessings of Desperation

After a blood test one Saturday morning, my doctor phoned that evening and urged me to go immediately to the emergency room. My numbers were way out of whack; he warned me that I was in crisis. But at that moment I felt fine. I spent the night at home and even preached the next morning. By that afternoon, I knew my doctor was right. My wife, Rebecca, took me to the ER for gallbladder surgery. I learned a lesson: it is possible to be in crisis even though, for the time being, you feel quite fine.

The evangelical church in America is in crisis but, for many people, it doesn't feel that way. But we have to stop pretending that we are a moral majority and face the fact that we are losing the culture war. Abortion, same-sex marriage, sex slavery, pornography, transgenderism, explicit sex education in schools—the floodgates have been opened. The god of secularism and uninhibited sexual idolatry appears to have won the battle; the God of the Bible has given way to the gods of paganism. The world looks at us with neither appreciation nor respect. We represent the God of bigotry, the God of the discredited past. Secularists are celebrating our defeat.

God who said He *sent* the Jews into exile is the God who *sends* us into the world.

Like the Jews who were constantly reminded that their God was a "loser," we are taunted by the secularists who delight in the supposed weakness of the church. And yet, the God who said He *sent* the Jews into exile is the God who *sends* us into a world that wants us to remain silent about our "antiquated" views. As Rod Dreher, senior editor of *The American Conservative*, writes, "The cultural left—which is to say, the American mainstream—has no intention of living in post-war peace. It is pressing forward with a harsh, relentless occupation, one that is aided by the cluelessness of Christians who don't understand what's happening."[12]

We have lost the culture war. The winners are drooling over the spoils. But we must remember that God didn't abandon the Jews to random fate, nor does Jesus abandon us to our own foolishness. Jesus promises us, "Behold, I am with you always, to the end of the age" (Matt. 28:20). Things are not what they appear. Temporary victories and defeats do not tell the whole story. *That story will only be written when Jesus returns to settle forever who the winners and losers are.*

Babylon, the United States, the Middle East, China— God is not intimidated by humanism, Islam, or American leftists. He will lead us if we seek Him. When we trust His care, there is no combination of Satan along with his demons that can permanently defeat us if God thinks we still have work to do.

Horrific suffering brought the Jews to a point of desperation. It took the destruction of their country to make them willing to turn from their idols. God knows, and we must agree, that only desperate people pray, only desperate people seek Him. God has humbled us as a church, exposing our weakness, compromises, and sins. Sometimes only *devastation* brings *desperation*.

Unacknowledged pride and self-confidence birth prayerlessness. As someone once said, "Prayerlessness is our Declaration of Independence."[13] Lack of prayer signals lack of humility. No wonder we stand powerless against the onslaught of evil in the media, in our schools, and even in our homes. We have to repent of many sins, among them, perhaps first among them, is *prayerlessness*.

Despite our great needs here in America, few evangelical churches have a regularly scheduled prayer meeting. When I asked a megachurch pastor if they had a prayer meeting and he replied, no, I asked a follow up question: "How bad would it have to get before you scheduled a regular prayer meeting?" He did not give me a clear answer.

What will it take?

The Encouragement of Divine Sovereignty

Let's face the question head-on: Is our God a loser? We cannot worship as long as we pessimistically believe our God is losing to the gods of our culture. To make my point, I must return to the conflict between God and Marduk. If you were to ask a Babylonian, "Whose God won?" they would confidently say Marduk. The evidence seemed unassailable. Just look around and see the weakened Jews cower in their subpar housing, forced to serve the Babylonians.

But make no mistake, Jehovah ruled victoriously even when His people suffered defeat! God—the God of the Jews—had the Babylonian armies in His hands. They could not have moved against Jerusalem without His express permission and direction. God is still in charge even when His people lose. He is there when His people are lied about; He is there when His people are taunted; He is there when His people are martyred. Martin Luther is quoted as saying, "Even the devil is God's devil."

The Jews returned to Jerusalem just as God predicted. Centuries later, another promise was fulfilled: the Messiah, who would offer His *shalom* to the world, was born in Bethlehem. "Peace I leave with you; my peace I give to you. Not as the world gives do I give to you. Let not your hearts be troubled, neither let them be afraid" (John 14:27).

The bottom line: Confidence in God's unassailable sovereignty fuels worship. Only those who see God even in their defeats can offer Him praise at all times just as the psalmist wrote, "I will bless the LORD at all times; his praise shall continually be in my mouth. My soul makes its boast in the LORD; let the humble hear and be glad. Oh, magnify the LORD with me, and let us exalt his name together!" (Ps. 34:1–3).

Even the defeated Jews can give God praise and worship!

The Rewards of Reasonable Risk

Jerusalem. Babylon. Chicago.

Living in Babylon had its risks. As evangelicals, we have often fled Babylon rather than redeem it. We don't have a good track record in seeking the *shalom* of our cities. We have either isolated ourselves from the obvious needs around us, or we have fled Babylon entirely.

D. L. Moody had a heart for Chicago and was a risk taker. He said, "Cities are the centers of influence. Water runs downhill, and the highest hills in America are the great cities. If we can stir them we shall stir the whole country."[14] He founded The Moody Church in 1864 because he needed a place where the street-toughened children of his Sunday school would be welcome. The churches of the day didn't appreciate him bringing children into church who were rowdy, fidgety, and often dirty. From humble beginnings, The Moody Church was founded, and later, the Moody Bible Institute was founded. The impact of the church and the school in the heart of Chicago for the past 150 years cannot be calculated. Moody used to say, "If God is your partner, make your plans big!"[15]

D. L. Moody is long gone, but God has raised up a new generation that carries on his legacy in the city. One of our members, Donnita Travis, volunteered through The Moody Church to help students from a notorious housing project with their homework. Struck by a love for the kids, she felt led to start a holistic after-school program with the vision of helping children from Chicago's high-risk, inner-city neighborhoods experience the abundant life Jesus promised (John 10:10). In 2001, she launched what is now known as By The Hand Club For Kids.[16] Beginning with sixteen students, the ministry has grown to nearly 1,400 kids from four of the most underresourced and crime-ridden neighborhoods.

Donnita, along with hundreds of volunteers and a paid staff, literally and figuratively take kids by the hand and walk alongside them from the time they enroll all the way through college. By The Hand takes a holistic approach to child development, caring for the children mind, body, and soul. Each child is mentored and tutored. The ministry is so successful that 82 percent of By The Hand freshmen have gone on to graduate from high school. And 88 percent of its high school

graduates have enrolled in a college or technical school, compared to only 40 percent for Chicago Public Schools. Many
have come to trust Christ as their Savior and Lord.

Let me also challenge us with the story of Brian Dye and
his wife, Heidi, who live in Garfield Park, which a few years
ago, had the distinction of having more murders than any of
the other seventy-seven neighborhoods in Chicago.

For several years, Brian has been involved in planning
Legacy Conferences that train and equip thousands of young
adults from cities across America to make disciples in their
own communities. Along with this, the Dyes are providing
leadership to the Legacy Christian Fellowship whose mission is to establish house churches, all led by bivocational
pastors, in each of Chicago's neighborhoods.[17]

The strategy of the entire ministry can be simply stated: Life-on-Life training. Over lunch in Brian and Heidi's
home, they explained to me that they have no biological
children but have had dozens of "children" live with them
throughout the years (somewhere between 150–175). Their
house has rooms for as many as eight guests. Presently, six
young men from the neighborhood are living with them—all
in different stages of spiritual growth.

The Dyes have walked alongside men who have no family, those who struggle with addictions, and those who have
experienced abuse. When I was there, a twentysomething
young man told me that, without the Dyes, he would have
been dead a long time ago. He volunteered that he was not
yet saved, because "he loved sin too much." The Dyes have
stories to tell of men who came to Christ as they were, despite their love of sin, and have gone on to live for God and

make a difference for the kingdom.

I asked the Dyes whether stealing might be a problem. "Yes. That has happened." One Christmas, when they were gone, their television set and computer were stolen. So they decided they would not replace these items (they do have laptops), and there would be little worth stealing in their house. Although there are regular reports of random violence in the neighborhood, they sit with friends on their front porch during the summer and are a welcoming committee for all who walk by. What impressed me most is the obvious joy they had in "doing life" with those who really can contribute nothing in return for their service.

I'd like to think that many of the Jews in Babylon had a similar ministry with their pagan neighbors. Selflessly meeting the needs of others—loving people without holding their sin against them and showing them a better way—has always been and always will be the most important doorway for sharing our faith.

There are dozens of faithful pastors here in Chicago who live in the neediest and crime-ridden neighborhoods, doing ministry, life on life, giving hope to their communities. I'm glad to report that some of the most high-need neighborhoods in Chicago have a credible witness to the gospel, lived out in the lives of His faithful servants.

They tell us that there are great risks, but also great rewards.

THE CROSS PLANTED IN THE TOWN SQUARE

Let us read every word of this challenge from George Mac-Leod, a twentieth-century Scottish clergyman, who reminds us where the cross of Christ should be planted. We can't change the world from a distance:

> *I simply argue that the Cross be raised again at the centre of the market-place as well as on the steeple of the church. I am recovering the claim that Jesus was not crucified in a cathedral between two candles, but on a cross between two thieves; on the town garbage-heap; at a crossroad so cosmopolitan that they had to write his title in Hebrew and in Latin and in Greek . . . at the kind of place where cynics talk smut, and thieves curse, and soldiers gamble. Because that is where churchmen should be and what churchmanship should be about.*[18]

There is no quick fix. We can worship in beautiful cathedrals; we can have glorious music and great preaching. But Jesus modeled life-on-life training. And we will not impact the cities and towns of our world unless we live among those who need to hear the gospel through an authentic witness. It is not only the church *gathered* that will win the world, but the church *scattered* that will show the beauty of Jesus to a world that is short on hope. Our impact will be marginal as long as we play safe; Jesus didn't and neither can we.

Jesus prayed, "I have given them your word, and the world has hated them because they are not of the world, just as I am not of the world. I do not ask that you take them out of the world, but that you keep them from the evil one" (John 17:14–15).

The church must be *in* Babylon but not *of* Babylon.

CHAPTER 3

CONFLICTS OF CONSCIENCE

Keeping the Faith in a Hostile Work Environment

The old adage is true: God won't put you where He can't keep you.

No one proved that more than Daniel who was conscripted to work for King Nebuchadnezzar, a pagan whose armies threw Jewish babies against rocks. Daniel sought the well-being of this king who was steeped in the occult and wanted those who served him to have the same training. There's no way to explain Daniel and his friends except for this: they had to personally prove that the presence of God was more powerful than the presence of evil.

Daniel and his three friends (whom we shall meet in a moment) remind us that when God judges a nation, the righteous suffer along with the wicked. These four men (I'm sure there were many others) had a heart for God and were obedient to His will. But when the Babylonians came, those devout men experienced the same earthly consequences as did all the newly arrived refugees.

These four men had deep convictions. But they introduce us to the question: How far can we engage our culture without compromising our convictions? Where do we draw the line? These are questions committed Christians are asking, and the church must be prepared to give some answers. At least we must find principles that guide us.

Devout Jews and Christians have often been lawbreakers; from midwives who refused to kill male babies in the days of Moses to the apostles who refused to obey an order against preaching the gospel, those who are godly have often faced the choice of whether to obey God or man. And sometimes the answer is not clear. As Russell Moore put it, "A Christianity that is without friction in the culture is a Christianity that dies."[1]

There are several kinds of conflicts we can have with our culture.

Sometimes conflicts arise because of state or federal laws. American Christians have had to wrestle with many questions in this arena. A recent debate involved whether Christian businesses had to participate in a national health care program that funds abortions and subsidizes contraceptives or the abortion pill.

I also think of the numerous examples of florists, photographers, and bakers who, on religious grounds, have a deep conviction that they should not bake cakes, provide flowers for, or photograph a same-sex wedding. They feel that such participation would show support for the homosexual life-style and, thus, go against the clear biblical teaching about homosexual conduct. Yet they have been pressured to conform or have been severely penalized for standing for their convictions. We can be grateful for the Supreme Court ruling in the *Masterpiece Cakeshop* case in June 2018, when it ruled in favor of the baker Jack Phillips, who refused to bake a cake for a same-sex wedding because of his religious convictions. But no doubt this ruling will soon be challenged. This is only a narrow, temporary victory.

We also find conflicts in the workplace. Our church received an email from a teacher who was told that he had to call students with the pronoun of their personal preference. For example, a biologically male student might identify as a girl so he should be addressed as "she" in the classroom. At home, he might be Bert, but at school, he's Bernice. This teacher was told by his principal, that for the parent/teacher conference, however, "she" must be referred to as "he," since Bert's parents were unaware that he is Bernice in school. The parents had no right to know that their son is transgender. Now the question or conflict is this: should a Christian teacher play this deceptive game?

There are other workplace rules that insist that employees be silent about their religious beliefs Bibles have been banned from desks and employees are told they cannot wear crosses as jewelry because it might offend other employees. Our military chaplains have been told they are not free to share biblical convictions that might offend certain service personnel, especially as it pertains to sexuality.

Then, of course, there are personal, domestic issues that

create conflicts of conscience. For example, I received emails from two separate mothers. One was asking whether or not she should go to the wedding of her son who is marrying a woman who is part of a cult; to make matters worse, the bride's father is a prominent leader in the cult and wields a great deal of authority.

The other mother wrote that her daughter is marrying a same-sex partner, and her family is divided on whether they should attend the wedding. Some argue yes, they should participate so that they don't lose connection with the daughter; other family members say no, because attending the wedding is a sign of approval.

What should a family do?

WHAT SHOULD OUR ATTITUDE BE?

How do we respond to conflicts of conscience in a pagan culture? In the previous chapter, we learned that one way is to continually oppose the culture. We can self-righteously shout to the people around us to get off our moral turf; we can even become angry evangelicals—angry because our freedoms are being taken away, angry because of corrupt politicians, angry because of judges who legislate their own bias rather than taking the Constitution seriously. In short, we can be angry because our culture often needlessly forces us into an ethical corner whether we like it or not.

Of course we have to take a stand against the culture, but we must do it in a way that never loses sight of Jesus. We stand against the culture with a redemptive mindset. We have to take account of culture, to be aware of what is going on in our world, and to accept it as far as our conscience allows, but then we have to draw the line and say, "This far but no further."

Or, alternatively, we can assimilate and blend in with the culture. We can go with the flow, arguing that we all have to live and that we should never become known for "what we are against." We can justify our compliance in the interest of love and our families, or by saying it's best for our career, or by pointing to others who have made similar world-affirming choices. Cowardice is very attractive in an oppressive culture.

Interestingly, God didn't ask Daniel and his three friends to distance themselves from their pagan surroundings; He asked them to engage with it. As we have already learned, they were to "seek the *shalom* of the city." God would give them wisdom as to where to draw the line, and eventually, they would have to prove their loyalty to God by risking their lives. But for now, they were to connect and help a pagan government—not run from it.

They teach us that you can even serve a person who is evil if you are mature and know where to draw the line! Not everyone is capable of handling such a delicate assignment, but they knew that Nebuchadnezzar needed to be introduced to the true God.

CULTURAL SENSITIVITY TRAINING

The Babylonians knew that they could take advantage of the hapless immigrants whom they had captured. They found four young Hebrew men who were swift learners and could be trusted advisors to the king.

> *Then the king commanded Ashpenaz, his chief eunuch [his chief of staff], to bring some of the people of Israel, both of the royal family and of the nobility, youths without blemish, of good appearance and skillful in all wisdom, endowed with knowledge, understanding learning, and competent to stand in the king's palace, and to teach them the literature and language of the Chaldeans.*

(DAN. 1:3–4)

In other words, they were to be immersed in Babylonian culture in order to serve Nebuchadnezzar!

By all accounts, the king set a high bar for those chosen to work with him in his government. He assigned them a daily portion of the food and wine that he himself ate and drank. "They were to be educated for three years, and at the end of that time they were to stand before the king. Among these were Daniel, Hananiah, Mishael, and Azariah [better known as Shadrach, Meshach, and Abednego] of the tribe of Judah" (Dan. 1:5–6). After three years they would know the Akkadian language and understand the religious and political culture of Babylon.

Nebuchadnezzar was not a considerate king to work for. In his conquests, he sanctioned one atrocity after another. But he did have the good sense to enlist brilliant and wise Hebrews to be employed in his court. Under his direction, his associates prepared the young men for their important political and social assignments. The four young men accepted the king's offer; they were willing to help the king in advisory positions.

For three years, they were educated in Nebuchadnezzar's

court; they were introduced to the literature and customs of Babylon. They were inundated with various kinds of pagan ideas regarding sexuality, the meaning of life, and all of the "wisdom" found in Babylonian mythology. The intention was to brainwash them for future service so that they could be trusted to benefit the pagan kingdom. Basically, they became experts in Babylonian protocol.

Larry Osborne in his book *Thriving in Babylon*, writes: "Babylon was also known for its demonic influences. The state-sponsored religion was satanic, and the core curriculum in the schools of higher learning included a large dose of astrology and the occult."[2] Yet these three young men endured pagan indoctrination without losing their faith. They knew that this would take resolve, but it would be possible. We wish we knew more about how they managed to live out their faith without being contaminated by the culture, but they succeeded.

The Indoctrination Continues

The king decided to change their Jewish names, which reflected some aspect of God's nature, to the names of pagan gods. So Nebuchadnezzar had his chief of the eunuchs rename them. Daniel, meaning "God is my judge," was renamed Belteshazzar, meaning "Bel's prince" (Dan. 1:7). Bel was a title for their demonic god Marduk. It would be like having your name changed to "Satan's prince." In the same way, the names of the others were changed, each reflecting the religious culture of the day. These four friends endured the name change to bless their pagan culture and seek the *shalom* of their city.

One other note: I agree with Osborne, who writes that almost certainly these four men suffered through the humiliation and agony of castration. Though not recorded explicitly, there are two reasons to believe it was so. First, the king's right hand man was "the *chief eunuch*" (Dan. 1:3), and this means that those who served with him would themselves be eunuchs. After all, the king had a harem of many beautiful women, and to keep the men who served in his palace from becoming involved with them, castration was routinely practiced.

Secondly, there is no reference to these men's wives or their genealogy or offspring. Knowing the importance of marriage and of keeping genealogies in Jewish culture, we would be surprised that they would not be documented.[3]

These men had every reason to hate Nebuchadnezzar: for his cruelty, for stealing their freedoms, for trashing their own faith commitment. But God said, in effect, "Don't be angry for *I have appointed you to be a witness where you are.*"

Think of it: get over your hatred and serve your enemy!

We have no idea how many dreams died in these men when they found themselves in Babylon. Dreams of a family, dreams of having a home in their beloved city of Jerusalem. God would replace their dreams with His dreams that they be faithful to Him, no matter the cost.

DRAWING THE LINE

But there was a limit to their concessions to pagan culture. "But Daniel resolved that he would not defile himself" (Dan. 1:8). What a critical statement! The King James translation that I memorized years ago reads, "Daniel purposed in his heart."

One of our interns at The Moody Church told me that it was that statement, "Daniel purposed in his heart to not defile himself," that kept his life pure in the midst of the temptations of Chicago. He *purposed*, he *resolved*, in his heart that he would not defile himself.

One of the lines drawn by these four youths dealt with food. Daniel would not eat the "gurma" food that was set before him. Interestingly, we don't know exactly what they found unacceptable about the food. However, we can say with a high degree of confidence that the food was not kosher; it probably also had been offered to idols. It likely signified the "good" life, a life of revelry that Daniel didn't want to be associated with. For whatever reason, Daniel said, "I draw the line here," and so he spoke to the chief of staff and said, "I don't want to eat this food. And I don't want to drink the king's wine."

It's not necessary for us to know exactly why the food was unacceptable in order for us to appreciate the fact that Daniel and his friends lived out their convictions no matter the cost. Matters of conscience can vary from culture to culture, but each of us must purpose in our hearts that we will not allow culture to dictate our values.

Keep in mind that Daniel didn't just say no to the food, he had the wisdom to suggest an alternate possibility. He knew that the intention of the king was their good health, so Daniel said in effect, "Feed us vegetables for ten days, and if we are not as healthy as all those who are eating the king's food, then we will concede that you have a point." Nebuchadnezzar's chief of staff agreed with the test. At the end of ten days, the four Jewish boys' faces glowed, and they were healthier than those who ate the king's food (see 1:12–16).

By no means is this the only place where Daniel drew the line! Subsequently we learn that he also became an advisor to the new king named Darius. Some of the king's cohorts hated Daniel and his God so they prodded the king to make an edict that would entrap Daniel. The king—God bless him—perhaps did not even understand why he was pressured into this new decree. It read in effect, "Whoever prays to any other God other than the king must be thrown in the lions' den" (see Dan. 6:7).

Daniel refused to be intimidated. He continued to pray with his window open toward Jerusalem. Three times a day he knelt and prayed to God, and refused to pray to the king. He was thrown into the den of lions, but the lions' mouths were closed, and no matter how hungry they were, they didn't touch Daniel. He was released unharmed (read the story in Daniel chapter 6).

Did Daniel know that he would be delivered from the lions by an angel? Absolutely not! We can assume he expected to be torn to shreds. Centuries later, Christians would be thrown to the lions in Rome. They would not be as fortunate. They are proof that it is not necessary to experience a miracle to be faithful to God.

Daniel's convictions were rock solid. He had made compromises he could live with, but some matters were nonnegotiable. "I can help the king, I can advise the king, but I will not compromise my faith in Jehovah. It is all a matter of *resolve*."

I certainly don't want to give the impression that I think we can imitate Daniel and his friends in being indoctrinated with an occult education. My point is that we should never underestimate God's commitment to keep us where He plants us. There is much in pagan society that you can conscientiously be associated with; but there is much that we must stay away from. That line might not be drawn in the same place for everyone. May God give us the wisdom to know where it should be drawn for us.

COLLEGE STUDENTS LOSE THEIR FAITH

Why do so many of our young people fail where these four Hebrews succeeded? Why, after their second semester, do many college students who attended church all their lives, memorized all the right verses, and sang the right songs say they no longer believe the gospel? Why is it that between 60 and 80 percent of "previously engaged Christian youth become disengaged with their faith as they transition into college"?[4]

Three reasons come to mind.

Recently, I spoke to a young woman who said she was having doubts about God, and for the time, at least, she had become agnostic. Rather than confront her intellectual questions, I asked if I could hear her story. Turns out that her doubts about God sprang from disappointment and anger toward God because of the rejection she experienced growing up. I'm glad that I was able to share with her that as long as her doubts were honest, God would meet her need. I have learned that doubts are often based on emotional struggles rather than intellectual arguments. If God does not seem to be meeting our need, we begin to have doubts. Atheism is often rooted in anger and disappointment with God.

A second reason students lose their faith is because of moral pressure, peer pressure, falling into sexual relationships outside of marriage, and not knowing how to bounce back from guilt and failure. So, having fallen into a moral rut, they write home and tell their parents that they no longer attend church because they have become "atheists."

A woman who has had a long track record with Inter-Varsity Christian Fellowship said she "unquestionably agreed" with me that the pressure in universities is so overwhelming that Christian young people lose their resolve, fall into immorality, and then find all kinds of intellectual reasons why they are abandoning their faith. They are not prepared for co-ed dorms and the morally depraved "annual sex week," along with friends and professors who encourage all forms of sexual expression as if there were no severe consequences to such behavior. I've heard it said that most college students are not *talked* out of their faith, they are *mocked* out of it.

Shamed into silence.

That's not to say that intellectual arguments are unimportant; there are good answers available to combat these attacks against Christianity. But when your worldview is shattered because you are plagued with guilt and addictions, then the intellectual questions serve to affirm your lifestyle. Centuries ago, Martin Luther's colleague Philip Melanchthon offered

> Most college students are not talked out of their faith, they are mocked out of it.

this clear insight, "What the heart loves, the will chooses and the mind justifies."[5]

There is a third reason young people lose their faith. We *teach* them in our churches, but we don't *train* them. We think that hearing the truth is sufficient; we think that as long as they have "accepted Jesus" they are ready for the sex-saturated, evolution-istic, anti-Christian bias they'll encounter in many colleges.

Training involves immersion in real-life situations with extensive feedback from students to make sure that they both understand and can articulate their convictions. Topics that should be included are the reliability of Scripture, the advantages of creationism over evolution, and the rationality of the Christian worldview of ethics, sexuality, and personal values. Training means anticipating the future by interact-ing with those who have actually weathered the cultural and moral storms of a secular college education. Without realis-tic training, our students are blindsided by the indoctrination they are about to receive.

And they need to be told that their first few weeks in college will almost certainly determine the direction their lifestyle will take. Without seeking out other Christians, without finding a gospel-empowered church and the resolve needed to withstand the pressure, they will be swept away and may even walk away from their faith. Early on, they must self-identify as Christians and be spiritually and mentally ready for the consequences.

Listening to a youth pastor, teacher, or a thirty-minute sermon once a week hardly prepares our young people for the spiritual conflict they will encounter in college. I agree with a person who said that "we are trying to give swimming lessons on dry land."

Although little is said about how these Hebrew youths were able to maintain their faith in a pagan environment, I can imagine they had fellowship together. I can imagine them meeting for prayer and discussing the duress they faced each day in their work environment. And they most likely encouraged each other in their fellowship with God.

OUR CULTURAL CHALLENGES

As we struggle to know where to draw the line, here are some principles to follow.

We Must See God, Not Marduk

I return to the theme I introduced in the last chapter, and that is the conflict between Jehovah and Marduk.

Nebuchadnezzar was convinced that Marduk answered prayers. When he dedicated his famous temple, the king prayed, "O merciful Marduk, may the house that I have built endure forever, may I be satiated with its splendor . . . and receive therein tribute of the kings of all regions, from all mankind."[6] In what appears to be an answer to the king's prayer, when his triumphant armies left Jerusalem, they took with them "some of the vessels of the house of God" and Nebuchadnezzar placed them in "the house of his god . . . in the treasury of his god" (Dan. 1:2).

Every day Daniel and his friends walked into the temple to advise the king, they walked past the vessels taken from the temple in Jerusalem. This, to the populace, was visual proof that Marduk triumphed over Jehovah.

Let's pause and think about this.

Of course, we know that Marduk did not actually win. Note how the book of Daniel begins, "The *Lord gave* Jehoiakim king of Judah into his [Nebuchadnezzar's] hand" (Dan. 1:2). Notice the phase "The *Lord gave*." We continue to read, "And *God gave* Daniel favor" (Dan. 1:9).

> God is sovereign internationally, but He is also sovereign personally.

Let's put these phrases together: GOD GAVE the Jews into the hand of their enemies. And GOD GAVE Daniel favor. And we continue reading, "As for these four youths, GOD GAVE them learning and skill in all literature and wisdom, and Daniel had understanding in all visions and dreams" (Dan. 1:17). Clearly, nothing happened without God's personal permission. Jehovah called all the shots!

To quote Ed Stetzer, "The world's illegal rebellion is illegitimate. It certainly *feels* real, of course— IS real—but it doesn't change the reality that God is still Ruler of everything. Though people may *think* they have rebelled, they have not—and cannot—ultimately escape the fact that King Jesus still is sovereign."[7]

God is sovereign internationally. He is the God of the nations, but He is also sovereign personally; indeed the hairs of our head are numbered. If all that we can see in our defeats is Marduk (Satan), we will be discouraged. Let us be assured that if Satan does win, it's only by God's sovereign decree. The devil's victories are temporary and only gain for him greater torment in the fires of hell. What appears to be a satanic victory is in reality a huge, eternal defeat.

Either because of our failings or because of God's hidden purposes, we are where we are by God's divine will (some might want to call it His *permissive* will). That's why we can face our present dilemmas with confidence and triumph. If we seek God in humility and repentance, we can count on His favor. We don't hang our heads in shame, but rather hold our heads in triumph.

Marduk is a loser. King Jesus reigns.

God knows the longitude and latitude of our little boat as we cross the tempestuous sea. He knows the strength of every board. He knows the trajectory of the wind and its speed. Let us never say there are so many disturbing trends in our society that we must simply blend in with the culture as best we can. Nor should we withdraw from our culture, abandoning it to its well-deserved fate. Let us not divorce God from our predicament, but rather see God in it. The promises of God for His people are still in place!

> *But you are a chosen race, a royal priesthood, a holy nation, a people for his own possession, that you may proclaim the excellencies of him who called you out of darkness into his marvelous light.*
>
> (1 PETER 2:9)

Even in the chambers of an evil king, these four Hebrew men saw themselves as agents of God. And to us Jesus says, "You are the light of the world. A city set on a hill cannot be hidden" (Matt. 5:14). Let us joyfully heed the call.

Let us give thanks that our God is in charge. Joyful worship is our first responsibility and privilege.

We Must Distinguish "Association With" and "Participation In"

These four Jewish men could be associated with an evil ruler and even help him as long as they didn't participate in his evils. God gave these four men the wisdom they needed to navigate this issue of conscience. When asked to eat the king's food, they said no; they correctly read the intentions of the king and suggested an alternative diet that would work just as well. Or better.

Sometimes when we're confronted with a conflict of conscience, we have to ask ourselves if there's an alternative that would be acceptable. Parents may be able to suggest a reasonable alternative to having their children participate in a sex education class in school. Stuart Briscoe, a name that is familiar to many (he and his wife, Jill, encourage missionaries all over the world), tells the story of how when he was in England, working at a bank, the manager wanted his staff to do what was basically dishonest; in effect, it was stealing from their customers. Briscoe, maintaining his convictions told the manager, "If you want me to steal *for* you, what makes you think that I would not steal *from* you if I had the opportunity?" Apparently, the manager was satisfied with that answer and accepted the validity of Briscoe's honesty. Sometimes we can retain our convictions without alienating a relationship.

A Christian doctor can associate with an abortionist; that

is not the same as participating in an abortion. A teacher can associate with colleagues who disagree with him/her on matters of sexuality; what the Christian teacher cannot do is teach ideas that are clearly contrary to Scripture. Paul said we should not associate with Christians who are living in obvious willful sin, but he made clear that this does not apply to fellowship with the unconverted sexually immoral people of the world, or those who were greedy, swindlers, or idolaters "for then you would have to go out of the world" (1 Cor. 5:9–10 NASB). If we say we will associate only with "good people," our circle of influence would be very small. We all need to broaden our friendships and yet determine where we draw the line.

Friendship, yes; participation, no.

When faced with a decision, here is a promise we can rely on: "If any of you lacks wisdom, let him ask God, who gives generously to all without reproach, and it will be given him," (James 1:5). Let our dilemmas be another reason to call on God for help and wisdom.

Where is *your* line in the sand?

We Must Appreciate Latitude of Conscience

In the Bible, there are some things listed that are always wrong under any circumstance. There are also some things that are always right under any circumstance. And then there are some things in the middle over which we can respectfully disagree.

Should you attend your daughter's same-sex wedding? Let us think carefully before giving an answer that applies to everyone. Christians may have legitimate differences of opinion on this matter. In Romans 14, the apostle Paul devoted a chapter to conflicts of conscience. Some Christians, without a twinge of conscience, were able to eat meat that had been sacrificed to idols; others were equally convinced that this was, on the face of it, a compromise with paganism.

If I could summarize, Paul says in effect, "Give yourselves some space because no one can legislate for the other on these matters; one person's conscience is more sensitive than another on this point; don't be quick to judge each other" (see especially verses 10–13).

Let us respect the mother who says, "I cannot attend my daughter's same-sex wedding. I will explain my convictions to her and assure her of my continued love." Let us also respect the parent who says, "I will attend, not because I agree with this sinful union, but because she is my child and I want to show my love for her even though she knows I disagree with her actions."

Even the decision of bakers or flower shop owners may legitimately differ on same-sex weddings. Many would argue (correctly in my opinion) that baking a cake or being the photographer for a wedding is a participatory, even a celebratory, act that indicates approval and a rejoicing with the couple to be married. Whether a Christian does or does not agree to give these services to same-sex couples, this should remain a matter of conscience and not be finally decided by any one of us.

We have to explain to this generation that love and truth are not in conflict, that a conscience informed by truth can be very loving even though it draws a line and says, "I refuse to do this."

No matter what my personal conviction is, love should

always abound, even when I refuse to compromise my convictions. And we remember, "For whatever does not proceed from faith is sin" (Rom. 14:23). Contrary to popular culture, love can say *no*.

What we cannot do is let the world tell us where we should draw the line; the world should not tell us what we can do and can't. Our cultural elites tell us that if we were "loving," we would do what they think we should. But we derive our definition of love from God's Word, not from the vicissitudes of the cultural currents.

We Must Have Deep Personal Convictions

We need an army of Daniels today.

Martin Luther had similar resolve. He affirmed, "Here I stand. I can do no other. To go against conscience is neither right nor safe." Luther said this even though he believed that his stand would cost him his life. As a result of his declaration, the emperor, Charles V, said, in effect, "Anyone who finds Luther can kill him without reprisal." God did spare Luther's life, but he lived the rest of his days anticipating his assassination at any moment.

We must teach our young people to have deep convictions. "I refuse to be defiled. I will respect those who differ from me, but I refuse to compromise my faith to get a better grade, even if it means failure or expulsion. I will not be defiled by the sexual pressure I face daily."

My wife, Rebecca, and I toured East Germany, back when it was still behind the Berlin Wall, under the rule of communism. A pastor there told us that the communists warned the people, "If you go to church, your kids can't go to university. You won't get any promotions, and you will be given the poorest paying jobs." For the most part, the people buckled under the pressure, thinking of their children and families. They said, "If that's the price of living and giving my kids a good education, we'll surrender and obey the State." According to one study, only 13 percent of people in that part of Germany say they have always believed in God.[8]

But there were some courageous Christians who said, "We will not stop associating with other Christians. We will go to church. We will trust God and not surrender to the communists' intimidations." The communists kept their promises. Devout Christians were marginalized, they were given the poorest paying jobs, and their children were denied a good education. As you know, in some communist countries, Christians were imprisoned, tortured, and/or put to death.

Let me ask this: A hundred years from now—in fact, much less than a hundred years from now—which family made the best decision? Is it not those who refused to be intimidated? As a parent, I think I understand how hard it would be for my children to be shunned by their friends and by the authorities. I can't even imagine the hardship of families scrounging for food. But those who trusted God found Him to be faithful, meeting their needs, and most importantly, giving them grace to endure their persecution. But will they not be honored by God for being faithful, no matter the cost?

We Must Commit to Radical Obedience

God had a twofold purpose in bringing the Jews to Babylon. One was to humble them so they might learn how much He hates idolatry. Second, He brought them there to be a light to the Babylonians so that He could be revealed as a promise keeper.

He kept His word, and after seventy years, the Jews returned to Jerusalem, and He gave them "a future and a hope." In essence, God said, "I brought you here not to destroy you, but to refine you. I want to humble you, not forsake you."

Is this also not God's agenda for the church today? Everything that has been nailed down is being torn up. Every day on the news, some new domino falls. The question is, what do we do? Perhaps God is saying, "I am humbling you. I am letting you be defeated so that you might have the opportunity for ultimate triumph."

Meanwhile, we are called to be His witnesses.

Pastor Tim Keller, who is known for his understanding of both the church and culture, warns that we must not just be focused on our culture, but on ourselves. We must see our own failures more clearly than the failures of the world. He writes:

> *Christians should be humbled before the new pagan pluralistic situation. Just as with the exiles, the situation is due in large part to our own failings. The Church did not lose its position of privilege simply because of evil enemies of the faith. We lost our position as part of God's judgment on our pride, our hypocrisy, our love of power, our prejudice, our bigotry and failure to hold onto the truth. This is the way in which God gets people's attention.*

[Then Keller adds a rebuke we all need to hear.]

> *We must be far harder on ourselves in gracious, humble repentance, than we are on the unbelieving culture*

around us. That was a major lesson for the exiles and for us. Our first response should be repentance. We should be very understanding toward people who have failed to believe in Christ because of the weakness of the Church's testimony. A lot of what is happening in our culture today may be more our fault than we are willing to admit.[9]

Jesus was crucified in weakness. He died as an exile, not just from the Jewish community, but from His own followers who were too fearful to be identified with their despised leader. But the seed fell into the ground and bore marvelous fruit. In the very same way, as a church today, we are culturally weak. Oftentimes we are despised, sometimes for good reason, sometimes not. The question is, are we willing to confess our weakness, seek God, and pay the price of living for the gospel? God wants us to represent Him even at a time when He appears to be losing.

Our weakness puts no limits on God's strength. If we acknowledge our helplessness and seek God, His strength will be perfected in our weakness. We can win even when we appear to lose.

"Here I stand, I can do no other, so help me God."

CHAPTER 4

WHEN THE STATE
BECOMES GOD

Standing Strong While Others Bow

Caesar often competes with God for our allegiance. Under ideal conditions, the responsibility of the state is to protect its citizens and to enact laws that will enable them to flourish. But the state often overreaches with laws that conflict with individual freedoms. As a nation drifts from God, pressure builds as the state encroaches on religious liberty and plays the role of God.

Before we begin to talk about the United States, let's review a bit of history. When Jesus held a coin in His hand and said, "Render to Caesar the things that are Caesar's, and to God the things that are God's" (Matt. 22:21), He was teaching that we have two responsibilities: one to God and one to the state. In an ideal context, we can fulfill our responsibility to both; however, conflict between the two has been the primary subject of 2,000 years of church history.

The Roman government was convinced that the unity of the state depended on religious agreement. Refusing to say "Caesar is Lord" was an act of disloyalty to the state—in other words, treason. Caesar competed with God for allegiance, and many who did not bow to Caesar were executed.

After Constantine "Christianized" the Roman Empire (the process began in AD 314), the shoe was on the other foot. Christians were now in charge and implemented the same ideology as the pagans. Soon it became illegal for a person to refuse conversion to Christianity. But even Christians suffered under the rule of this "Christian state." A group of Christians called Donatists believed that the church should be separate from the state and insisted on their freedoms. After years of conflict, the Donatists were persecuted, deemed heretics, and killed. As Bishop of Hippo, Augustine, who for many reasons can be admired as a theologian and philosopher, nonetheless said that God gave the church two swords: the sword of the Word of God and the sword of steel. The latter sword was often used for anyone deemed a heretic.

Charlemagne, who was crowned by the pope on Christmas day in AD 800, decreed that all parents who did not have their infants baptized must be put to death. It was not a matter of theology. The Catholic Church saw infant baptism as a symbol of the unity of Christendom; it was a ritual that gave legitimacy to members of the Holy Roman Empire. Infant baptism was not only the rite that made a child a Christian, but also the rite by which he/she became a citizen of the Empire. So parents had to have their children baptized, or they were put to death. The state played God.

Communism and Fascism are more contemporary examples of regimes where freedom of religion is subservient to the dictum of the state. If churches are allowed to exist at all, they have to obey the laws and regulations of the state. The state may tell families that they cannot homeschool their children, and pastors may be told what they can and cannot say from the pulpit. We all know that Christians have been and are denied freedom of religious expression in such countries, and many over the years have paid dearly for their convictions by imprisonment, marginalization in society, and even death.

The United States of America was different. It was founded on the novel idea that a country can be unified, not on the basis of a common religion, but by a constitution. Thus we have the "separation of church and state." This meant that the state was not to interfere with religious practices. There would not be a state church to which all had to belong. There would not be a litmus test of an approved religion for employment or entrance into the American way of life.

Along with this came the important right of freedom of speech. Unfortunately, the dictum, "I disagree with what you say, but I will fight to the death to defend your right to say it" no longer applies. A Pew Research study found that 40 percent of millennials believe the government should be able to prevent people from publicly making statements that minority groups may find offensive.[1]

Let's be clear that as Christians, we are to speak the truth in love, as Paul admonishes us in Ephesians 4:15. Of course we are not to speak words that come from a place of anger or unkindness; but think about this: in the context of the government being able to limit statements that some groups find offensive, sharing the gospel could potentially fall under such restrictions.

Some fear that freedom of speech, protected by the First Amendment, will allow others to say something that offends them. University students often will protest a campus speaker with whom they don't agree, and many of them believe it is acceptable to silence a speaker by shouting or even resorting to violence.[2]

Here is the irony. The censurers, who are all too ready to deny freedom to those who disagree with them, are perceived by our culture as "tolerant," whereas those who express differing views are "intolerant." In other words, the philosophy of the left is *preach tolerance, but practice intolerance against anyone who has the courage to express an opposing point of view.*

Because of the First Amendment, it's difficult to legally limit freedom of speech. There are those who say that the best way to limit free speech in America is to publicly shame those who express opposition with the present cultural "mainstream," especially as it relates to sexuality. Shaming produces silence.

Hate speech legislation, which has been enacted in Europe and Canada, has rightly protected some but has also limited the freedom of others to be critical of the actions and tenets of certain groups or religions, such as Islam. The Canadian Parliament, by a vote of 201–91, passed Motion 103, which condemns "Islamophobia," the meaning of which is left undefined. Yet, no other religion is protected under this motion.[3] That means that anyone who speaks out against Islam—even radical Islam—is not immune from censure or prosecution. Defenders of Motion 103 say that it is "nonbinding," and therefore not a threat to freedom of speech.

But for many years, Canada has had hate speech laws. Sections 318, 319, and 320 of the criminal code forbid "Hate Propaganda," which can be variously applied. For instance, Pastor Mark Harding was found guilty of this crime because he opposed the promotion of Islam in the schools in his district, a privilege not given to Christianity, Hinduism, or Buddhism. His punishment was two years of probation, and he was subjected to more than three hundred hours of indoctrination by an imam as punishment.[4]

The loss of our freedoms can take an unusual twist. The lawsuit *Christian Legal Society v. Martinez* arose when Hastings University insisted that the Christian Legal Society could not require its leaders to adhere to a certain set of beliefs and behaviors, but it had to be open to all students, without discrimination. This means, among other things, that an atheist could become president of the Christian Legal Society. This action on the part of the university is a denial of freedom of association and the free exercise of religion. The notion that student groups at the university can have no religious, political, or moral requirements for leadership defies common sense and defeats the very purpose of such groups.[5]

One of our greatest threats to freedom of speech today are the proposals to add sexual orientation and gender identity as protected classifications in the law. These proposals, called SOGIs (Sexual Orientation and Gender Identity), "threaten constitutionally protected freedoms of conscience and speech, violate citizens' privacy rights and dignity interests, and expose citizens with sincere, deeply held religious beliefs to significant legal and financial liability if they seek to practice those beliefs in the public square."[6]

Christian schools might have to abandon their policy of opposition to homosexual practices in order to maintain their accreditation. Churches are being told that if they rent out their facilities to outsiders for weddings, they will have to do so for same-sex couples or face a lawsuit. Employers in Christian bookstores or businesses would have to employ any combination of LGBTQ employees to meet the state guidelines.

The church is to equip its members to be obedient to God alone.

Freedom of religion in America is not what it used to be!

In a recent trip to Israel, we visited Masada, where more than nine hundred Jews died holding out against the Roman armies. We learned that these defiant Jews took Roman coins, and over the image of Caesar, they stamped their own Jewish symbols such as the Menorah. They were making an important statement: our loyalty to God trumps loyalty to Caesar. And they died standing behind that belief.

I believe it's the responsibility of the church to equip its members to withstand the heavy arm of the state and be obedient to God alone, despite the consequences. We can take heart. The people of God have encountered this encroachment before; in fact, throughout most of the church's history, believers have always had to choose between God and Caesar.

The early church never prayed that they would be exempt

from persecution, but they did pray for boldness to stand for Christ and endurance when persecution came.

Now for an example that will encourage us.

NEBUCHADNEZZAR, IDOLATRY, AND GOD

When the Jews arrived in Babylon, they were forced to live in a powerful country that took prerogatives that belonged to God alone. In the last chapter, we learned that Daniel, along with Shadrach, Meshach, and Abednego, worked in the Babylonian government and served the state with integrity and divine favor. That was before their faith confronted a serious crisis.

King Nebuchadnezzar had a dream of a man with a head of gold. Daniel was called in to interpret the dream. He told the king that he (Nebuchadnezzar) was the head of gold; as for the other body parts of the man, his chest, torso, legs, and feet represented other kingdoms that were still to arise. It's one of the greatest predictive dreams of history, and it proved to be true (see Dan. 2).

Nebuchadnezzar could not get this image out of his mind. He decided to set up an image of a man (almost certainly an image of himself) that was ninety feet high, set on a base that was nine feet in diameter, and placed in the plain of Dura.

And now for some high drama.

A New Law Regarding Religious Practice

All the inhabitants of Babylon were brought to the plain to stand beneath the tall statue. Then the king issued a new law.

"You are commanded, O peoples, nations, and languages, that when you hear the sound of the horn, pipe, lyre, trigon, harp, bagpipe, and every kind of music, you are to fall down and worship the golden image that King Nebuchadnezzar has set up" (Dan. 3:4–5).

Nebuchadnezzar became the "divine lawgiver," and with his new law came heightened consequences for disobedience. Those who wouldn't bow before the image were to be thrown alive into a fiery furnace!

The orchestra sounded, the music began, and thousands of people bowed on cue. But three men remained standing! (We don't know where Daniel was that day, but if he had been there, he most assuredly would have joined his friends in defiance.)

Someone who resented these three young, "stubborn" Jews told the king that Shadrach, Meshach, and Abednego had refused to bow to the image. Enraged by their refusal, the king called them in for a personal conversation. Paraphrasing his speech in the vernacular of our day, he said, "Perhaps you didn't get the memo—everyone is to worship the image when the music begins. Maybe you didn't understand, so I will give you a second chance. We will have a redo, and I expect you to comply" (see Dan. 3:13–15).

Their reply was immediate.

"O Nebuchadnezzar, we have no need to answer you in this matter. If this be so, our God whom we serve is able to deliver us from the burning fiery furnace, and he will deliver us out of your hand, O king. But if not, be it

known to you, O king, that we will not serve your gods or worship the golden image that you have set up."

(DAN. 3:16–18)

This is one of the greatest expressions of faith found in all of the Bible. *We believe our God will deliver us, but if He doesn't, we will not bow before your image. We will bow but only before the God of heaven!*

Nebuchadnezzar was livid: "Then Nebuchadnezzar was filled with fury, and the expression of his face was changed against Shadrach, Meshach, and Abednego. He ordered the furnace heated seven times more than it was usually heated" (Dan. 3:19).

Then he ordered some of the mighty men of his army to bind the three men and throw them into the burning, fiery furnace. We read, "Then these men were bound in their cloaks, their tunics, their hats, and their other garments, and they were thrown into the burning fiery furnace" (Dan. 3:21).

Here we get a glimpse into Nebuchadnezzar's evil heart. These three men were his advisors; they had survived his rigorous indoctrination program; they had served with integrity—surely their religious convictions should not be penalized by death. But such tolerance was not to be.

The men who threw the three Jewish men into the furnace were themselves consumed by the flames. To his astonishment, Nebuchadnezzar saw that the three bound men were walking around in the flames unsinged! He was incredulous, "Did we not cast three men bound into the fire? . . . But I see four men unbound, walking in the midst of the fire, and they are not hurt; and the appearance of the fourth is like a son of the gods" (Dan. 3:24–25).

THE QUESTION FOR US

Here's what we'd like to know: How did Shadrach, Meshach, and Abednego have the courage to remain true to their convictions? They expressed the hope that they'd be delivered, but they were prepared to be reduced to ashes. "You can throw us into the fire, but we'll not deny our God."

Whence their courage?

They Trusted the Promises of God

Shadrach, Meshach, and Abednego trusted the promises of God. We don't know how acquainted they were with the prophet Isaiah, but almost certainly they knew that God said to Israel:

> "But now thus says the LORD,
> he who created you, O Jacob,
>   he who formed you, O Israel:
> "Fear not, for I have redeemed you;
>   I have called you by name, you are mine.
> When you pass through the waters, I will be with you;
>   and through the rivers, they shall not overwhelm you;
> when you walk through fire you shall not be burned,
>   and the flame shall not consume you.
> For I am the LORD your God,
>   the Holy One of Israel, your Savior."
>
> (ISA. 43:1–3)

Of course they were likely wise enough not to interpret this promise as an assurance of their deliverance, nor should we. There have been plenty of martyrs who were burned at the stake. This promise found in Isaiah was to affirm the perpetual existence of the nation of Israel—not a promise that any individual would be delivered from the flames. But this much they knew: *delivered or not, they could count on the presence of God.*

Perhaps these three men remembered Psalm 73 when it was read in the synagogue back in Jerusalem.

> *Nevertheless, I am continually with you;*
> * you hold my right hand.*
> *You guide me with your counsel,*
> * and afterward you will receive me to glory.*
> *Whom have I in heaven but you?*
> * And there is nothing on earth that I desire besides you.*
> *My flesh and my heart may fail,*
> * but God is the strength of my heart and my portion*
> *forever.*
>
> (PS 73:23–26)

The pressure to compromise our own faith comes down to this: Is God faithful to what He has promised? Is it true that He will never leave us nor forsake us (see Heb. 13:5)? *The question is not whether we will escape the fire, but whether He will walk with us through it.*

In America, we haven't had to be concerned about being thrown into a furnace, but we do have to be concerned about whether we can still preach the gospel and its implications in our churches. We have to be concerned about whether chaplains in the military can share the gospel. We have to be concerned whether our churches are legally compelled to be rented out for same-sex weddings. We have to be concerned about the sexualizing of our children in the public schools.

We have to get back to the basics: Are God's promises valid or not?

They Trusted the Providence of God

Shadrach, Meshach, and Abednego so confidently trusted God that they left the choice as to whether they lived or died in His capable hands. We know how the story ended, but they didn't. When they were thrown into the fire, as far as they knew, they were going to be incinerated; they were destined for the ash heap. But they believed their responsibility was to be faithful to God; the outcome was His.

One lesson we should *not* take from this story is that God always delivers His people from the fire or that He always sends an angel to close the mouths of hungry lions. Church history is filled with stories of faithful believers being burned at the stake or thrown to the lions; even today, hundreds of Christians are killed each month for their faith. They die without divine intervention.

Hebrews 11 is often called the great catalog of the Heroes of Faith, but this chapter wasn't written to teach us how to do miracles like Moses, Elijah, and Daniel. Instead, it points us to a more profound truth: those who suffer and die without seeing any form of deliverance are heroes of faith; they also are heroes because they kept on believing even when there was no empirical evidence that God cared about them!

Don't miss this. Hebrews 11 has a radical change of tone

in verse 36. After listing many miracles in the first thirty-five verses, we suddenly read, "*Others* suffered mocking and flogging." Then follows a list of horrors that those other believers endured. There was no "fourth man" delivering them from the flames, no intervening angels to close the mouths of lions; no parting of a Red Sea—these others suffered without a hand from heaven. Yet, these nameless ones are also deserving of great reward.

In Acts 12, James and Peter were in prison. King Herod chose to kill James. Peter was told he was next. Peter fell asleep the night before his expected execution (perhaps because he wanted to arrive in heaven rested!), but unexpectedly, an angel woke him and opened the doors of the prison to lead him to a prayer meeting where all of his friends had gathered.

My point: we simply don't know why one person is allowed to live while the other is martyred. Those mysteries are hidden in the mind of God; we call it *providence*.

We don't live by explanations but by promises.

Blessed is the person who prays, "God, we know you are able to deliver this young mother from cancer. But if You don't, we won't swerve in our devotion and faith in your name." Our heavenly Father is unpredictable. He sometimes delivers us out of the fire; at other times He lets us be burned in the flames. Either way, He is with us; we are not abandoned in this life or the next. We might not see a miracle of deliverance on earth, but heaven awaits us. Meanwhile we don't live by explanations but by promises.

We don't just suffer for ourselves; we also suffer for those who see us. Jesus warned His disciples that they'd be persecuted for His sake: "and you will be dragged before governors and kings *for my sake*, to bear witness before them and the Gentiles" (Matt. 10:18). I'd like to think that many ISIS members have come to personal faith in Christ after witnessing the death of Christians they have martyred. The apostle Paul recalled the impact that Stephen's martyrdom had on him (see Acts 22:17–20).

It is said that just as some Christians were being torn to shreds by lions, they were not just looking into the sky, it was as if they could see something or *Someone*. Perhaps like the first martyr, Stephen, they already saw Jesus welcoming them at the right hand of God the Father.

The "fourth man," who delivered Shadrach, Meshach, and Abednego, walks with us, even when we don't see Him. We don't have to be delivered in order for us to experience His presence.

Let's agree that we will stop trying to read God's purposes through an envelope. We might see a phrase or two, but we don't understand the full sentence nor the total eternal picture. I have stopped trying to predict what God will do in a certain situation. He has surprised me too many times!

TRANSFORMING LESSONS FOR US

Perhaps we won't be thrown into a furnace, but some among us might lose our jobs because we won't sanction same-sex unions or we express our disagreement with sharia law. Or we might lose customers or friends for violating an accepted dictum of political correctness.

Opposition Is to Be Expected

We need to embrace our predicament and to do so with joy. Peter, writing to believers living under the intolerant Roman Empire, said:

> *Beloved, do not be surprised at the fiery trial when it comes upon you to test you, as though something strange were happening to you. But rejoice insofar as you share Christ's sufferings, that you may also rejoice and be glad when his glory is revealed. If you are insulted for the name of Christ, you are blessed, because the Spirit of glory and of God rests upon you.*
>
> (1 PETER 4:12–14)

When faced with obedience to either the state or Jesus, we must always choose Jesus. Several years ago, many evangelicals (along with some leaders who were not specifically evangelicals) signed a document called the "Manhattan Declaration: A Call of Christian Conscience," which affirmed our commitment in the face of growing opposition from state interference. Part of it read:

> *We will not . . . bend to any rule purporting to force us to bless immoral sexual partnerships, treat them as marriages or the equivalent, or refrain from proclaiming the truth, as we know it, about morality and immorality and marriage and the family. We will fully and ungrudgingly render to Caesar what is Caesar's. But under no circumstances will we render to Caesar what is God's.*[7]

We must "purpose in our hearts" to stand for liberty of conscience, not just for ourselves, but for those who disagree with us. This is why the phrase "separation of church and state" is so essential. We insist on the freedom to live out our personal convictions as guided by Scripture.

Fear and anger are not options for Christians. We must be able to emulate the early church, which considered it a privilege to be identified with Jesus within a hostile culture.

Let's not be surprised when the next shoe drops.

We Must Learn to Stand Alone

Weren't there about 10,000 Jews who made the trek from Judah to Babylon? Did all of them bow before the image? Maybe they were on the other side of the plain and nobody saw them standing instead of bowing. But I think it's more likely that they bowed when the music began. They said to themselves, "In our hearts we know we are not bowing to the image, we are bowing to Jehovah. So we'll bow, but God knows that in our hearts we are still standing up."

What would we have done?

Because some gay rights groups target those who oppose same-sex marriage, one evangelical church I'm aware of has contemplated removing the names of its elder board from its church website. The fear is that activists may target elders for harassment, which could include pressuring employers to dismiss these men for adhering to the sanctity of biblical marriage.

I understand the pressure, but are we as a church going to buckle because of threats, harassment, or even the loss of our livelihood? Should Shadrach, Meshach, and Abednego have

114

bowed with their bodies but not with their hearts? I pray that the church in America will live up to its convictions and accept the consequences. Anything less discredits the power of the gospel we profess to believe.

There are Christian men and women who will not bow their heads in a cafeteria or restaurant to give thanks to our heavenly Father because they don't want to be identified as a Christ follower. Yet Jesus said, "For whoever is ashamed of me and of my words in this adulterous and sinful generation, of him will the Son of Man also be ashamed when he comes in the glory of his Father with the holy angels" (Mark 8:36).

The majority of the Jews bowed to the golden image because *they feared the furnace more than they feared God.* From our more recent history, we don't remember many names of those who opposed Hitler, but we do remember Dietrich Bonhoeffer and Martin Niemöller and a few others. We remember them for one reason: they did not bow to an earthly agenda. At times, they stood almost entirely alone. Cowards are not long remembered.

Don't misunderstand. Of course there are many heroes who are unknown to us, but they are known to God. We think of millions of nameless Christians who have been shunned, ostracized, and martyred who will be especially honored because of their faithfulness. Whether known or unknown on earth, heroes calculate the long-range consequences, preferring to be honored in eternity rather than on earth.

The resolutions of Jonathan Edwards, an influential eighteenth-century theologian, are sometimes summed up this way: "Resolution One: I will live for God. Resolution Two: If no one else does, I still will."[8]

It Is Not Necessary for Us to Have Freedom to Be Faithful

Study the history of the church and you will be surprised that our freedoms in the West are an anomaly: for most of the last 2,000 years, the church has not had freedom of religion. The story of Christianity is filled with those who were sent to prison, burned at the stake, drowned, or made to dig their own graves and then buried alive.

Let us also never forget that it's unnecessary for us to win in this life in order to win in the life to come. We think, for example, of John Hus, who in 1415 was burned at the stake in Constance for preaching the gospel in Prague. He lost in this life, but he won in the life to come. We think of Polycarp, who died in Smyrna in the early centuries; we think of the many martyrs in our generation, especially those in closed countries, who will receive special honors for dying well for the sake of the gospel.

There is a day coming when the state will defiantly replace God. Regarding the coming evil beast, we read that he blasphemes the God of heaven "and authority was given it over every tribe and people and language and nation, and all who dwell on earth will worship it, everyone whose name has not been written before the foundation of the world in the book of life of the Lamb who was slain" (Rev. 13:7–8).

Imagine! Authority over every tribe, people, language, and nation! Most will bow to the beast, but there will be a remnant that won't, and they'll be given special honor for all of eternity. They are described above as those whose names were written in the Book of Life before the foundation of the world.

While in California, a friend took us to see the grave of

Frank Sinatra, which is marked with a lyric from one of his songs: "The Best Is Yet to Come." That, of course, is true for believers in Christ, but not for unbelievers. Theirs could read: "The Worst Is Yet to Come."

What a difference an eternal perspective makes!

The Power of an Authentic Witness

Incredibly, cruel King Nebuchadnezzar, the very man whose armies captured Jerusalem, the man who sought the worship of all of his subjects and intended to incinerate those who refused, the man who prayed to Marduk—*that* man came to trust in the living and true God!

You weren't expecting that, were you?

After witnessing the deliverance of the three men in the furnace, the king sent out a decree that only the God of Shadrach, Meshach, and Abednego was to be worshiped. Anyone who spoke against their God was to be punished "for there is no other god who is able to rescue in this way," (Dan. 3:29).

And there's more.

Nebuchadnezzar, whose ego knew no bounds, bragged about his accomplishments. But God humbled him by sending him to live with animals and even eat as they do. "He was driven from among men and ate grass like an ox, and his body was wet with the dew of heaven till his hair grew as long as eagles' feathers, and his nails were like birds' claws" (Dan. 4:33).

This humiliation resulted in his apparent conversion to the God of heaven. He affirmed the sovereignty of God over all peoples and nations: "Now I, Nebuchadnezzar, praise and extol and honor the King of heaven, for all his works are right and his ways are just; and those who walk in pride he is able to humble" (Dan. 4:37).

Michael Rydelnik, professor of Jewish studies at Moody Bible Institute, believes we have solid reasons to believe that Nebuchadnezzar genuinely repented and submitted himself to the God of heaven and therefore will be among the redeemed![9]

We know that Daniel prayed three times a day, most probably for the two kings he served. His witness along with that of Shadrach, Meshach, and Abednego bore fruit. The ruthless king for whom they worked, the king who had been an enemy of the Jews, *this king* was converted and gave powerful evidence that he exclusively worshiped the God of heaven.

God sometimes surprises us by saving the worst of sinners, the most unlikely infidel. Who is the Nebuchadnezzar in your life for whom you are praying and witnessing?

FROM A PASTOR'S HEART

Chrysostom was a preacher in ancient Constantinople (today called Istanbul). He was run out of town and hounded by the authorities because they detested his preaching against the abuse of wealth and power.[10] His people wanted to defend their pastor, and so they took up sticks and stones, but of course, they were no match for the growing opposition. Just like today, we often feel powerless in the wake of our cultural opposition.

Nevertheless, the congregation gathered in the church for his last sermon before he was exiled to die. Let me give you a paragraph of what he said:

Numerous are the waves, and great the tossing of the sea, but we have no fear of going down, for we stand upon the rock. Let the ocean rage as it will, it is powerless to break the rock. Let the waves roll, they cannot sink the bark of Jesus. Tell me, what should we fear? Death? To me to live is Christ and to die gain. *Is it exile perchance? The earth is the Lord's, and the fullness of it. Is it confiscation of property? We brought nothing with us into this world, and it is clear that we can take nothing away with us. I despise what the world fears, and hold its good things in derision. I do not fear poverty, nor do I desire riches. I am not afraid of death; I do not pray to live, if it be not for your good. This is why I speak of what is now taking place, and exhort your charity to be of good cheer.*[11]

And so it is, we can be of good cheer because our enemies are limited by God's purposes in what they can do. Someday the strongest political power this world has ever seen will rule through the Antichrist as described in Revelation 12 and 13. This future dictator will usurp the place of God and demand worship from all who live on the face of the earth. How will the saints withstand this powerful worldwide geopolitical regime?

"They conquered him by the blood of the Lamb and by the word of their testimony; for they did not love their lives to the point of death" (Rev. 12:11 csb).

CHAPTER 5

THE CHURCH, TECHNOLOGY, AND PURITY

The Courage to Confront a Deadly Enemy

The church has a responsibility to be involved in culture, but today, culture comes—often uninvited—into our homes, our bedrooms, and our hearts. And this "culture" wars against our souls; it opposes our quest for purity and personal holiness. Its influence is insidious and often evil.

Let's suppose you woke one morning to discover that someone had stolen your children while you were sleeping. They were abducted so silently that you never woke up. You frantically search for your kids while you speed dial the police. If you had the good fortune of discovering your children unharmed, you'd take maximum precautions, doubling the locks on your doors, barring your windows, and installing a high-tech, ultrasensitive security system.

But what if we already have a monster in our homes that doesn't steal our child's body, but does steal something even more valuable—the child's soul? You are left with the obligation to clothe and feed your child, but his or her heart would be owned by another master. Think of the conflict, the struggles, and the arguments that would ensue as you tend to the child's physical needs, but his or her devotion is to a monster that has the potential to mislead, deceive, and otherwise destroy your son or daughter.

This monster is, of course, *technology*.

Even as I write this chapter, my fear is that many people who read it will completely agree with what I am about to say but will do nothing about the negative impact that technology is having in their personal lives and the lives of their families. They'll deem this monster too powerful and too seductive to confront. "The demon is in too deep." And the excuses are many.

Yes, I know that technology is being used for good purposes. At The Moody Church, our media ministry harnesses the internet to reach people all over the world. Thanks to technology, Islam itself has been forced to weaken its grip on its subjects because they have access to Western news outlets and Christian programming. Technology can be used for either good or evil. A knife in the hand of an angry man can be devastating, but the same knife in the hands of a surgeon is valuable indeed.

But we make a mistake to emphasize the benefits of technology without confronting its dark and destructive influences. The church today has to go head-to-head with this issue and give families the tools they need to protect their children from these addictive influences.

Rebecca and I are friends with a couple who shared this story about their son whom we shall call Brett. He became addicted to video games; sometimes he would scarcely eat, and his grades began to drop at school. His parents suspected this addiction, but whenever they confronted him, he was defensive and denied that he spent excessive time on his computer. One day when his parents left the house, they set up a hidden video camera. When they returned home, they confronted him, and he again lied, saying he had been doing his homework. The video camera proved otherwise, and he was forced to admit the truth. He began crying, "Mom and Dad, I'm addicted! There's no way out!"

They wisely took his computer out of their house for several days, and when it was brought back, they put severe limits on its use. Eventually, he was delivered from the immediate addiction to his computer; but make no mistake, when certain desires are awakened within us, the temptation to recreate those feelings stay with us and probably will for the rest of our lives. This explains why those who are caught by the allure of violent games or pornography may be freed, but find powerful temptations to return to their former ways.

MYTHS ABOUT TECHNOLOGY

We want to believe the lie that technology is harmless without facing the fact that if not held in check, it's almost instantly addictive. Teens are not the only ones who come under its spell. Many adults spend hours on end scrolling through Facebook, Instagram, or other social media feeds. We have turned a blind eye to what is happening by accepting some myths about technology.

First, we've accepted the lie that technology is neutral, not realizing that it is weighted against a pure mind and Christ-honoring lifestyle. The late Neil Postman, educator and author of *Amusing Ourselves to Death*, wrote a harsh rebuke to those who believe technology is neutral. "To be unaware that a technology comes equipped with a program for social change, to maintain that technology is neutral, to make the assumption that technology is always a friend to culture is, at this late hour, stupidity plain and simple."[1]

Postman argued that every technology has a bias; it has an agenda. That's especially true about the internet. Just click on a news site, and you'll see provocative pictures that arrest our attention; yes, nothing is sent to us without a bias, often a very tempting one. The media opposes us at almost every turn. It is not neutral! By and large, it is opposed to our core values.

Second, there is the myth that what we watch doesn't affect us. However, various studies have shown that violent video games and other media can produce both short-term and long-term aggressive behavior in adolescents and adults;[2] and we hardly need a study to prove the degenerative effects of pornography use on everything from marital relationships to how young people view sex. Why would advertisers spend billions for ads if what we see doesn't affect our behavior? Let me put it even more strongly: *we become what we enjoy looking at*.

A third myth is that we can control technology by simply

telling people to hit the "off" button. Many people cannot turn off the television, the computer, their tablets, or their smartphones because of the addictive power of these technologies. As a result, marriages and homes are being destroyed. One man told me that he and his wife come home from work, eat a hastily prepared dinner, then she sits at her computer and enters a chat room with her friends till about 11 p.m. They have no meaningful communication, make no new friends, and each evening repeat the same routine. When he tries to talk with her about it, she becomes defensive and blames him for the boring existence they have together.

According to psychiatrist Thomas Kersting, author of the book *Disconnected: How to Reconnect Our Digitally Distracted Young People*, addiction to technology is not only widespread but it rewires our brains. He sees many children in his practice and has noted that the use of technology affects their ability to flourish while also producing anxiety, depression, and attention issues.[3]

I can't imagine life without email, but as for the internet itself, when I was told that its growth worldwide has been fueled by pornography, I think it would have been better if it had not been invented. The internet has become a recruiting tool for anarchists and a platform for bloggers who pontificate on various matters with no accountability for their supposed facts or moral judgments.

SOCIAL MEDIA, WHERE VENGEANCE IS DISGUISED AS JUSTICE

I am grieved by the way in which social media is being used (or rather misused) in today's overheated and angry culture. Christians are falling into the snare of sniping at each other in ungodly ways, all "for the sake of truth." I am reminded of Paul's words in Galatians: "through love serve one another. . . . But if you bite and devour one another, watch out that you are not consumed by one another" (Gal. 5:13, 15). Yes, we now have a platform where we can, if we wish, bite and devour others.

Of course there are responsible bloggers, but as I read some blogs and comments written by Christians, I have noticed the following:

First, whatever the perceived fault that is being exposed, it is often exaggerated and put into the worst possible light. No one seems to be willing to give a fellow believer the benefit of the doubt. Responses come in attack mode, with exaggerated comments, embellishments, and distortion. The sniping and accusations among Christians after the 2016 election made me wonder whether we had forgotten that we are citizens of a larger kingdom. As fallen creatures, all of us are prone to believe the worst about others rather than to believe the best. Of that, let us repent.

Second, I often find very little charity, but rather anger and self-righteous rhetoric with no concern about any reconciliation or love that might "cover a multitude of sins." Matters that should be dealt with privately are exposed for the whole world to see. Many online pontificate with an air of self-assurance as if they have the responsibility of bringing somebody down because of some perceived indiscretion. This is a long way from Paul's admonition: "Brothers, if anyone is caught in any transgression, you who are spiritual should restore him in a spirit of gentleness. Keep watch on yourself, lest you too be tempted" (Gal. 6:1).

Is there a place for exposing facts and situations for the wider Christian world? I think there is, but I suggest the following guidelines going forward.

Why do you think that your proposed exposé is necessary to bring glory to God? What God-honoring goal do you have in mind?

Have you gone to this person and/or institution to make sure that your facts are not only correct but also in balance and in context?

If you are writing about a particular person, would you say these things to their face? Or do you find it safe to shoot arrows from a distance, immune from uncomfortable personal interaction?

Do you write with the goal of bringing about restoration and/or reconciliation whenever possible? Or are you writing out of a spirit of anger and personal hurt?

Are you under the authority of a church or Christian institution to whom you owe accountability for your own life and actions?

My plea to my fellow believers: Let's dial down the rhetoric. Let's not tell ourselves that all the faults of others should be exposed; let's not write about each other out of a spirit of revenge or anger and then call it justice. Let us believe the best about each other and be reluctant to believe the worst. Let's treat others the way we would want them to treat us.

Long before the rise of social media, Paul wrote, "Let no corrupting talk come out of your mouths, but only such as is good for building up, as fits the occasion, that it may give grace to those who hear" (Eph. 4:29).

Those are words this generation needs to hear.

HEARTS DRAWN AWAY FROM GOD

The verse for this generation is Proverbs 4:23, "Keep your heart with all vigilance, for from it flow the springs of life." Your heart is the place where life makes up its mind. Little wonder so many teenagers—yes, I'm speaking about Christian teenagers—often find it difficult to focus on their relationship with God. YouTube seems to have more excitement than the Bible, and Facebook does more to stroke the ego than a devotional book.

The smartphone in the palm of our hand brings the knowledge of the world to us. Its capacities challenge our imaginations. Today, young people get more of their education about sex and other issues of life from the media than they do their parents or church. The average child spends hours each day using a smartphone, computer, television, or tablet.

One evening at a youth conference, I walked to the back of the auditorium and noticed the many students who were on their cellphones. No, they were not looking up Scripture, because the speaker had not, at that point, announced any Scripture passage.

I agree with those who say that media may constitute the most powerful education systems known to man. Cultural critic Ken Myers sees the media onslaught on our culture as more insidious than persecution. He writes, "Enemies that come loudly and visibly are usually much easier to fight than those that are undetectable . . . but the erosion of character, the spoiling of innocent pleasures and the cheapening of life itself that often accompany modern popular culture can occur so subtly that we believe nothing has happened."[4] Remember, the goal of much of the media is to ensnare your child (or *you*, for that matter) into various forms of sensuality. The goal is always to enliven the appetite for "more." I agree with Ravi Zacharias that we are "a generation that listens with its eyes and thinks with its feelings."[5]

Today kids are being raised by television, computers, and iPads. In one week, I interacted with two sets of parents who discovered that their teenager (age sixteen in both instances), knew how to bypass any filtering systems on their computer and smartphones. A year later, one of them discovered that their teen was secretly downloading explicit pornography, and the other learned that their teen was into demonic mind games. Both are dealing with teenagers who are angry, depressed, and even threatening.

Technology has the power to seduce, to enslave, and to destroy human decency. Like a lighted match thrown into a can of kerosene, our sexual desires can be easily awakened, and those desires keep demanding more and more. In each of us, there's a small voice that tells us we are about to embark on a destructive path, but we think we can control the consequences. We're lying to ourselves—and we know it. It's frightening to realize that one bad choice can set you spiraling down a path of destruction.

I shall never forget what a man who had been arrested for child pornography told me: "Once you start down that path, you end up going to places you never thought you'd ever go." *Once you start down that path, you end up going to places you thought you'd never go!*

It has been said that the ultimate test of a moral society is the kind of world it leaves to its children. We have to fight for ourselves and for future generations.

The world is using technology to vie for our lifelong devotion. A parent recently said to me, "In retrospect, giving my daughter a cellphone was like giving her her first shot of heroin."

THE CRITICAL ROLE OF THE CHURCH

Fighting against the negative effect of technology is an important responsibility of the church. The reason can be simply stated: walking in obedience and fellowship with God is always a communal enterprise, and when it's necessary to help people overcome the destructive effects of repetitive sin, the church must be available, open, and ready to help. I know of no one who has successfully fought and won these personal battles alone. We don't need anyone's help to get into the swamp—we do that perfectly well on our own—but we cannot crawl out of it without the help of others.

At The Moody Church, we launched a ministry we call the 5:8 Ministry, based on the words of Jesus, "Blessed are the pure in heart, for they shall see God" (Matt. 5:8). With the help of video instruction and personal testimony, many men have been freed from internet addiction through instruction, accountability, and corporate prayer. There are other kinds of models of ministry available; each church must find the one leadership believes will be best.

Unfortunately, there are many pastors who simply ignore the dangers of the media. They are willing to affirm the old adage that "technology is neutral and it just depends what you use it for." And with that, they are lulled into a peaceful sleep, a quiet satisfaction that the destructive effects of media won't affect their home, their congregations, or even themselves. Evidently they think that if they look the other way, it'll eventually go away. Meanwhile, the inner core of the church is being contaminated by the presence of this secret monster. The rot is well hidden, but it is everywhere.

A youth pastor in California said that he assumes that every young person who joins their group is addicted to pornography. If he finds someone who isn't, then he's grateful, but he has to operate on that assumption given the widespread use of computers, tablets, smartphones, and other kinds of technology. The temptations are immediately accessible, powerful, and unrelenting. Perhaps his assumptions are a bit over the top, but let's give this young man credit for recognizing the elephant in the room, an elephant that some pastors will not even talk about.

Jesus, speaking personally to the church in Thyatira, chided the congregation about their lax approach to sexual sin. He commends them for all of the good work that the church was doing, but then says, "But I have this against you, that you tolerate that woman Jezebel, who calls herself a prophetess and is teaching and seducing my servants to practice sexual immorality" (Rev. 2:20).

Jesus is not finished. He goes on to say, "I will strike her children dead. And all the churches will know that *I am he who searches mind and heart,* and I will give to each of you according to your works" (Rev. 2:23). Imagine, He searches our minds and hearts and the hard drives of our computers!

If the first-century church could not avoid the sensual spirit of Jezebel, how can the twenty-first-century church avoid the greater temptation of a Jezebel that stalks every home through ubiquitous media outlets? Jezebel is now at our fingertips.

Church leadership must take an active role in helping those who find themselves grasping for help. The church should not turn away from the silent suffering of those who don't know where to turn and are too ashamed to find the help they need. These personal struggles never resolve themselves on their own.

How can we as a church ignore the heart of Jesus who seeks a pure bride? We need one another. And in the fellowship of believers, there is hope.

THE SPIRITUAL BATTLE

Back one night in the 1990s, the same day we hooked up to America Online, I had a demonic dream. Three demons were pinning me against a wall, and I felt powerless. What a relief it was when I realized that, indeed, it was just a dream. I interpreted this dream as God's gift to me: He was saying, in effect, "You now have an enemy in your home that will try to destroy you."

Maintaining mental and spiritual purity while surrounded by the temptations of technology thrusts us into a new level of satanic warfare. The church should be helping all of us realize that we are in a spiritual battle. The Bible says that Satan "prowls around like a roaring lion, seeking someone to devour." If you watch Animal Planet, you already know that a lion does not roar when he's on the hunt for prey. He roars to mark his territory. He lets every other competitor know that "this territory is mine." He dares another lion to contest it. I believe it's not too strong to say that Satan has marked technology as his territory. He says, "*This is mine; here I rule.*"

> Satan has marked technology as his territory. He says, "This is mine; here I rule."

There is a battle raging in the invisible world. The minute you begin to win some victories, the opposition intensifies. Satan's one desire is to draw our souls away from God; then he substitutes pleasure, guilt, self-condemnation, and anger in God's place. The devil wants us to continue to violate what we know to be right and so fills our minds with a list of rationalizations. Satan doesn't respond to sweet reason, he doesn't play by the rules, and he won't go down without a fight. Churches need to help, guide, and encourage their people to confront the enemy. There is nowhere to hide. This is not a war that can be won without prayer, earnest prayer, and intercessory prayer. And accountability.

While you are reading this chapter, some people were awake all last night trying to invent new ways to hook your child and make them slaves to the latest video game, movie, or sensual images. When the late Hugh Hefner began his pornographic "empire," he relied on a new crop of boys each year to become addicted. And we have to admit, he was successful. He fulfilled his dream by destroying the dreams of millions of others who ended up with immorality, broken marriages, unrelenting shame, and hearts indifferent toward God.

I write the rest of this chapter to help parents think through their critical role as gatekeepers in the lives of their families.

THE HOME, THE GATEKEEPER

Let us hear the Word of the Lord: "[The priests of Israel] have done violence to my law and have profaned my holy things. They have made no distinction between the holy and the common, neither have they taught the difference between the unclean and the clean" (Ezek. 22:26).

What an interesting indictment!

It's the responsibility of the parents, most importantly the father, to teach children the difference between the clean and unclean. The father has the responsibility to protect himself and his family from would-be intruders. And if there is no father in the home, then some other gatekeeper, probably the mother, has to take charge. To reference the message of the late Mark Bubeck, we are faced with the challenge of raising lambs among wolves.[6]

Peter wrote these words before the internet and smartphones: "Beloved, I urge you as sojourners and exiles to abstain from the passions of the flesh, which wage war against your soul" (1 Peter 2:11). We've all experienced that war, sometimes losing, sometimes winning.

Surveys show that most parents have no idea what their children are watching. Add to that the fact that fathers are often clueless about the great influence they have in their homes. One said, "Don't blame me for the fact that all of our kids are messed up. I'm never home!"

Let's Begin with Ourselves, the Parents

As parents, we have to prepare our own lives for personal holiness. Parents who are addicted to technology and all its temptations lose their moral authority to discipline their children. Many a father has found himself tongue-tied, unable to admonish or discipline his son because he (the father) is guilty of the same behavioral pattern. Unconquered sin makes parents angry and passive, unable to speak to moral issues that need resolution.

I don't know what God will demand of you to be victorious over your own issues of anger, disrespect, or lust. But Jesus said, "If your right eye causes you to sin, tear it out and throw it away. For it is better that you lose one of your members than that your whole body be thrown into hell. And if your right hand causes you to sin, cut it off and throw it away. For it is better that you lose one of your members than that your whole body go into hell" (Matt. 5:29–30). Of course, He wasn't speaking literally. You could gouge out your right eye and still lust with the left. But Jesus *is* saying, "Do what is drastic . . . do whatever you have to in order to find the help you need to be delivered from the snare of sensuality."

135

As parents, we must model Christian behavior. If you don't want your children to watch certain programs, then *you* don't watch them. And if you're watching something and a risqué advertisement comes on, you switch channels and discuss with your child why you did that. Talk about the power of sensuality and how the advertising industry thrives on it. We can't expect them to live one way if we are living another. Make use of teachable moments.

If father and mother are angry with each other and disagree on principles of discipline and rules, children will take advantage of the confusion. Parents, at all costs, must be unified. They *must* be unified if they intend to protect their children from these distracting forces within the home. And let us not forget that shaming only fuels addiction; only an open, understanding attitude can create an atmosphere of help and moral sanity.

To the single parent: God bless you. You mothers, you have to be a mother and a father to your child; you fathers, you must also be a mother to your child. But all isn't lost; God is on your team. God is greater than our brokenness and loss, greater than families affected by divorce, unplanned pregnancies, or death.

Taking Critical Steps

Let these words form an image: "A man without self-control is like a city broken into and left without walls" (Prov. 25:28). What a picture of a life without safeguards. Whatever enemy is outside the walls can enter in, whether invited or uninvited. Without self-control, our heart is like an open door that welcomes every enticing image or idea that carries us off to the world of worthless imaginations.

What specifically should parents do?

Establish a healthy and workable relationship with their child

Author and speaker Josh McDowell frequently says, "Rules without relationship leads to rebellion."[7] As a parent, if you only condemn your children for what they're doing or seeing on their electronic devices, that will put an end to all communication. You must enter into your child's world, not to condemn, but to understand, to guide, and to "connect." And after you have won a hearing, you can be more direct, more helpful.

Parents must remember that their child is a sexual creature, created in the image of God as either male or female. God built into our natures a deep and unrelenting desire to connect with the opposite sex. This desire is innate, it seeks satisfaction, and it will not take "no" for an answer. This urge is not to be condemned, but it must be controlled and channeled.

Unfortunately, you will almost certainly be unable to keep your child from seeing explicit material, either at home, at school, or at a friend's house. Only a good relationship with a parent or guardian can give the child perspective and alternatives to this seductive, bottomless pit.

Become educated about the resources available to block material on an electronic device or television

Allow computers, tablets, and other such devices to be used only in public spaces in the home and absolutely never allowed in the child's bedroom! The number of children who stay awake spending time on their favorite addiction instead of sleeping is high. Past research has shown that 70 percent of teenagers "accidently" come across pornography on the internet, and we can be sure far more children are exposed once they intentionally seek it out.[8] Yes, you have to set ground rules regarding when and how computers and electronic devices can be used, and teach the child what to do if they stumble on a pornographic site. Filters of various kinds should be installed. And check your child's browser logs regularly to see where they've been surfing.

What do you say to a child who argues, "You don't trust me," when you insist that there be no electronic device in the bedroom, especially at night? Respond by saying, "No, I don't trust you, because I don't even trust myself!" Children should never have an unrestricted right to privacy in a home. Interaction should always be respectful but clear.

Avoid a herd mentality. Just because "all fourth graders" are getting their own smartphones doesn't mean your child should have one. Your child may hate you for your strictness but grow to love you even more when they are older and realize what you spared them from.

Be watchful for what your child is learning and seeing in school

Public schools should protect children, but given the climate and pressure of politics and the culture, they're often doing the opposite. Parents must realize that in many cases, sex education classes expose children to topics parents would never imagine and teach children about sexual relationships apart from the moral values necessary to undergird such knowledge.

Tammy Bruce, who was the head of the National Organization for Women (NOW) in Los Angeles, has, for the past twenty years, been writing many excellent books that expose the leftist agenda that she knows all too well. She was able to witness firsthand the left's attempts to undermine our millennia-old code of morals and values.

She watched as the leadership of NOW drifted from its original purpose of fighting for women's rights and degenerated into an organization that sought to undercut all distinctions between right and wrong in order to foist their own amoral agenda on the country. In this crusade, NOW was joined by other groups with the intent of reordering society as we know it. These groups, she says, have the intention of *bending society to mirror their warped view of the world.*

She points out that, for radicals, it's not a matter of accepting homosexuality but rather "eliminating the lines of decency and morality across the board. Instead of being about tolerance and equal treatment under the law, today's gay movement, in the hands of extremists, now uses the language of rights to demand acceptance of the depraved, the damaged, and the malignantly narcissistic."[9]

I shall quote one of her passages at length. It deserves a careful read:

> *Today's gay activists have carried the campaign a step further, invading children's lives by wrapping themselves in the banner of tolerance. It is literally the equivalent of the wolf coming to your door dressed as your grandmother. The radicals in control of the gay establishment want children in their world of moral decay, lack of self-restraint, and moral relativism. Why? How better to truly belong to the majority (when you're really on the*

fringe) than by taking possession of the next generation?
By targeting children, you can start indoctrinating the
next generation with the false construct that gay people
deserve special treatment and special laws. How else can
the gay establishment actually get society to believe, bor-
rowing from George Orwell, that gay people are indeed
more equal than others? Of course, the only way to get
that idea accepted is to condition people into a nihilism
that forbids morality and judgment.[10]

Bruce believes the reason these ideas are widely accepted
is that "sexualizing children," as she calls it, guarantees control of the culture for future generations. She writes, "It also
promises sex-addicted future consumers on which the porn
industry relies. By destroying those lives, they strike the final
blow to family, faith, tradition, decency, and judgment."[11]

Bruce devotes an entire chapter of her book to Judith
Levine's *Harmful to Minors: The Perils of Protecting Children*
from Sex. We might dismiss this book as the work of a disengaged activist who speaks for no one but herself. Sadly, this
is not so. Levine is respected in many circles and is highly
regarded in academia.

Certainly the majority of homosexual men and women
would, I'm sure, disagree with Levine's book. But we must be
aware that lying at the core of the radical homosexual movement is the desire to "sexualize children" for the purpose of
control and conditioning. This "grab for children by sexually
confused adults" as Bruce describes it, is the most serious
problem our culture faces today.[12]

Francis Schaeffer, who helped awaken the evangelical
church to its cultural responsibilities back in the 1970s,

would not be surprised were he to step into our world today. He presciently wrote:

There is a "thinkable" and an "un-thinkable" in every era. One era is quite certain intellectually and emotionally about what is acceptable. Yet another era decides that these "certainties" are unacceptable and puts another set of values into practice. On a humanistic base, people drift along from generation to generation, and the morally unthinkable becomes thinkable as the years move on.[13]

> **We are watching as the unthinkable is becoming thinkable right before our eyes.**

Writing in the 1970s, he said that what was regarded as unthinkable back then would become thinkable in the '80s and '90s; and what was unthinkable in the '80s and '90s would eventually be thinkable beyond that. He concludes with this clincher: "Yet—since they do not have some overriding principle that takes them beyond relativistic thinking. . . . *They will slide into each new thinkable without a jolt.*"[14]

Forty years after that was written, many forms of deviancy are now normalized and worthy of special respect. We are watching as the unthinkable is becoming thinkable right before our eyes. Parents must wake up to the new reality that their children must be both protected and instructed to discern between the clean and the unclean. That is a difficult but possible assignment in an era of smartphones, iPads, and computers.

Just because your child is attending a Christian school doesn't mean that he/she is exempt from the corrupting opportunities of technology. And don't ever think that the friends that they have are Christian friends, and therefore that their friends' homes are okay.

You can't take anything for granted; all of us would be surprised at what happens and what is watched even in "Christian" homes. Become well acquainted with your children's friends at school. Do you know where they go after school or where they hang out? Establish rules that your child must follow when they are with other children—and check up on them. Each home is different and will require different rules, but this is important and must be done.

We must prepare our children for the battles they face

You can't be with your children 24/7. In strict homes, parents often pride themselves because they are running a "tight ship" and think if they do all the right things, the child will automatically follow biblical models of self-restraint and holiness. But these well-meaning parents often create resentment in the life of a child who then leaves home and makes up for all the sins he was not allowed to commit when he was under his parents' authority. Then surprised parents turn to preaching at the child, warning, admonishing, shaming, but the child isn't listening because that child's heart is somewhere else. Without a willing heart, there can be no listening ear. The child becomes more secretive and the addiction more destructive.

To help the children understand what they will likely encounter, talk through some situations: what to do if you are invited to see a risqué movie; what to do if your boyfriend/girlfriend wants to initiate a sexual relationship; how to respond when a party gets out of hand; or what to do when called names because you don't do what the "cool" students do.

Share your own struggles with your children. We, as parents, have to get over the idea that in order for our kids to respect us we have to give the illusion of always walking in victory, as if we've never been where they are in the thick of the battle. In an age-appropriate way, parents must talk about their own failures. Haven't we all done things of which we are ashamed? Nothing will open up the lines of communication like the childlike humility on the part of the parent. The children need to know, "Mom and Dad are human. Mom and Dad understand."

Help your family correctly interpret guilt

The purpose of guilt is not to drive us away from God, but it is God reaching out to us to receive His grace for a new beginning. We must remember that God is a restoring God—a God of reconciliation, a God of the second chance. Sin always takes us further than we wanted to go, keeps us longer than we intended to stay, and costs us more than we intended to pay. But, thanks to grace, there are plenty of exceptions to this general rule. There are people who have fallen into every sin imaginable, and they've ended up living good, productive, wholesome lives because of grace. God is indeed the God of the second chance, and the third, and . . .

> **God is indeed the God of the second chance, and the third, and . . .**

"Rejoice not over me, O my enemy; when I fall, I shall rise; when I sit in darkness, the LORD will be a light to me" (Mic. 7:8).

Realize that only God can change the heart of your child

What do you do with a child who is still at home, but whose heart is elsewhere? There's no easy answer. After you have confessed any failures on your side of the ledger, you must simply commit the child to God and wait on Him. You might be able to change his behavior, but only God can change his heart.

We must love God more than we love our sin.

Refuse to enter into arguments. Remember sin is inherently irrational. Teenagers who drink or do drugs have their own skewed version of reality. If the child is so incorrigible that they can no longer live at home, remember the story of the prodigal son: he came to his senses in a pigpen.

We cannot determine God's timetable for bringing prodigals back home. Even when we do all that we can do, let us remember that we must depend on God for all that He can do. "I waited patiently for the LORD; he inclined to me and heard my cry. He drew me up from the pit of destruction, out of the miry bog, and set my feet upon a rock, making my steps secure" (Ps. 40:1–2).

LOVING GOD MORE THAN LOVING SIN

The bottom line is that we must love God more than we love our sin. But this love cannot be manufactured; it cannot be turned on and off like a faucet. The love we have for God must be God-given, the result of conversion. And this love is nurtured through the Word of God and the fellowship of God's people. It grows in response to what God has done for us.

> *See what kind of love the Father has given to us, that we should be called children of God; and so we are. . . . Beloved, we are God's children now, and what we will be has not yet appeared; but we know that when he appears we shall be like him, because we shall see him as he is. And everyone who thus hopes in him purifies himself as he is pure.*
>
> (1 JOHN 3:1-3)

We shall be like Him . . . and *we must purify ourselves even as He is pure.* We all fail in the struggle, but we do not give up. Here is a promise as we face the future:

> *His divine power has granted to us all things that pertain to life and godliness, through the knowledge of him who called us to his own glory and excellence, by which he has granted to us his precious and very great promises, so that through them you may become partakers of the divine nature, having escaped from the corruption that is in the world because of sinful desire.*
>
> (2 PETER 1:3-4)

"Blessed are the pure in heart, for they shall see God" (Matt. 5:8).

CHAPTER 6

TRANSGENDERISM, SEXUALITY, AND THE CHURCH

Calling Out the Lies of the Culture

"Oh that my head were waters, and my eyes a fountain of tears, that I might weep day and night for the slain of the daughter of my people!" (Jer. 9:1).

Let us weep for a nation that has lost its way in its understanding of sexuality. Let us pray for sensitivity and sanity; for help and healing. George Orwell has been quoted as saying, "In a time of universal deceit, telling the truth is a revolutionary act." Let us join together in telling the truth to this generation.

However, if we do not guard our hearts, a discussion of

both homosexuality and the transgenderism debate can readily lead to a self-righteous attitude among those of us who have never had such aptitudes or desires. It's easy to portray those who struggle with gender dysphoria (or identify with the opposite gender rather than their biological sex) as somehow belonging "out there" and forgetting that we're all members of a fallen humanity and humbly grateful for God's undeserved mercy toward us.

We must compassionately see people who are trying to fix themselves.

I write not with a judgmental spirit, but with sadness. The issue of gender dysphoria is theoretical—unless it's your son who tells you that he wants to be girl, or your daughter who tells you that she's a boy trapped in a girl's body. These scenarios are happening more often than we think, and yes, also among Christian families.

Our churches should be welcoming beacons of hope in a world that is broken. We must compassionately see people who are trying to fix themselves, trying to manage emptiness, pain, and loneliness. Like any of us, they're looking for ways to find meaning for their lives, to find a semblance of peace. And they are going to great lengths to do it.

I disagree with those pastors who refuse to discuss these issues because they think that transgender people and homosexuals exist only outside the church, not within its walls. If we claim that the gospel is for everyone and speaks to the whole of life, then we have something to say about these cultural currents that are swirling around us. Let us walk alongside those who tell us that they struggle with various forms of sexual expression.

A SAFE PLACE

Just recently, a distraught grandmother told me that her thirteen-year-old granddaughter came home from school and asked, "Why should we not welcome people who are transgender into whatever bathroom they identify with?" And, "What's wrong with two men loving each other and wanting to be married?"

These are questions that deserve answers within our homes and churches. What our young people (and adults, too) need is a safe place where matters of sexuality can be discussed with openness and freedom from judgment. Parents must provide godly guidance as their children navigate the often confusing journey of development and maturation.

As Christians, we must be willing to engage our culture with compassion and a listening ear, not with condemnation. If all parents can do is quote passages from the Bible without seeking understanding and listening to their child's story, this will only increase the guilt and shame the child may feel. It may push them further, perhaps even to the point of alienation—from their parents, from their church, and from God. Every person wants to be listened to and heard.

We must distinguish between accepting a person and approving of his or her conduct and attitudes. Every human being is created in the image of God and deserves respect; but not every human being deserves our approval of their conduct and lifestyle.

As the prophet Isaiah said, "Come now, let us reason together, says the LORD" (Isa. 1:18). The purpose of this chapter is to awaken all of us to the destructive effects of the sexual revolution and, above all, to provide some direction for our churches and the parents and family members of teenagers who are bombarded with transgender and same-sex indoctrination. If this chapter sparks dialogue and further research into these issues, it will have been worthwhile.

THE CHALLENGES BEFORE US

I was introduced to the reality of transgenderism about thirty years ago when a woman in our congregation told me that she returned home unexpectedly from work only to discover her husband dressed in women's clothing and, in her words, "prancing around the basement." Then she discovered an entire box of women's clothes, including undergarments. Thinking his wife would not be home, this man was caught going through what, for him, was a familiar routine.

The husband would not come for counseling or discussion about his gender identity. The woman told me sometime later that they eventually divorced. Back in those days, such men were known as "cross-dressers," but today, those who may choose to do so have at their disposal the option of body-altering surgery. Their hope in taking this drastic measure is that their body will match their mind.

This was not my only encounter with transgenderism, but it introduced me to the reality of the conflict some families experience when gender is no longer conferred by the Creator but is determined by an individual. The modern man says, "If I *think* or *feel* I am a woman, then I am a woman." And a woman says, "If I *think* or *feel* I am a man, I am a man."

With an air of defiance, many in our generation say, "God did not determine who I am; *I* determine who I am."

Really?

GOD'S WORD AND HUMAN WISDOM

Let's start from the beginning. "Then God said, 'Let us make man in our image, after our likeness. And let them have dominion over the fish of the sea and over the birds of the heavens and over the livestock and over all the earth and over every creeping thing that creeps on the earth.' So God created man in his own image, in the image of God he created him; *male and female* he created them" (Gen. 1:26–27).

God created only two sexes who are to complement each other in marital love, resulting in the development of families that populate this world. If you are a man, you will always have male chromosomes; if you are a woman, you will always have female chromosomes. Every cell in the body is programmed to be male or female. Every person, no matter their sexual orientation, had both a mother and a father; they would not exist otherwise.

So, what exactly is gender rebellion? To put it simply, it's an attempt to blur gender distinctions by saying that it's not your physical anatomy that defines gender, but rather it's what you *feel* or *think* you are. While the roots of gender rebellion are in atheistic evolution, it is being pushed to the forefront of today's society through initiatives such as the feminist movement whose goal is "to reform or eliminate traditional gender roles."[1] This attempt to "reform" gender is destroying families and young people, and it affects us all. It is indeed a time to weep.

WE BEGIN WITH CHILDREN

After reading a *Time* magazine article in 2015 titled, "Meet the New Generation of Gender-Creative Kids," I knew I had to do more research and speak on the topic. The article describes a retreat for gender nonconforming children, ages six to twelve. Among them were biological boys who loved to wear girls' clothing. These boys don't know what gender they'll eventually be—maybe transgender or gender conforming or gender fluid. They don't know, and so the camp wanted to provide a place for "gender-variant children" where they would know they were not alone.[2]

Then there was a study in the UK conducted by Maria do Mar Pereira from the University of Warwick's Department of Sociology. Tara Culp-Ressler, in an article for ThinkProgress.org, summed the research up this way: "Raising children in societies that adhere to rigid gender roles, with fixed ideas about what should be considered 'masculine' and 'feminine,' can actually be detrimental to their physical and mental health, according to a study that observed 14-year-olds' interactions over a three month period."[3]

Pereira observed that the "restrictive norms . . . are harmful to children of both genders . . . men have to be dominant over women . . . boys feel constantly anxious and under pressure to prove their power—namely by fighting, drinking, sexually harassing, refusing to ask for help, and repressing their emotions." While girls "feel they must downplay their own abilities, pretending to be less intelligent than they actually are, not speaking out against harassment, and withdrawing from hobbies, sports and activities that might seem 'unfeminine.'"[4]

The June 2015 *Chicago Magazine* article "The Change Agent" highlights a doctor who helps his clients switch sexes. These clients range in age from eighteen to as young as four. Rob Garofalo says he's "helping them become their authentic selves" by using drugs to stop the natural maturation process so that the children can make the switch more easily.[5] He also has three therapists on staff at his clinic to help the children overcome anxiety and depression.

Aside from the emotional issues, there are the physical issues. When handing a fifteen-year-old patient and his mother a three-page consent form that will allow the doctor to administer estrogen to the young boy, Garofalo admits, "There haven't been many studies on the long-term effects of estrogen on young people . . . there's just so much that we don't know yet."[6] Even though there is still "so much to know," this doctor, and others like him, are preparing to mutilate the bodies of children in an attempt to make them "who they really are."

In the article, "Don't Let the Doctor Do This to Your Newborn," activist Christin Milloy, the first transgender person to run for provincial office in Canada, suggests that your doctor shouldn't tell you whether your newborn baby is a boy or a girl because:

With infant gender assignment, in a single moment your baby's life is instantly and brutally reduced from such infinite potentials down to one concrete set of expectations and stereotypes, and any behavioral deviation from that will be severely punished—both intentionally through bigotry, and unintentionally through ignorance. That doctor (and the power structure behind him) plays a pivotal role in imposing those limits on helpless infants, without their consent, and without your informed consent as a parent.[7]

Remember, these folks are serious in what they write and say.

THE RUSH TO AVOID MISGENDERING

This is what our teenagers just might encounter when they leave our churches for college.

On December 31, 2016, I received a news blurb from the Associated Press about the University of Kansas. They were offering gender pronoun buttons to students so that they could make their preferred gender clear to all and so that transgendered students would feel welcome. A sign at the university's library reads, "Because gender is, itself, fluid and up to the individual. . . . Each person has the right to identify their own pronouns, and we encourage you to ask before assuming someone's gender. Pronouns matter!" It continues, "Misgendering someone can have lasting consequences, and using the incorrect pronoun can be hurtful, disrespectful, and invalidate someone's identity."[8]

The pressure to support transgenderism is growing. Kenneth Zucker, a psychiatrist, who, for decades, led the Child Youth and Family Gender Identity clinic at the Centre of Addictions and Mental Health in Toronto, was fired for suggesting that doctors should take a cautious approach when it comes to children because feelings usually don't persist into adulthood. He encouraged therapists to explore the possibility of helping children become secure with their birth sex. Activists railed against him until the center announced it was winding down its gender identity clinic, which meant Zucker was out of a job and the clinic apologized for being not "in step with the latest thinking."[9]

Zucker's firing put a chill over other therapists who fear for their jobs. John Whitehall, professor of pediatrics at Western Sydney University, wrote, "In fifty years I have not witnessed such a reluctance to express an opinion among my colleagues." He said he polled twenty-eight medical professionals who thought that the rush to change children's bodies was ridiculous, but none wanted to go on record.[10]

At one conference promoting transgenderism, the delegates insisted that those who don't call people by their "preferred" gender should be fired. A nurse was complimented for finally switching gender pronouns for a pregnant mother. Rather than calling her a "she," the nurse finally stated, "*His* cervix and bloodwork look healthy." The patient was so happy because the nurse had finally "gotten it."[11] We also are being told we should "get it."

At this time, all but a few states allow a person—depending on certain criteria—to rewrite history by changing their birth certificate to reflect a change of gender.[12] States where it is not yet allowed may be accused of being hateful and intolerant. Go figure.

GAINING UNDERSTANDING

In *The New Atlantis* Fall 2016 report on sexuality and gender, Lawrence S. Mayer and Paul R. McHugh looked at findings from the fields of biology, psychology, and social sciences. Let me make sure you understand their qualifications before I tell you about their findings. Lawrence S. Mayer, MB, MS, PhD is a scholar in residence at Johns Hopkins University School of Medicine in their Department of Psychiatry, as well as a professor of statistics and biostatistics at Arizona State University.

Paul R. McHugh, MD, was a professor of psychiatry and behavioral sciences at Johns Hopkins University School of Medicine, and for twenty-five years, was the psychiatrist-in-chief at Johns Hopkins Hospital. He has written six books, has over one hundred peer-reviewed articles, and is considered one of the leading psychiatrists in the world.

These two men combined have written five hundred peer-reviewed scientific articles and studies, and explored research done across a variety of scientific fields including epidemiology, genetics, endocrinology, psychiatry, neuroscience, embryology, and pediatrics, as well as empirical studies done in various fields of the social sciences.

Here are just a few of their findings that should make us stop and think before we go rushing into the fray of transgenderism.

- Members of the transgender population are at higher risk of a variety of mental health problems.
- Compared to the general population, adults who have undergone sex-reassignment surgery continue to have a higher risk of experiencing poor mental health out-

comes. One study found that, compared to controls, sex-reassigned individuals were about five times more likely to attempt suicide and about nineteen times more likely to die by suicide.

- Only a minority of children who experience cross-gender identification will continue to do so into adolescence or adulthood. [This should give hope to parents whose children report that they think they are transgender.]
- There is little scientific evidence for the therapeutic value of interventions that delay puberty . . . There is no evidence that all those children who express gender-atypical thoughts or behavior should be encouraged to become transgender.[13]

Keep in mind that transgender surgery can never change anyone's sex. "You are never changing the sex of a patient. Never. Every cell in the body is programmed to be male or female," writes Quentin Van Meter, a pediatric endocrinologist.[14] That is why McHugh labels transgender surgery of minors "child abuse."

LIVING AUTHENTICALLY?

Transgendered people tell us that their bodies don't match their internal reality. The trans movement believes that relief from this dysphoria can only come if the outer "false" appearance is changed to match the inner "true" state of the person. In Bruce Jenner's case, he puts it this way, "Bruce Jenner . . . was 'always telling lies.' Caitlyn Jenner . . . 'doesn't have any lies.' . . . Caitlyn Jenner has the possibility to make it right."[15]

What do we say to those who say they must live according to their feelings or orientation and not according to their biological anatomy? After all, they tell us, they want to live "authentically." Shouldn't people always be "true to who they feel they are"?

What do we say to those who say they must live according to their orientation?

The legendary UCLA head coach John Wooden once said: "Being true to ourselves doesn't make us people of integrity. Charles Manson [now deceased] was true to himself, and as a result, he rightly is spending the rest of his life in prison. Ultimately, being true to our Creator gives us the purest form of integrity."[16]

Sex-reassignment surgery doesn't address the fundamental psychological issues that underlie transgenderism, which McHugh defines as a mental illness. He believes that "to surgically alter someone's genitalia is to enable a disorder," according to one article that outlines some of his findings and conclusions from his book *The Mind Has Mountains: Reflections on Society and Psychiatry*:

> *I have witnessed a great deal of damage from sex reassignment. . . . The children transformed from their male constitution into female roles suffered prolonged distress and misery as they sensed their natural attitudes as males develop. . . . We have wasted scientific and technical resources and damaged our professional credibility by collaborating with madness rather than trying to study, cure, and ultimately prevent it.*[17]

This "madness" brings us to the topic of transableism. Transableism refers to thinking that you're born with body parts that you don't feel belong to you, and so you must rid yourself of these parts to live authentically. In Canada, a man studied how he could amputate his arm without bleeding to death because he always felt that his arm wasn't really part of his body. He cut off his healthy arm because it wasn't part of who he perceived himself to be. As reported in a *National Post* article, he told the body modification website ModBlog, "My goal was to get the job done with no hope of reconstruction or re-attachment, and I wanted some method that I could actually bring myself to do."[18]

There are people who want to be made deaf or blind because these body parts don't really represent who they are. They, too, want to voluntarily disable themselves to be "authentic." The condition, known as Body Integrity Identity Disorder, is a "rare, infrequently studied and highly secretive condition in which there is a mismatch between the mental body image and the physical body," according to one study.[19]

And now there are those who claim to be trans age, such as a fifty-two-year-old man who identifies as a six-year-old girl. Stefonknee (formerly Paul) Wolscht says, "I can't deny I was married. I can't deny I have children . . . but I've moved forward now and I've gone back to being a child." So he left his wife and children in order to live "authentically" as a six-year-old. He continues, "Well, I have a mommy and daddy . . . who are totally comfortable with me being a little girl. And their children and grandchildren are totally supportive." Then this description: "They color and 'do kid's stuff. It's called play therapy.'"[20]

Should we be okay with letting him play with his "peers" in a kindergarten class? Should his family buy him dolls so that he can live "authentically"? After all, should we not applaud him for wanting to live in accordance with who he "really" is?

Absurd?

Of course it's absurd, but in a culture where reason and common sense no longer carry any weight, absurdity is no longer an argument against anything. Our society tells us that we should applaud people for having the courage to "become who they really are." You can't judge anyone as long as they are being true to themselves.

Joe Carter, in an article for The Gospel Coalition, writes, "When your mind has been so seared by acceptance of evil that you condone amputation of healthy body parts, it's not surprising that your ability to think logically has been hindered. If you start with the premise that radical mutilation of the body is an acceptable practice . . . you shouldn't be surprised to find it applied in ways that are different, yet equally disturbing."[21]

We should not be surprised that the Pro-Ana community believes that anorexia nervosa is a chosen lifestyle and should be respected by society. Starving yourself within an inch of death to make your body look like you think it should makes your "inner person" correspond to the "outer person." It's all okay as long as you're being true to yourself.[22]

THE CRUX OF THE MATTER

National Geographic magazine calls their January 2017 Special Edition, dedicated to the Gender Revolution, "historic."

It advocates the present cultural view that we need a radical proposal about the fluidity of gender even though it's at odds with both natural law and biblical anthropology.

In discussing this issue in the Witherspoon Institute's "Public Discourse," Andrew Walker and Denny Burk rightfully ask, "Why is it acceptable to surgically alter a child's body to match his sense of self but bigoted to try to change his sense of self to match his body? If it is wrong to attempt to change a child's gender identity (because [transgender activists say] it is fixed and meddling with it is harmful), then why is it morally acceptable to alter something as fixed as the reproductive anatomy of a minor?"[23]

Let me ask it this way: does a man who has a healthy arm surgically removed because he doesn't feel it is a rightful part of his body have a body problem or a mind problem? When a man who is fifty-two identifies as a six-year-old girl, does he have a body problem or a mind problem? Does a woman who has anorexia and starves herself to death have a body problem or a mind problem? Just so, when someone argues that they are transgender and, therefore, contemplating irreversible gender reassignment surgery, we must help them understand that they do not have a body problem, but a mind problem. It goes without saying that there is also a spiritual problem!

The middle-aged man should not be allowed to "authenticate" himself by living like a little girl; the man who thinks that his arm is not really a part of who he is should not have it amputated; and the transgender person should not have irreversible gender reassignment surgery. Those who struggle with these issues must seek help in reordering their mind.

Even if they never experience the realignment of the inner feelings with their outer body, as Christians, especially, they also must seek the transforming work of the Holy Spirit and commit themselves to holy living in their relationships.

In addition, we must tell this generation that a life of celibacy can have the special blessing of the Lord. People must be urged to not act on their feelings either by having gender reassignment surgery or entering into defiling sexual relationships. To best communicate this, the church must welcome them and help them find a home.

THE BLESSINGS OF CELIBACY

Years ago at The Moody Church, we had a conference on sexuality during which a married couple came to ask for advice. One partner was a man who had reassignment surgery and now identified as a woman. "She" was married to her husband, a man. Recently, they both had become Christians and knew immediately that what they had done was displeasing to God. The "woman" told me that she was willing to have another series of surgeries to become a man again, if this is what God wanted. But she added, "These surgeries are so traumatic, I think it would kill me." We discussed the problems in their sexual relationship, and I suggested that rather than "reverse surgeries," they consider the option of living celibate lives. We can't undo the past, but we can glorify God in whatever situation we find ourselves.

Let me commend to you the thoughtful book *Loving My LGBT Neighbor: Being Friends in Grace and Truth* by Glenn T. Stanton, who helps us break stereotypes and shows us how to love our Lesbian/Gay/Bisexual/Transgender friends. The advice he gives to Christians who struggle with same-sex attraction applies equally to those who are transgender. He writes, "There are untold thousands of faithful and beautiful saints in so many churches across the world who are same-sex attracted, struggling with those temptations, but have made the choice to live celibately because that is what God calls all people to when they have not entered into His plan for marriage."[24]

> Marriage is blessed in the Bible, but so is celibacy.

Marriage is blessed in the Bible, but so is celibacy. Jesus Himself spoke of eunuchs; that is, those men who have no natural attraction to women. He did not condemn them but said there were three kinds: (1) some are born that way, (2) some are made that way (by castration), and (3) some choose that lifestyle for the sake of the kingdom of heaven (Matt. 19:10–12).

In today's society, if a boy has no natural attraction for women, he's told he's gay. Not necessarily so. Many Christians who have same-sex attractions (as well as those who are attracted to the opposite sex) have chosen to live a life of singleness and holiness. To those committed to a life of holiness, God makes this remarkable promise, which, in principle, is applicable to all who live celibate lives:

> Let not the foreigner who has joined himself to the
> LORD say,
>   "The LORD will surely separate me from his people";
> and let not the eunuch say,

"Behold, I am a dry tree."
For thus says the LORD:
"To the eunuchs who keep my Sabbaths,
  who choose the things that please me
  and hold fast my covenant,
I will give in my house and within my walls
  a monument and a name
  better than sons and daughters;
I will give them an everlasting name
  that shall not be cut off."

(ISA. 56:3–5)

They will be given a name better than sons and daughters!
Men and women, who for various reasons choose celibacy,
can be confident that they have a rightful and blessed place
in God's kingdom. Some will be more content than others;
there will be those who struggle and must live with unful-
filled dreams, but God is there to help and to bless. Unful-
filled dreams are no obstacle for God's special blessing. If
those who struggle with gender dysphoria were to lean into
their pain, rather than trying to find ways to avoid it, they
would find spiritual strength. Grief is the one pain that God
often uses to heal other pains.

Of course, many testify that God has seen fit to transform
those who struggle with same-sex attraction or gender dysphoria; some have entered into satisfying, natural marriages. But
let us not forget that Jesus and Paul were also single. Paul spoke
about the benefits of singleness in 1 Corinthians 7:32–36. Let
the church not condemn but rather encourage all believers to
commit to a life of holiness. That is the will of God for us all.

CHURCH, WHERE ART THOU?

Kaeley Triller is a woman who, as a child, was sexually abused by a pedophile who destroyed her sense of self-worth. Her feelings of shame and worthlessness plunged her into a series of terrible choices that perpetuated the lies she believed about herself.

Her employer at the local YMCA asked her to draft talking points to sell a new policy that would open the organization's locker rooms and bathrooms on the basis of gender identity rather than biological sex. Kaeley refused. She thought of the little girls getting ready for swimming class exposed to a predatory male. How damaging it would be for girls to know that at any moment a man could invade their privacy. She had already encountered predators who were trying to gain access to girls' events. Most probably every pedophile in our nation is in favor of bathroom legislation that gives them access into the bathrooms of the opposite sex. Kaeley asked that the Christian men around her would defend her cause, but for that, she was fired.

Soon she was employed by the statewide campaign to repeal the open locker room law in the state of Washington. She knew she would need the help of the local church, but of 150 churches contacted, only seven said *yes*. All the others had the same response, "*We don't want to be perceived as being unloving to the broken.*" After she made her story known, she heard from hundreds of women with similar stories and the most recurring theme was: *When I asked the church to help me, no one would.*

When I asked the church to help, no one would!

Her understanding of our culture comes through in her

response to those churches: "But, dear church, our need to feel loving cannot supersede our responsibility to truly love well. The world has convinced too many of us that truth is bigotry, real love is hate, silence is golden, and if it feels good it is good."

She continues, "These battles require an army, not isolated soldiers. . . . We need the church's help. A church that intimately knows the heart of her King does not fear conflict with the world; she embraces the conflict as His vehicle to radical transformation."

And finally, "True love isn't defined by the world; it's defined by the One who laid down His life to redeem the world."[25]

The bottom line is that few churches were willing to explain to their constituencies why it was important to vote against this new law. We are told that the church should not get involved in politics, but are these issues political or moral?

We can articulate our concerns in a way that people understand the issues and see our stand is loving.

I've been a pastor for many years, and I know how difficult it is to walk the line between involvement in these issues and extending love to all who hurt. But I believe that, as pastors, we can articulate our concerns in a way that our people understand the issues and see that our stand is not unloving, but, in fact, is most loving. What could be more unloving than to give unrestricted bathroom rights to the few who claim they are "trans" and thus trample on the rights of boys and girls, men and women, who expect to have privacy in bathrooms and showers? As someone has said, *we expect our politicians to fix what we as pastors are not even willing to preach on!*

This is not a time for the church to give an uncertain sound; this is a time when we must speak with compassionate clarity about the issues at hand.

GOING FORWARD

We must listen with respect and seek understanding when people (particularly the young) report that they might be transgender or gay. As Christians, and as churches, we cannot dismiss the confusion—even suffering—some people experience when it comes to the issue of gender. A compassionate and understanding heart is what's needed to help them along. But we must also remember that our body is not our own—it belongs to Christ.

This suffering and confusion extends to the family members and friends of those either struggling with or fully embracing transgenderism. As a nine-year-old girl, Denise Shick, author of *It Is Well with My Soul: Finding God's Peace in the Transgender Storm,* was shocked by her father's admission that he wanted to become a woman. In an interview with Janet Parshall, host of Moody Radio's *In the Market with Janet Parshall,* Shick explained the devastating fallout of that first announcement and the years of living with her father after that.

Over the years, Shick said she questioned everything from her father's love for her, to her relationship with God, to God's wisdom. What if God had made a mistake in making her a girl? Even though she eventually embraced her gender, once she entered high school, her father's overt jealousy over her developing body caused her to downplay and hide her femininity, waiting until she got to school, for instance, before putting on makeup and the pretty clothes she enjoyed wearing.

Her father was so focused on his situation, she said, that he was not aware of the damage being done around him. Almost twenty years after dealing with her father's anger and behavior, Shick said she went through another grieving process as her father finally left her mother, as well as Shick and her young family, to pursue a life as "Becky."

After thirteen years, and little communication with her father, Shick learned that he was dying of cancer. She says God softened her heart toward this man who, as a child, had been sexually abused and raised by an alcoholic mother and mostly absent father. She spent the last six months of his life visiting him and sharing her faith with him.

Although Shick isn't sure if her father eventually accepted Christ, Shick went on to found Help4Families. This organization provides help with the emotional pain and spiritual confusion people face when a loved one experiences gender-identity confusion.

She also urged listeners to speak to those who identify as LGBT "with a caring heart and a softness in the words we choose." She said, "The fact is they are hurting, and we can't dismiss that."[26]

In the article "Suffer the Children," Jamie Dean writes, "To love transgenders we must work through the complicated layers of sin and pain—a process that requires the relational context churches can provide." The author goes on to quote Heath Lambert of the Association of Certified Biblical Counselors:

"It will be the death knell if we say 'this is wrong' but then we can't help."[27]

Only when we see the depth of Satanic deception are we able to help others see their problems from a divine perspective. Remember, those who walk in darkness do not see things as they are, but rather see things the way they want them to be. "The way of the wicked is like deep darkness; they do not know over what they stumble" (Prov. 4:19).

Let it be said, *it is better to be accused of being harsh than it is to tell lies with hushed tones of compassion, love, care, and thoughtfulness.*

We must also introduce our congregations to people who deeply regret undergoing transgender surgery and who are now sounding the alarm and pleading that others not make their mistake. Many of these people, however, are afraid to speak out because they'll be branded as haters, bigots, or obstructionists. One who is speaking out is Cari Stella who regrets her surgery and says that activists will not be able to ignore transgender regrets forever. "We exist . . . and our numbers are growing."[28]

In the article, "I Was a Transgender Woman," Walt Heyer tells how his grandmother wanted him to be a girl, so she dressed him in a purple chiffon dress. This set in motion that idea that he was born with the wrong body, so he struggled with gender dysphoria. Later in life, he discovered that his sex reassignment surgery was not the answer. He writes, "Hidden deep underneath the make-up and female clothing was the little boy carrying the hurts from traumatic childhood events, and he was making himself known. Being a female turned out to be only a cover-up, not healing. I knew I wasn't a real woman, no matter what my identification documents said . . . It was obviously a masquerade."[29]

Years later, he discovered that he had dissociative disorder due to his traumatic childhood. "The gender specialist never considered my difficult childhood or even my alcoholism and saw only transgender identity. It was a quick jump to prescribe hormones and irreversible surgery . . . . going to a gender specialist when I first had issues had been a big mistake," he explains. "I had to live with the reality that body parts were gone . . . [and] could not be restored."[30] You cannot change the confusion of the mind by altering the shape of the body. Outer changes are synthetic; only a change of heart can bring lasting peace.

In my opinion, the church is the last barrier against a total breakdown of sexual sanity. And, if we feel powerless against the media, the courts, and our politicians, let us remind ourselves Jesus is in the trenches with us. (A heads-up to church leadership: please be prepared with a pastoral and legal response when a male in your church wants to use the women's bathroom because he identifies as female. It is already happening.)

To a world blinded by pain and finding only emptiness, Jesus makes this promise: "Come unto me, all ye that labour and are heavy laden, and I will give you rest. Take my yoke upon you, and learn of me; for I am meek and lowly in heart: and ye shall find rest unto your souls" (Matt. 11:28–29 KJV).

Let us continue to introduce this Savior to a hurting world.

For further reading: *As Nature Made Him: The Boy Who Was Raised as a Girl* by John Colapinto

CHAPTER 7

ISLAM, IMMIGRATION, AND THE CHURCH

Balancing Compassion and Security

We have seen the images on television: hordes of refugees trudging—they know not where—to seek refuge from war, persecution, and starvation. If we are not moved by this spectacle, it only can be because many of us in the West—including Christians—have hardened hearts that turn away from basic compassion and the spirit of Christ. For many of us, however, it's not a matter of the lack of concern but of a feeling of helplessness, a feeling that there's nothing we can do to alleviate the suffering of these distressed people. Language, culture, distance, and even religion separate us from their plight.

The current Syrian refugee crisis, which at this writing numbers 5.5 million people,[1] is constantly in the news. And there are conflicting opinions as to what the United States should be doing, not just for refugees, but for immigrants from all over the world who seek to live among us. Many agree that US immigration policies are inconsistent and often fraught with red tape for those who want to legally gain entry into the United States and make it their home.

Regarding immigration and refugees, the role of the church is different from the role of the government.

The purpose of this chapter is narrow in its focus. I want to clarify that in the matter of immigration, as well as the entrance of refugees into the country, the role of the church is very different from the role of the government. There are some things that the church can do that a government cannot; and there's much that the government can do that is not within the jurisdiction of the church. In my opinion, many evangelicals are confused on this point, and this has led to disparaging comments and reactions on both sides of the immigration debate.

I also want to address the related issue of the role of Islam in America, because I believe it poses special concerns for us along with special opportunities. Certainly, the churches of this nation should welcome the privilege of building relationships with those who come to our shores from other countries, regardless of their religious backgrounds. Our opinion of Islam should not stand in the way of our commitment to befriend Muslims in ways big and small and show them the love of Christ. There was a time when we sent missionaries to the Muslim world; now God has brought more and more Muslims to our shores.

ISLAM AND IMMIGRATION

My intention is not to create fear but to help the church understand Islam's view of immigration and radical Islam's long-term agenda in relation to immigration in the United States. I also want to show how Islam's intentions can be an opportunity for the church.

Let me make clear that followers of Islam in America can be diverse, both in ethnicity and adherence. Many Muslims have integrated and have accepted the freedom of religion so valued here and practice tolerance and respect for other religions. However, there is also a vocal minority that attempts, and sometimes succeeds, to exert a great deal of influence among the Muslim population. These groups take the Quran and the Hadith (the sayings of Muhammad) literally and are committed to the supremacy of Islam in America.

Radical Muslims often condemn moderate Muslims who, in other countries, face imprisonment and even death for voicing opposition to certain teachings in the Quran. According to Pew Research, the majority of US Muslims say there is more than one true way to interpret Islam's teachings, while 31 percent say there is only one true way to interpret the faith.[2]

I have discovered that Islam has a well-developed doctrine of migration going back to the days of Muhammad, who migrated from Mecca to Medina in AD 622 to spread his new doctrine. In fact, the Muslim calendar begins not with the birth or death of Muhammad, but with the date of his migration, which illustrates the importance of spreading Islam by moving from one geographical location to another. This event became known as the Hijrah (migration). This model of migration is not for the purpose of assimilating into a new host nation, but for colonizing and transforming host countries.

In the Quran, a promise is given: "Those who believe, and adopt exile, and fight for the Faith in the cause of Allah. . . . for them is the forgiveness of sins and a provision most generous" (Surah 8:74).[3] The Hadith connects migration with jihad, "And I command you with five that Allah has commanded me: Listening, obeying, Jihad, Hijrah and Jama ah [community]."[4]

For Muslim extremists, the role of immigration is critical to advance their agenda; more so than through acts of terrorism. We can easily believe the false narrative that our main concern should be the prevention of terror attacks, although prevention is undoubtedly an important role of law enforcement. But by no means should we think that terrorism is radical Islam's most useful weapon. Indeed, many of these Islamic leaders decry terrorism in an effort to take the focus off of a more effective and insidious strategy, namely, to subdue the West by *civilizational jihad*.[5]

The Muslim Brotherhood (MB), the oldest political Islamist group in the Arab world, was founded in Egypt in 1928 by Hassan al-Banna. This Islamic scholar and teacher envisioned "a universal Islamic system of rule that could be attained by promoting Islamic laws and morals and by engaging society through offering social services."[6]

Although the US State Department has not officially designated the MB as a terrorist organization, Egypt did so in 2013; and in 2015, a British government review "concluded that membership of or links to it should be considered a possible indicator of extremism."[7] However, in 2003, the FBI uncovered the MB's multifaceted plan to dominate America through immigration, intimidation, education, community centers, mosques, political legitimacy, and establishing "interfaith dialogue" centers in our universities and colleges. A document confiscated by the FBI outlines a twelve-point strategy to establish an Islamic government on earth that is brought about by a flexible, long-term "cultural invasion" of the West. Their own plans teach us that "the intrusion of Islam will erupt in multiple locations using multiple means."[8]

But near the top of this strategy is immigration. To be more specific, the first major point in their strategy states: "To expand the Muslim presence by birth rate, immigration and a refusal to assimilate."[9] This strategy transformed Indonesia from a Buddhist and Hindu country to the largest Muslim dominated country in the world. As Europe has discovered, open borders for refugees may be viewed as a compassionate response to a catastrophic humanitarian crisis, but it has long-term risks and consequences. For example, in 2015, Europe experienced the biggest wave of displaced people since World War II. However, "the crisis abated after Turkey agreed to block the flow of people. But it exposed deep divisions within the 28-member European Union over how to handle asylum-seekers escaping conflict and poverty in the Middle East and Africa." And "balancing moral and legal obligations with anti-immigrant sentiment" has become a similar challenge in the United States.[10]

As early as the 1960s, MB ideologue Sayyid Qutb popularized Abul A'la Maududi's notion to "Islamize society."[11] Maududi, a leading scholar of Islam who wrote the book *Jihad in the Cause of Allah,* said, "Islam is a revolutionary program to alter the social order of the whole world and rebuild it in conformity with its own tenets and ideals. . . . The purpose of Islam is to set up a state on the basis of its own ideology and program."[12] They will fight in multiple ways to undermine the American Judeo-Christian values of democracy, freedom of religion, and the like.

Andrew McCarthy, former chief assistant US attorney, posits that American leftists have paired up with militant Islamists to undermine national security and the nation's liberties. He says that America's greatest threat is not terrorism, but rather a stealth strategy. He writes, "Leftists and Islamists are well aware that their designs for society—which for both involve drastic transformation—are anathema to most Americans. They have to advance their cause in stealth."[13]

In America, the Muslim Brotherhood has dozens of front organizations through which they operate. Such organizations are the troops on the ground, so to speak, that implement the Grand Jihad, as they call it.[14] The hope of the Brotherhood is that people in the West will be so focused on terrorism that they'll turn a blind eye to the inner transformation of America that is happening away from the headlines.

To again quote McCarthy, the man who has been decorated with the Justice Department's highest honors: "Policymakers won't come to grips with what Islamists are trying to accomplish. . . . Focused myopically on only one of the jihadist's means, violence, they mistakenly assume that ending the violence would perforce end Islamism's threat to our way of life."[15] He warns, it is "national suicide for a free, self-determining people to pretend that our problems are limited to Muslim terrorists."[16] So the threat of terrorism is but a foil for a more insidious campaign of deception and infiltration.

Although he later denied having made the statement to a reporter, Omar Ahmad, cofounder of Council on American-Islamic Relations (speaking for the Muslim Brotherhood) was quoted as saying, "Islam isn't in America to be equal to any other faith, but to become dominant. The Koran should be the highest authority in America, and Islam the only accepted religion on earth."[17] No wonder the Brotherhood's London publication had as its cover page slogan, "Our Mission: World Domination."[18]

Islam teaches that Allah, not Western democracy, has already provided the only law permitted: that is sharia.[19] The MB is clear on this point, "The shariah cannot be amended to conform to changing human values and standards. Rather, it is the absolute norm to which all human values and conduct must conform."[20] Their "radical" hope is that through Muslim immigration and population growth in the West, sharia law will eventually replace the United States' existing laws.

Despite the plans and actions of radical Islam—whether carried out through covert infiltration or through blatant violence—God is always in control of this world. We have only to look again to the story of Daniel where, during King Jehoiakim's reign, King Nebuchadnezzar of Babylon besieged Jerusalem and "*the Lord gave him victory*" (see Dan. 1:1–2 NLT). At the same time, God gave Daniel understanding, knowledge, favor, and the power to interpret the king's dreams.

Like Daniel, Christians have an opportunity, even in our own Babylon, to stand firm and serve God. For years, many of us have prayed for "closed countries" and sent missionaries to Muslim countries. What if a part of God's answer to our prayers for the Muslim world is to bring them to America to be introduced to genuine Christians and not the caricature promoted in their home countries? Muslim immigration presents potential risks, but may also present opportunity.

But before we speak about the role of the church in the immigration debate, let's clarify the role of government in protecting our borders.

THE ROLE OF THE GOVERNMENT IN IMMIGRATION

Today, we often find ourselves between two competing values: compassion and long-term security. Back in February of 2015, ISIS predicted that they would create such conflict that Europe would be flooded with 500,000 refugees as a "psychological weapon" to create instability and chaos.[21] The eventual goal of Islam is population displacement to win Europe to the Muslim religion. Many of the refugees are women and children who are looking for somewhere—anywhere—where they can have food, shelter, and enough clothing to survive. More than half of the refugee applicants in 2017 were children, with more than 43 percent under the age of fourteen.[22] But this very real refugee crisis can be "highjacked" for the cause of the Hijrah, which means "to emigrate in the cause of Allah," or in other words, to move to a new land in order to bring the Muslim faith to that region. This might explain why there are so many young men among the refugees. This is done in obedience to the Quran which says, "Whoever leaves his home as an emigrant to Allah and His Messenger and then death overtakes him [will be rewarded]" (4:100).[23] This is *jihad by immigration.*

The church says, "Whosoever will may come."

The mistake made by many well-meaning people is to transfer the role of the church to the role of the government. I heard one pastor say that restrictive immigration is contrary to the gospel. But the state's overarching role is to protect its citizens both in the present and, as far as possible, for future generations. The church says, "Whosoever will may come," but the state does not.

The Bible is often pressed into service on the part of those who would argue for what could almost be regarded as an open-borders policy with statements like, "Jesus and His family were refugees in Egypt." Or "God is undocumented," or "We are turning Jesus away." Some people argue that opening our borders is fulfilling the Great Commission. But I respectfully disagree.

Today, we hear that it's "un-American" to restrict immigration. But historically, the United States has had strict rules regarding immigration. Years ago, my family and I visited Ellis Island where more than twenty-one million immigrants landed between 1885 and 1954. All arrivals were asked twenty-nine questions, one of which was how much money they had so that they could support themselves for a time (they needed to have the equivalent of $600 in today's funds). Doctors watched people as they disembarked the ship; those with visible health problems or diseases were sent back on the next vessel. Some unskilled workers were turned away because they were feared to become "a public charge." In all, about 2 percent (about 120,000) were sent home, often with tearful goodbyes from family members who were allowed into the country while their relatives were not.[24] Sometimes families were divided with the mother being refused entry and the father remaining with their children. Please understand that I am not agreeing with these policies, I'm simply pointing out that the United States has always had a rather high bar for entry.

Muslims who are committed to living under the Constitution should be welcomed, but some may be vulnerable to radicalization. According to one theory, a contributing factor in radicalization could be "acculturation—the process of balancing two competing cultural influences."[25] In other words, if Muslims feel rejected in their host country, they may be more likely to radicalize and become attracted to jihadist movements and groups. Obviously, US immigration polices cannot predict what immigrants might do, but the government must continue to have reasonable policies to vet immigrants.

Nowhere in the Bible does the idea exist that a country does not have the right to control its borders or determine who will come to live within its home. When Abraham left the Promised Land to go to Egypt, he did so with Pharaoh's knowledge and permission; the same is true when Jacob and his extended family went to Egypt. Yes, Joseph and Mary fled to Egypt, but they almost certainly did so with the permission of those who guarded the borders, and when the crisis was over, they returned to their homeland. These biblical stories are descriptive but not meant to be a model for our nation's immigration policies.

There are several passages in the Old Testament where Israel is admonished to welcome strangers and foreigners (see Lev. 19:34), but these texts are certainly not to be applied to present-day immigration policies. For one thing, Israel lived under a theocracy, and so all who joined them were expected to assimilate by accepting Israel's culture and religion. This theocracy is not to be equated with the nation of America and with its freedoms. Such passages are instructive for the church, but they most assuredly cannot be the basis of the government's immigration policy.

Certainly the state should be compassionate whenever it can, but that is not its first consideration. The state is called to protect its citizens, preserve order, and mete out punishment. Can you imagine a state run by the commands in the New Testament that apply to us as Christians within the church? When a foreign power, figuratively speaking, smites the state, should the state turn the other cheek? Should the state bless the nation that curses it? Someone asked this question: Should the government be compassionate and forgive offenders 70 x 7 times?

There are several references to government in the New Testament; perhaps the best known is Romans 13:1–4. Although most of us have read it many times, we should reread it with new eyes. Paul wrote this during the rule of the cruel and ungodly Emperor Nero:

Let every person be subject to the governing authorities. For there is no authority except from God, and those that exist have been instituted by God. Therefore whoever resists

*the authorities resists what God has appointed, and those
who resist will incur judgment. For rulers are not a terror
to good conduct, but to bad . . . he is God's servant for
your good. But if you do wrong, be afraid, for he does not
bear the sword in vain. For he is the servant of God, an
avenger who carries out God's wrath on the wrongdoer.*

(ROM. 13:1–4)

The government is an avenger; it bears the sword. It should
be both respected and feared.

In the Capstone Report article "Repairing Evangelical
Political Theology," the writer comments: "For the Christian,
the state possesses and always has possessed the power over
who it allows into its borders. There is no inalienable right
to access a land or territory based on any Old or New Testament text."[26]

The state exists to create order so we can live in it safely.
One of America's founding fathers, Alexander Hamilton,
already foresaw the need to exercise care in admitting foreigners "indiscriminately." The following is an excerpt from
one of his speeches.

> *The safety of a republic depends essentially on the energy
> of a common national sentiment; on a uniformity of
> principles and habits. . . .*
>
> *The United States have already felt the evils of incorporating a large number of foreigners into their national
> mass. . . it has served very much to divide the community
> and to distract our councils. . . .*
>
> *To admit foreigners indiscriminately to the rights of*

citizens, the moment they put foot in our country . . .
would be nothing less than to admit the Grecian horse
into the citadel of our liberty and sovereignty.[27]

We gladly welcome foreigners into this country, but the government must do its best to make certain that they are people who are committed to American values and our "national sentiment," as Hamilton put it. The government has the responsibility of controlling the borders, both for causes of national security as well as long-term consequences that mass migration might bring.

I agree, that our present legal immigration system is broken; the process needs to be streamlined rather than fraught with red tape, fraud, delays, unacceptable costs, and inconsistencies. Untold numbers of people are suffering because of our government's gridlock and political alliances. But securing our borders must be the government's first priority.

Of course, the church can exert influence on our government leaders and lobby for laws that many Christians think should be changed. But ultimately the government must keep national priorities in mind.

Slanderous attacks are often leveled at those who are in favor of secure borders; they are often called racists, haters, unchristian, and worse. But there are good reasons to believe that secure borders and a strict legal immigration policy that punishes violators is best for the nation as a whole, and especially the best long term. We must continue to debate questions such as how many refugees or immigrants we can reasonably welcome each year and encourage our government to continue its thorough vetting process of refugees. As I write this, Congress is hotly debating the current US immigration policy, although I hold out little hope that they will work out a policy that both places high value on border security and lays out reasonable immigration laws going forward.

No matter what our leaders decide or where Christians stand on the issues, we can have our differences while behaving in a way that reflects Christ.

Meanwhile, as a church, we always have the privilege of welcoming anyone God brings to us. The symbol of the government is the *sword*; the symbol of the church is the *cross*.

THE ROLE OF THE CHURCH

Not unlike early European immigrants, many of the Muslims who have immigrated to America have made this country their home; they work hard, raise families, and worship freely without thought of their immigration as some kind of jihad.

> The church plays an entirely different role from the state; its symbol is the cross.

When I visited one of the mosques here in Chicago, an imam told me that only about 15 percent of the Muslim community take their faith seriously enough to attend Friday prayers, etc. In fact, some Muslims quietly disagree with the statements and ideology of Islam. In short, Christians have an opportunity to share the love of Christ with those who desire the freedoms of the West but are still bound by the chains of oppressive ideology.

The church plays an entirely different role from the state;

its symbol is the cross. Refugees, especially, are deserving of our special care and involvement. If we as Christians turn away from helping refugees from any nation or engaging with Muslim immigrants and citizens because of fear, we are denying our Lord who died unjustly on a Roman cross. Thankfully, fear did not keep Him from going into hostile territory. If we believe that God is sovereign over the nations, we must also realize that God has brought them to us. And for this, we should be grateful.

In His parable of the Good Samaritan, Jesus tells us that our neighbor is anyone who is in trouble, anyone we could help. When we encounter someone who is bleeding alongside of the road, we don't ask how they got there or whether they're here legally; we don't ask them what religion they belong to. We stop and help them, even at personal sacrifice.

In the excellent book *Seeking Refuge: On the Shores of the Global Refugee Crisis*, the authors tell of a pastor in Jordan who opened his church to Syrian refugee children and their mothers and offered life skills training and other activities. Sadly, many in his congregation didn't agree with the decision and left. But the pastor said by welcoming the refugees, his church changed for the better. He is quoted as saying, "For so many years we tried to share God's love to the people in Syria, but we were stopped. Now Syria has come to us and to our church.'"[28]

Perhaps it is best to have such ministries independent of any one church, but invite concerned Christians from various churches to unite for responding both strategically and with God's guidance. I am personally acquainted with a group of Christians who have done just that. For several months they met together with earnest prayer, seeking God's wisdom and help before blessing the Syrian refugees in their city. They have taken them food, welcomed them into their homes, and have helped them with their basic needs and services. Interestingly, the children of these refugees learn English quickly and serve as interpreters between these Christian and Muslim families. As the Christmas season approached, the Syrian families were invited to a meal and about 170 accepted. And those numbers are growing. Bridges are being built to form relationships of mutual respect and love. And caring.

Laypeople from a number of churches involved in this ministry say that the Muslims have reciprocated with love, hospitality, and deep appreciation. The Christians are regularly invited into Muslim homes and vice versa. Now Christians are praying in the Muslim homes in the name of Jesus and are welcomed to return.

Ministry leaders were disappointed that more area churches didn't get involved after being invited to participate. Apparently, some, at least, are so focused on their own programs and are comfortable with business as usual. As a pastor, I have found that congregations find it easier to send missionaries to foreign countries than meeting their Muslim neighbors face-to-face. On the other hand, churches, as well as individual believers, that have caught the vision and are meaningfully involved, find that they are blessed in return. Ministry to Muslims in America could be the church's finest hour.

One thread that runs throughout the testimony of Muslims who come to faith in Christ is this: the testimony of Christian love drew them to Christ. As one former Muslim put it, "Here I was convinced I had the right religion, but my religion taught me only to hate and to seek revenge. These people had the wrong religion and all they did was show me love." Little wonder he came to saving faith in Christ.

Because Islam denies the very heart of the Christian faith—namely the divinity of Jesus, His death on the cross, and His resurrection—and because Islam has been so successful in overpowering Christianity in many countries, we must recognize that it is empowered by deceptive and dark forces. But we also must see many Muslims as living in fear of apostasy and threatened by excommunication or even death if they convert to another religion.

Let me reemphasize that Christians who have a credible ministry to Muslims are *praying* Christians. These are Christians who walk in humble repentance with a God-given burden for those who don't know our heavenly Father. They are Christians who understand the spiritual battle going on. Only a loving relationship with our neighbors, empowered by the Holy Spirit, will overcome these barriers.

Jesus calls us to a loving relationship that rejects fear and does not shrink from sacrifice. He came from heaven to earth, not to play it safe, but to use His own suffering and death to redeem us and also to serve as an example for His followers. If we have the opportunity, we have no legitimate excuses not to be involved.

I'll end this chapter with one overriding thought from *Seeking Refuge*: "If we respond to Muslims with love and respect, we have a remarkable opportunity to point them to Jesus. To the contrary, if we demonize or shun them, we not only risk falling into the sin of slander, we also minimize the chance that they would ever consider following Jesus, and

The church must be the welcoming committee for strangers.

we play into the plans of extremist groups that want marginalized Muslims to view Christians as their enemy."[29]

The government must do what the church cannot: protect its people and preserve order. Likewise, the church must do what the government cannot: be the welcoming committee for strangers in our land. *We must see Jesus on our doorstep.* And we must live the truth of His words: "Truly, truly, I say to you, whoever receives the one I send receives me, and whoever receives me receives the one who sent me" (John 13:20).

CHAPTER 8

FIVE FALSE GOSPELS WITHIN THE EVANGELICAL CHURCH

Defending the Faith Once Delivered to the Saints

The church has always been tempted to dull the sharp edges of the Christian faith, to abandon hard truths in the face of cultural and religious pressure. Passing a vibrant faith to the next generation is always a challenge, especially without the support of the government, the courts, the media, public schools, and the national *zeitgeist* that insists that we simply flow with the raging river of cultural opinion.

The empty churches of Europe testify to what happens when the clear gospel witness becomes beholden to political correctness, submission to culture, and a willingness to unite with other religions under the banner of tolerance and love. The loss of a Christian consensus and the diminishing witness of the true evangelical faith reminds us that we cannot take the future of our own churches for granted.

Peter Marshall, who, for many years was chaplain to the US Senate, told the story of "The Keepers of the Springs," about a town in Europe that sat at the foot of a great mountain range [paraphrased here]:

High up in the hills above the village, an old man served as the Keeper of the Springs. He patrolled the mountainside and made sure that the spring that fed the village below was always clear of silt, leaves, and dead animals.

Each day the water tumbled down to the town, cold and pure. Gardens were refreshed, lawns turned green, and people had their thirst quenched. Summer and winter the townspeople drank from its coolness and washed in its freshness.

But the town faced a crisis. Times were hard and the council had a budget to cut. Someone noticed a small amount of money committed to the salary of the Keeper of the Springs. They decided that they would release him of his duties and end his salary because most people seldom saw him, and therefore, they didn't even know who he was. They also persisted in the hope that the water would probably stay just as pure without this unknown guardian.

For the first few weeks, the water seemed to be the same: clear and pure. But gradually a green scum developed on its surface and leaves clogged with dirt and debris floated on the water. After a while, sickness came to the village, and soon an epidemic raged, reaching into every home.

The town council met again in an emergency session. They realized they had made a bad mistake so they appointed a delegation to climb up the mountain, find the old man, and beg him to resume his former labors. Before long, pure water flowed down to the village again; children laughed and played on the banks of the stream as they had in days gone by.[1]

In the New Testament, church leaders are charged with the responsibility of keeping the water pure. We stand at the headwaters of the stream keeping it free of pollution and calling out when the central message of the gospel is either ignored or even a little smudged. *We are called to be the Keepers of the Springs.*

This chapter deals with just five of the many doctrinal temptations the church faces. If we waver, it's my conviction that the witness of the church will be severely compromised. In the end, it will have little to say to a world that desperately needs to hear a word from God.

There are many false teachers in mainline churches where the gospel is redefined, miracles are denied, and Christ is stripped of His deity. As H. Richard Niebuhr described liberalism, "A God without wrath brought men without sin into a kingdom without judgment through the ministrations of a Christ without a cross."[2] The gospel of liberalism inspires people, but it saves no one from God's coming judgment.

In this chapter, I am focusing on the false teachings present in many evangelical churches. Many people found *The Shack*, by author William Paul Young, to be a blessing because it presents God as accessible to those who are in pain. Others found the theological beliefs represented in the book to be reprehensible. At any rate, in his book *Lies We Believe About God*, Young denies almost every doctrine of historic Christianity, including original sin, the sovereignty of God, Christ's sacrifice for sinners, the existence of an eternal hell, and instead affirms universalism—the doctrine that all will be saved.[3] Despite these heresies, I saw *Lies We Believe About God* promoted on a Christian television network as a refreshing book that will be a great encouragement in your walk with God!

Some of our evangelical churches are teaching a shrunken —or even a distorted—gospel but their congregations may not be aware of it. As long as the Bible is used in a sermon, that is sufficient. But the narrow road is often indistinguishable from the broad road, which always offers plenty of company. And with the loss of the gospel comes a loss of power. Each of the following five doctrinal errors will be exposed far too briefly, but space forbids a longer analysis of each.

THE GOSPEL OF PERMISSIVE GRACE

Let me begin by giving thanks to God that in many churches grace is being emphasized to the benefit of the congregation. Many people have been rescued out of sterile, joyless, and performance-based Christianity when they learn that we are not only saved by grace, we are also daily renewed and accepted by grace. They have been delivered from a life of rules without relationship and outward compliance without joyful obedience. Grace, once understood, is truly amazing, not just for great sinners but also for struggling saints. Spiritual victory comes not by putting people back under the law, but by introducing them to the completeness of Christ's work and

His grace toward us. Believers do not have to earn God's favor, for we have been permanently accepted by Christ. No wonder Paul revels in what he calls "abounding" grace (see Rom. 5:20).

It's difficult for me to be critical of those with whom I have so much in common, for I am also a lover of grace. But today we are witnessing a perversion of grace in what we can call the Grace Movement. Perhaps the best book that exposes this false notion of grace is *Hyper-Grace: Exposing the Dangers of the Modern Grace Message* by Michael Brown.[4] His research confirms what I've been seeing and hearing in the past decade: teachers and preachers who offer people grace in advance, even before they are convinced they need it.

In times past, we preached the law. Once people were convicted of their sin, we explained the wonders of God's grace. But today, many preachers say that "God loves you unconditionally" and "God loves you just as you are." The person listening hears, "I can continue to sleep with my girlfriend; I can continue to be in love with my addictions, but thankfully, I am pleasing to the Lord because of Jesus." So, the reasoning is, "I love to sin, God loves to forgive, so I can pretty well do as I please." *Unconditional love* is interpreted as *unconditional acceptance of one's lifestyle.*

God does not love everyone in the same way. He loves His people, those who are "in Christ" unconditionally, even as He loves His Son (John 17:20–23). But this does not mean that God is always pleased with our conduct; nor does it mean that God does not discipline us for our waywardness. Although God is kindly disposed to everyone and loves the world (John 3:16), "it is a fearful thing to fall into the hands of the living God" (Heb. 10:31). And again, "Therefore let us be grateful for receiving a kingdom that cannot be shaken, and thus let us offer to God acceptable worship, with reverence and awe, for our God is a consuming fire" (Heb. 12:28–29). No wonder even believers, knowing the holiness of God, are told to "conduct yourselves with fear throughout the time of your exile" (1 Peter 1:17).

According to Brown, some grace teachers affirm that God is always in a good mood. He points out that in Benjamin Dunn's book *The Happy Gospel: Effortless Union with a Happy God*, Dunn presents God as always being joyful.[5] In the same vein, Pastor Chuck Crisco asks, "What if God is in party mode all the time?"[6] God in party mode? All the time?

Well, if these authors mean that He is always good, kind, and righteous, then, yes, God is always in a good mood. But if you mean He is never angry, then, no, God is not always in a good or joyful mood. I find it impossible to ignore dozens of references to God's wrath and anger, not just in the Old Testament but in the New Testament as well. Remember the flood, Sodom and Gomorrah, and Israel's own severe judgment for their idolatry? And if you say, as many grace preachers do, that all of this was under the old covenant, then think about the coming of the Great Tribulation, and eventually, eternal hell. Just read the judgments described in the book of Revelation, and you should be convinced that not everyone is loved unconditionally, and God is not always "in a good mood."

We have to stop preaching that God loves everyone unconditionally. The Bible says that God is angry with the wicked every day (Ps. 7:11) and that the wicked are an abomination to Him: "For all who do such things, all who act dishonestly, are an abomination to the LORD your God" (Deut. 25:16).

He rages against sin and gives this warning to all the unrepentant who would presume upon His love: "But because of your hard and impenitent heart you are storing up wrath for yourself on the day of wrath when God's righteous judgment will be revealed" (Rom. 2:5). To even say that "God loves the sinner but hates the sin" might be misleading. As the late R. C. Sproul has pointed out, God doesn't send the sin to hell; he sends the *sinner*.[7] Yes, let us gladly tell people that God loves them, but to say that God loves everyone unconditionally, or to imply that His love means we need not fear coming judgment, is to give cover to unrepentant sinners.

Teachers in the modern Grace Movement may say that they believe in the wrath of God, but it's noticeably absent in their preaching and in their books. When they do make reference to it, they once again say that this was true under the old covenant, but not the new. Joseph Prince says, "God is not judging America (or any country in the world today). America and its sins have already been judged! Where? At the cross of Jesus! Sin has been judged at the cross!"

Incredibly, Prince, who is the most famous of the grace preachers, believes that even unbelievers cannot be under God's wrath because all sin was judged at the cross.[8] This idea flatly contradicts Paul's words, written under the new covenant, "For the wrath of God is revealed from heaven against all ungodliness and unrighteousness of men, who by their unrighteousness suppress the truth" (Rom. 1:18). Paul then follows up with a list of sins committed by the ungodly for which they are judged, both in the present and the future.

I long to hear a message by a modern grace preacher on this passage of Scripture:

> *. . . when the Lord Jesus is revealed from heaven with his mighty angels in flaming fire, inflicting vengeance on those who do not know God and on those who do not obey the gospel of our Lord Jesus. They will suffer the punishment of eternal destruction, away from the presence of the Lord and from the glory of his might.*
>
> (2 THESS. 1:7–9)

God is a very complex being—love and justice, truth and wrath are held in balance.

If the first characteristic of the new grace teachers is a refusal to acknowledge God's present and future wrath against sinners, the second is that the law is presented as an enemy of grace. Brown tells about meeting a man who had served a well-known "hyper grace" leader. This man wrote that in the movement, "You are legalistic if you EVER tell someone to 'not' do things . . . that's legalism or 'do-do' Christianity as they call it."[9] In their thinking, grace must be completely divorced from law; to feel obligated to obey any commands is to put us back under law. Even the commands of the New Testament (such as in Romans 12) are downplayed, or it is said that these will be followed naturally if we are under grace. In their estimation, even the disciplines of the Christian life put us back on a "saved by works" footing.

I am not saying that the preachers in the Grace Movement encourage sin; they would say that it is their message of grace that delivers people from their sins. But historically, their complete rejection of the law has been called *antinomianism*, which in many instances has led to the justification of worldly living. I heard one preacher say, in effect, "It does not matter what I do because I am standing in the perfection of Christ before the Father." Jude speaks about those who "pervert the grace of our God into sensuality" (v. 4).

Paul warned the Galatians about the danger of putting themselves back under law. But—and this is critical—this should not be interpreted to mean that we cannot be instructed by the law. We are not putting ourselves under law if we seek to obey the New Testament commands of Scripture; we are putting ourselves under the law when we think that obedience, without a heart change, is all that God requires. Paul knew that his message of grace could be misunderstood so he warned, "For you were called to freedom, brothers. Only do not use your freedom as an opportunity for the flesh, but through love serve one another" (Gal. 5:13).

Third, these grace teachers say that Christians need never confess their sin. Since Jesus has forgiven us past, present, and future, if we sin, we need only acknowledge we have already been forgiven. They adamantly deny that the Lord's Prayer is a model for us because it asks for forgiveness, something we need never do. And as for the well-known verse 1 John 1:9—"If we confess our sins . . ."—this is not for Christians but for the unsaved. In their view, if we teach that Christians must also repent, we are being legalistic Pharisees.[10] Jesus evidently disagreed when He asked five of the seven churches of Revelation to repent!

We should not be surprised that, as Brown has shown, this teaching of grace sometimes leads to the acceptance of homosexual behavior and even the radical heresy that in the end all will be saved.[11] Some of these teachers allege that to attend a church where this grace message is not taught means that we are falling under the control of "tyrants and manipulators."[12]

Biblical grace fights against sin; permissive grace allows contentment with your sin. New Testament grace trains us for righteousness. "For the grace of God has appeared, bringing salvation for all people, training us to renounce ungodliness and worldly passions, and to live self-controlled, upright, and godly lives in the present age, waiting for our blessed hope, the appearing of the glory of our great God and Savior Jesus Christ" (Titus 2:11–13).

In previous chapters, we encountered the false prophets of Jeremiah's day who preached their one-sided emphasis that God had chosen the nation, and therefore, they could expect His unending favor despite their lifestyle. The false prophets said that the people could unconditionally depend on the Lord's favor, but then God gave His evaluation: "They have healed the wound of my people lightly, saying, 'Peace, peace,' when there is no peace" (Jer. 6:14).

I will say it again: turning the grace of God into sensuality gives the impression that it is safe to sin because we are under grace. When we emphasize grace to the exclusion of God's discipline and judgment, when we speak only of heaven and never of hell, Jeremiah would say to us, "You are treating the wound of our people too lightly."

Seventeenth-century Puritan pastor Thomas Watson said it well: "Until sin be bitter—Christ will not be sweet."[13]

THE GOSPEL OF SOCIAL JUSTICE

"What are you preaching on these days?" I asked a pastor in the Midwest.

He replied, "Right now, I'm doing a series on the gospel of the kingdom, the gospel of social justice." Thankfully, I knew him well enough to know that he also believed in the necessity of individual conversion through faith in Christ. But I also knew him well enough to know that the gospel of personal conversion is near the bottom of his list of priorities.

"Social justice" can mean many different things to different people. For some, it is the gospel of socialism, the Marxist notion that resources have to be equally distributed through government intervention, control, and ownership. This, in their minds, results in a just and fair society; only then can the oppressed experience "social justice." Others would define it in terms of liberation theology that sees salvation as freedom from economic and social oppression. Same-sex marriage is often defined as a social justice issue. Some universities are dedicated promoters of various social justice theories, affirming that minorities should demand justice, however they would define it. Alternate, more moderate voices are stifled, sometimes with violence motivated by dictums of extreme political correctness.

On the other side, there are many evangelicals who stand apart from the culture, praying for revival but uninvolved in combating poverty, racism, and injustice. We should applaud the younger generation for having a social conscience and living out the gospel through community involvement, helping the poor, the oppressed, and the needy without abandoning the gospel of grace. Christians always have had, and should have, a strong commitment to alleviating human misery and injustice wherever it is found. Many of the hospitals in Africa were built by Christian ministries.

But dangers lie ahead.

We all know that in the early twentieth century, many churches left off preaching the cross of Christ and replaced it with "doing good to their fellow man." They justified their stance with verses of Scripture from the Old Testament, such as "bring justice to the fatherless, plead the widow's cause" (Isa. 1:17) and similar texts in the New Testament, where Jesus taught that when we visit His followers in prison, we are visiting Him (Matt. 25:35–40). Thus, social concerns replaced the finished work of Christ who died and rose again to save sinners. In fact, the gospel of God saving us from sin was almost entirely neglected. In reaction, fundamentalists rejected the social gospel and, for the most part, confined themselves to the urgent need for individual conversion, neglecting the social implications of the gospel.

History is repeating itself today, but with a different twist. Many millennials, feeling as if they don't fit with evangelicalism's romance with conservative politics, have chosen to devote themselves to social justice, and sadly, many of them have abandoned the doctrine of personal repentance and opted for what they see as a more practical gospel, helping the poor and needy, "The Gospel of Social Justice."

I know a church that fits this description exactly. It challenges its people to be involved in many different forms of social work, but it has long since neglected the gospel of God's redemption in Christ. One other example of this is the Emerging Church movement where, for the most part, the concerns of earth replace the concerns of eternity. These churches talk about *justice* but not *judgment*.[14]

One leader describing how his denomination came to abandon the gospel explained how our first generation preached the gospel and then worked out the social implications of the gospel. The second generation assumed the gospel, neglected it, and continued with the social implications. The third generation totally ignored and even rejected the gospel but continues with the social implications.

Two missionaries who have sought to bring the gospel to Africa have written that the evangelical missionaries there no longer come to do church planting but "are focused on social relief, with the church tacked on as a theological addendum. By all appearances, there has been a mega-shift in evangelical missions away from church planting and leadership training toward social justice or social action."[15]

We are commanded to live radically like Christ, committing ourselves to the needs of others, body, soul, and spirit. The gospel comes not in words only, but through authentic, caring Christians who are willing to sacrifice it all for others. But we must serve with a redemptive mindset, always seeking for opportunities to build bridges that will lead them to eternal life. But if we don't see that the message of the gospel is singularly important, we substitute a temporal body for an eternal soul.

To quote author and popular blogger Trevin Wax, "I fear that the evangelical distaste for heaven/hell conversation has less to do with the Bible and more to do with the current cultural climate. People today are far less likely to be concerned with eternity. Many people go through much of their lives without considering death, much less judgment."[16] Imagine living your entire life with scarcely a thought about your eternal future.

Evangelicals have to return to our biblical roots and talk about heaven and warn against hell. We need gospel-driven social work that serves people because they are needy and because we want them to trust in Christ. And yes, of course, we should continue to serve them whether they believe in Christ or not; but our heart's cry is for them to believe the gospel and be saved. If compassion motivates us to help alleviate the suffering in this present world, how much more should compassion motivate us to share the good news to alleviate their suffering in the world to come?

The gospel is not what we can do for Jesus, but what Jesus has done for us.

My friend Pastor Colin Smith says that you can tell whether you are preaching the gospel by asking yourself: Would this message get me thrown out of a synagogue or mosque? If you could preach in a Mormon temple and not stir up anger, you have not preached the gospel. The gospel urges men and women to repent of their sins and put their faith in Christ alone for their eternal salvation.

Let us remember that the gospel is not what we can do for Jesus, but what Jesus has done for us. We must tell this generation that *social justice, even at its best, is not the gospel*!

What would happen if Satan took over a city? Presbyterian pastor Donald Grey Barnhouse speculated that if Satan were to take over Philadelphia, the bars would be closed, pornography banished, and pristine streets would be filled with tidy pedestrians who smiled at each other. There would be no swearing. The children would say, "Yes, sir" and "No, madam" and churches would be full every Sunday . . . *where Christ would not be preached.*[17]

"And there is salvation in no one else, for there is no other name under heaven given among men by which we must be saved" (Acts 4:12).

Eternity is at stake.

THE GOSPEL OF NEW AGE SPIRITUALITY

Many younger evangelicals do not feel at home in church. They gravitate to groups where they can be personally involved in honest sharing, caring for the poor, and ongoing relationships. They are more open, more vulnerable, and less inclined to follow the dictates of "organized religion." Predictable formal worship services that follow a script often lack the vitality some of them are looking for. They are often more accepting of marginalized people who don't meet the standards of decorum that some churches appear to demand. They would probably prefer meeting in a gym than a stately church. They are a "seeking" generation and uncomfortable with being told what to believe but are committed to finding a faith that is right for them.

Despite many admirable qualities, this generation is open to seek spiritual experiences independently of Bible doctrine. Thus, in order to be more relevant, New Age spirituality, which is widely accepted in our culture, is often taught alongside biblical teaching in our evangelical churches and seminaries.

We can be heartened that classes in spiritual formation are being offered in churches, seminaries, and Christian colleges. However, in many instances, the textbooks used contain New Age teachings based on mystical experiences of God rather than the Scriptures. For example, one author, whose book is sometimes used in spiritual formation classes, refers to what Jesus said about paying attention to the lilies of the field, and then makes this comment: "Whoever wrote this stuff believed that people could learn as much about the ways of God from paying attention to the world as they could from paying attention to scripture."[18]

Scripture must be believed whether we experience God or not.

Such books and others like them are popular because they present God as more accessible, more easily experienced without much need for specific Bible doctrines. However, we have to teach our people that the only sure knowledge we have of God is based on Scripture, which must be believed whether we experience God or not.

Martin Luther, the evening before his confrontation at the Diet of Worms, had no experience of God at all. He begged God to help him, but there was only silence. The next day with nothing to guide him except God's bare Word, Luther refused to recant, and we still refer to that event as an important turning point in church history.[19]

My point: we might learn some things about God when we experience the world, but only in the Scriptures do we have a reliable guide to lead us to encounter God and salvation. Sometimes we have no experience of God at all but,

"We walk by faith, not by sight" (2 Cor. 5:7). Teaching students how to study the Bible, walk in the Spirit, and grow in biblical faith would be a better option when teaching spiritual formation.

Let's move on to the subject of contemplative prayer. Like meditation, contemplation is a much needed discipline in today's stressful world. Yes, I believe in scriptural, contemplative prayer. But there is a unique twist that is often associated with contemplative prayer, namely to return to the mysticism of the "desert fathers," a way of praying that relies heavily on Catholic teachers who tell us that we must learn the ancient art of centering prayer. This is attractive to Christians who want to "go deeper" in their relationship with God. They are convinced that, through "contemplation," they can connect with God in the soul of their being. Some begin by centering, that is, focusing their minds on a word or phrase that helps them connect with the divine within them. Before they know it, they may be having a spiritual experience that is divorced from theology and encountering their mystical center, which they think is God. To no one's surprise, soon they are imbibing the general tone and techniques of Eastern religions.

Incredibly, Barna Research shows that practicing Christians find the lure of this New Spirituality enticing, "perhaps because it holds a positive view of religion, emphasizes the supernatural and simultaneously feeds into a growing dissatisfaction with institutions." About 28 percent of practicing Christians strongly agree that "all people pray to the same god or spirit, no matter what name they use for that spiritual being." Furthermore, the same number believe that "meaning and purpose come from becoming one with all that is."[20] No need for specific doctrine or biblical teaching; what matters is a technique to access the "god" within. New Age Christianity is an attractive haven for those who have been disappointed by the church for a variety of reasons.

People want spirituality, but not religion. According to professor of religion Jerome P. Blaggett, people are saying, "Yes, I want to have a connection to the sacred, but I want to do it on my own terms—terms that honour who I am as a discerning, thoughtful agent and that affirm my day-to-day life."[21]

Religion on *my* terms!

Some of the leaders who are often mentioned as authorities in helping people find God on their own terms are teachers like Thomas Merton, a Catholic who was so greatly influenced by Eastern religion that some who knew him well said he was more Buddhist than Christian. Henry Nouwen in *Pray to Live* says that Merton was "able to uncover the stream where the wisdom of East and West merge and flow together beyond dogma, in the depths of inner experience . . . Merton embraced the spiritual philosophies of the East and integrated this wisdom into his own life by direct practice."[22]

Merton himself writes that "at the center of our being is a point of nothingness which is untouched by sin and illusion, a point of pure truth. . . . This little point of nothingness . . . is the pure glory of God in us. . . . It is in everybody."[23]

Is there truly a place within us that is untouched by sin and is the pure glory of God in us? In everybody?

Merton also wrote that "it is a glorious destiny to be a member of the human race. . . . Now I realize what we all are. . . . if only [people] could see themselves as they really *are*.

. . . I suppose the big problem would be that we would fall down and worship each other."[24]

If we saw each other as we are, we would fall down and worship each other! Really?

There are dozens of New Age teachers, but when several people told me that evangelicals are flocking to read the writings of Father Richard Rohr, I decided I would read his book *The Divine Dance: The Trinity and Your Transformation*, which is dedicated "to all the unsuspecting folks who do not know that they are already within the divine flow."[25] The forward was written by William Paul Young, author of *The Shack*, and it is endorsed by authors like Rob Bell of *Love Wins* fame. Surprisingly, Rohr was told by his publisher that his greatest reading demographic is young evangelicals who are helping make his books bestsellers.

Rohr's book is not about the Trinity, but rather Rohr imaginatively uses Trinitarian language in order to give a backdrop to his own eclectic spiritual teaching. The book uses the language of the Trinity as a pretext for describing the "divine flow" in which everyone participates.

There is much to say, but space necessitates a brief response.

First, this book, and others like it, exalts human nature, our "divineness," and our ability to meet God without doctrine or the teachings of religion. There is no emphasis on repenting from sin or seeing who we are in the presence of a Holy God. By no means is Christ the only way to the Father. After all, no matter your religion or where you are on your spiritual journey, "you are already in the flow."

Second, all the themes of Eastern religion are in Rohr's

book: pantheism, God is "the flow" and all creation (not just humanity) is part of that flow, and "creation is thus 'the fourth person of the Blessed Trinity.'"[26] He promotes universalism[27] and says there is no doctrinal or lifestyle test to enter "the flow," you only have to realize that you're already in it.[28] No need to worry about accountability to God. Rohr writes, "To sum it all up, I do not believe there is any wrath in God whatsoever—it's theologically impossible when God is Trinity."[29]

No wonder the book ends with various prayers in which all faith traditions can participate. As you find God in the depths of your soul, your consciousness ends up being "god." Everyone, yes, everyone has "god" already within them.

Someone has said, "We don't want a father in heaven. We want a grandfather in heaven, a grandfather who watches the kids play, and even if they are mischievous, he enjoys it all, and at the end of the day he says, 'A good time was had by all.'"

What is so attractive about New Age spirituality? *At last people have a god who agrees with them about everything!* They want a god who does not embarrass them; a god who thinks just like they do. They want a theology that diminishes the horrors of sin and magnifies how good we as human beings actually are! Self-salvation has many forms and is very attractive. We want a god who is as broadminded as we are.

The apostle Paul has a word for us: "For the time is coming when people will not endure sound teaching, but having itching ears they will accumulate for themselves teachers to suit their own passions, and will turn away from listening to the truth and wander off into myths" (2 Tim. 4:3–4).

That day is here.

THE GOSPEL OF MY SEXUAL PREFERENCE

Is the evangelical church willing to practice the biblical teachings about church discipline? Most would say *no*. I spoke to one pastor who said they allow people into their membership wherever they are at in their spiritual journey; unmarried couples who are living together, a homosexual couple with children, etc., are allowed to become members despite the church's opposition to these lifestyles. But that church has concluded that those who become members must join in order to grow in their faith rather than saying, "Membership is not for you." In short, this church was reluctant to raise the bar of church membership beyond vague generalities.

There is another reason why churches are reluctant to administer church discipline. They know the power of being shamed, despised, and targeted. They don't want to be accused of being hateful rather than loving. They don't want to be vilified in the evening news.

Same-Sex Marriage and Church Discipline

We applaud Reverend Byron Brazier, pastor of Chicago's Apostolic Church of God for his courage, his fidelity to the Scriptures, and his willingness to do what is right and pay the price. On Sunday, July 30, 2017, he explained to his congregation that a woman had her membership removed after they learned that she married her same-sex partner. Brazier had spoken to the woman personally and explained the church's position. She understood and apparently accepted the church's verdict. But when word got out, others became upset at the church for shaming this woman (though her name was not publicly released), and rejecting her for who she was. "Love" should always win.

About fifty people showed up outside the church to protest what one spokesperson called the "public shaming . . . [of] LGBTQ congregational members." Predictably, the demonstrators called Brazier hateful and chanted, "Hey, hey ho! Hate has to go!" The demonstrators began their meeting with the reading of Scripture, prayer, and the singing of a hymn. These protesters were from a progressive church that welcomed same-sex couples under the banner of "love and inclusion" not "hate and exclusion."

One speaker addressed the issue of religious freedom. She said that the LGBTQ community never expected churches to give up their religious freedom. In her words, "Communities of faith do not have to discriminate in order to survive . . . religious freedom *requires* the liberation of LGBTQ people."

Reread that statement again if you have to. Religious freedom turns out to be agreeing with what the progressives believe about sexuality and religious practice. In effect, "Religious freedom should be limited by *my* lifestyle and beliefs."

Another speaker said, "If we can challenge what the writers of Scripture have to say about women . . . about slavery, then surely we can challenge the writers of Scripture as to what they say about homosexuality." The demonstrators ended their meeting outside the church by singing, "O how I love Jesus."[30]

Conclusion: the biblical teaching about homosexuality can be set aside. Homosexual relationships are not a sin but an alternate expression of one's humanity. Jesus was all about love, not hate; to follow Him is to take the path of helping people, not hurting and shaming.

When Brazier was asked to defend what he had done in light of the fact that our churches are filled with other sinners who are guilty of a host of various sins, he agreed that, yes, there were other sinners and no one is perfect, "But what we must realize is that we cannot institutionalize that which the Lord has already condemned." In other words, yes, we are all sinners, but to condone a deliberate act that attacks God's establishment of the family is to cross a clear line. We are called to be a welcoming community without affirming such lifestyles.

> To condone a deliberate act that attacks God's establishment of the family is to cross a clear line.

Truth and Love

Earlier I spoke about millennials who are caught between two worlds; they hear echoes of the past but also are tuned to the much louder voices of our present culture. They have gay friends who are caring and thoughtful, so when asked to choose between the Bible and culture, they side with culture and take the next step and feel compelled to endorse same-sex marriage. But we must distinguish between homosexual inclinations and acting on them. We must also distinguish between respect for all people and agreeing with their behavior.

We must also counter the widespread notion that those who accept the LGBT lifestyle agenda have taken the moral high road; they, after all, are all about "inclusion" and not "exclusion." They represent "love," not "hate." We as evangelicals must show that these basic premises are wrong, *very* wrong. You cannot attack natural law without ongoing negative consequences. God is not a neutral bystander in this discussion.

Caleb Kaltenbach, who grew up immersed in the LGBT community and is now the lead pastor of Discovery Church in Simi Valley, California, says there is a "tension that arises in engaging with LGBT people . . . between acceptance and approval, and how to challenge people well. There is a tension between grace and truth. We have to own the fact that it isn't our job to change somebody's sexual orientation. It is our job to speak truth into people's lives."[31] Agreed.

In September of 2017, a document was released to the press called The "Nashville Statement" (so called because those who met to draft it did so in Nashville).[32] It was an expression of fourteen affirmations and denials and, in essence, set forth the biblical teaching about sexuality. The bottom line is that marriage is between one man and one woman and that homosexual relationships are sinful.

The negative reaction, even by those who claim to be evangelicals, was severe and immediate. Evangelicals who embrace same-sex relationships quickly appealed to love and compassion. One so-called evangelical blogger wrote that "the demagoguery on display is nauseating" and those who signed it were modern-day Pharisees. Thus the Nashville Statement was condemned as unloving and judgmental.

Be warned: we are living at a time when words such as *unity*, *love*, *acceptance*, and *inclusion* are being defined in ways that defy Scripture. We are forgetting that God is a jealous God who often exercises intolerant love. We have to get over the idea that God agrees with us about everything. Under cultural pressure, evangelicals are susceptible to jettison biblical teaching and fall in line with our culture's expectations.

And it could get far worse.

An attempt will be made for biblically based Christian colleges to close unless they drop their insistence that natural marriage is the only kind that God sanctions. And churches will have to choose between biblical convictions or the heavy "boot" of the state bent on squelching every bit of religious freedom about matters of sexuality. The LGBT community has already proven that their convictions trump religious freedom and, clearly, they have veto power over laws they do not favor.

The day might come when child protection services will be called in to monitor children who are homeschooled and, if necessary, remove them from the care of parents who have been diagnosed with acute "intolerant personality disorder."[33] For Christians who object to such actions, they'll be vilified as siding with hopelessly entrenched, bigoted cultists. They might be declared mentally incompetent.

> It is better to be accused of harshness than of lying with hushed tones of compassion.

My fellow brothers and sisters, we need to get over our fear of being called bigots, intolerant, or racists, and make it perfectly clear to both church and society that no Christian can truly follow Christ and endorse self-harm (as in gender re-assignment surgery) and same-sex relationships. We cannot show a godly love for our neighbor if our silence is interpreted as submission to Satan's objective of destroying God's temple. Let me repeat, *it is better to be accused of being harsh than it is to tell lies with hushed tones of compassion, love, care, and thoughtfulness.*

Let us hear again the words of Jesus, "Blessed are you when people hate you and when they exclude you and revile you and spurn your name as evil, on account of the Son of Man! Rejoice in that day, and leap for joy, for behold, your reward is great in heaven; for so their fathers did to the prophets" (Luke 6:22–23).

The Evangelical Divide

"Was he against it, before he was for it? Is he really against it now?"

That is the opening question that Al Mohler asked about the strange story of Eugene Peterson.[34] Peterson, retired since 1991, was asked if he would perform a same-sex wedding if he was still pastoring today. He answered, "Yes." After the ensuing firestorm and the threat of having his books pulled from Christian book markets, he changed his mind and now says he believes that marriage should just be between a man and a woman. What he really believes, we may never know.

This is the watershed issue of evangelicalism. As Mohler says, "Those who have fled for security to the house of evasion must know that the structure has crumbled. It always does."[35] There is no place to hide.

To all those pastors who fear that a loving but firm stand against same-sex relationships would brand your church as a hate group, and thus do damage to the gospel, put yourself in the shoes of the apostle Paul: just reread Romans 1:18–32, and remember he was writing to a church within a culture that was rife with defiling sexual sins of every sort. Yet he wrote candidly about God's view of homosexual relationships, knowing his letter would be read publicly to the congregation. He knew that truth hurts, but it also heals (1 Cor. 6:9–11).

After Martin Niemöller came out courageously in oppos-ing Hitler's agenda, his fellow pastors strongly condemned him, saying that they thought that sensitive political matters could be handled more diplomatically. He replied, "What does it matter how we look in Germany compared with how we look in heaven?"[36]

A good question. So, how does the church of Jesus Christ look in heaven?

"Yet you have still a few names in Sardis, people who have not soiled their garments, and they will walk with me in white, for they are worthy" (Rev. 3:4).

THE GOSPEL OF INTERFAITH DIALOGUE

I write this with a heavy heart and great concern for the "faith once delivered to the saints." Our culture has chosen to submit to Islam, and there's pressure on the church to follow suit. Let me say from the outset that I am not opposed to those who engage Muslims in conversations about the dif-ference between the two religions outside the setting of the pulpit. I have enjoyed such exchanges. However, under the guise of tolerance, love, and some would even say, evange-lism, Muslims are being invited into churches to present a special revised version of Islam.

As emphasized in a previous chapter, becoming friends with Muslims is a privilege given to us by the Lord. And, for the sake of the record, I am opposed to arguing, trying to prove who is right, and expressing words of condemnation. We should not attempt to win an argument but to win trust and show respect and caring. In fact, I've heard testimonies from Muslims who converted to Christianity, and all of these stories have the same theme: unexpected love and caring from Christians.

However, this chapter has to do with "interfaith dialogue," a planned and organized forum that is employed by some Muslims or Muslim groups to present a more palatable version of Islam. Stephen Coughlin, a concerned Catholic, exposes the acceptance of Islam among liberal Catholics. He grieves that Catholics "are willing to submerge their own core beliefs in favor of seductive relationships with interfaith partners whose approval and false friendship they foolishly come to prioritize over fealty to their own faith."[37]

Coughlin writes that through this subversion of the interfaith community, the Muslim Brotherhood, in particular, seeks to manipulate other religions in further dislocation of their faith. What has been so effective in America's universities and colleges is now entering our churches. Coughlin explains, "For the brotherhood, the interfaith venue represents an optimal platform for penetration into the leadership circles of religious organizations."[38]

Interfaith dialogue in the church gives Muslim leaders an uncontested platform to speak publicly and invites them to present a version of Islam that simply does not exist in Muslim countries. Nor is it based on Islam's history or its foundational writings.

The Goal of Interfaith Dialogue

From the Muslim point of view, the goal of interfaith dialogue is stated by the late Sayyid Qutb, a leading member of the Egyptian Muslim Brotherhood: "The chasm between Islam and Jahiliyyah [the society of unbelievers] is great and a bridge is not to be built across so that people on the two sides may mix with each other, *but only so that people of Jahiliyyah may come over to Islam.*"[39]

In this same vein, Omar Ahmad, founder of the Council on American Islamic Relations, was reported as saying, ". . . the media person among us [members of the Muslim Brotherhood] will know *that you send two messages, one to the Americans and one to the Muslims.*"[40]

The book *Interfaith Dialogue: a Guide for Muslims* by Muhammad Shafiq and Mohammed Abu-Nimer, speaks in neutral tones, many of which Christians would find acceptable. The authors talk about fairness, politeness, careful listening, and the need for coexistence.[41]

In brief, it was written to present a sanitized version of Islam to non-Muslims by reinterpreting its sacred texts and its history without discussing sharia law and issues such as the harsh penalties for apostates, or Muslims who renounce their faith. Nor does it refer to Islam's historic violence against Christians, particularly in the Middle East.

Muslims should encourage a spirit of *trust* but should not forget that "the Qur'an becomes the purified text that restores the prophetic concept of pure monotheism."[42]

Read this carefully: "Each dialogue partner has the right to define his or her own religion and beliefs [so that] the rest can only describe what it looks like to them from the outside."[43] And again: "These seminars should address both Christian and Muslim beliefs and provide a comparative view of each, without attempting to judge between the two."[44]

The bottom line: Muslim participants in interfaith dialogue want an uncontested platform where they can present a version of Islam without undesirable references from the Quran or discussion about Islam's mistreatment of its own people, especially those who disagree with its teachings.

Each dialogue participant should take the other's words at face value. In other words, a critical analysis of the respective religions is discouraged. They believe a friendly atmosphere is important if Islam is to be seen as open and tolerant.

Let's Listen In

Imagine you are a Christian in Iraq, Iran, Egypt, or Saudi Arabia and have witnessed oppression and persecution firsthand. You might not recognize this revised version of Islam. Here are six quotes from *Interfaith Dialogue* to instruct the Muslim speaker on how to present Islam to Americans:

Islam should be presented as "protecting and enhancing civil rights."[45]

"Muslim participants can emphasize that Islam stands for protecting the rights of both men and women."[46]

"Many people in the West believe that Islam is a religion of revenge because they do not know that its core teachings are forgiveness and mercy."[47]

"Muslims should avoid saying that Jews, Christians, Hindus, Buddhists, or others will end up in hell."[48] Such conversations should be avoided. And if not, then this should be stated in a way that is least offensive, because "peaceful living and coexistence are at the very center of what Islam enjoins on all Muslims."[49]

"Muhammad . . . built an interfaith confederation that included Jews, Christians, Muslims, and pagans. His goal was to find a way for everyone to live together in peace. . . . [Muhammad] always used the Islamic principles of forgiveness and mercy to reconcile differences between individuals."[50]

Perhaps now we understand the value of interfaith dialogue for the Muslim community. Little wonder we read, "Interfaith dialogues are perfect settings not only for nurturing positive and constructive Muslim and non-Muslim relations, but also for spreading them abroad and allowing such relationships to be the guiding model for interaction."[51]

Muslims look for Christian leaders who will play by these interfaith dialogue rules and who will accept the Muslim narrative uncritically, even at the expense of their own Christian beliefs.

Frank Gaffney, one of America's most knowledgeable scholars on Islam says, "The Catholic church in particular has proven especially susceptible to a sophisticated strategy of manipulation whose goal is the dislocation of faith to advance submission to Islamic Law (shariah) under cover of cherished leftists, liberal values of acceptance, inclusion and acceptance."[52] Protestant churches—even evangelical churches—are following suit.

Unfortunately, Muslims who present their version of Islam can count on a ready American audience that longs to believe that groups like the Muslim Brotherhood are tolerant, peaceful, and respectful of other religions. They can count on the fact that they are speaking to people who have never read the Quran and the Hadith; they can be quite sure that many have never studied the history of Islam and also have willingly ignored all the statements of the Brotherhood leaders who say that their intention is to destroy Western civilization from within.

No matter the professed goals of the Brotherhood, no matter the number of terrorist attacks carried out by radical Muslims, no matter the history of Islam, and no matter the growing insistence that we curtail our freedoms in favor of Muslim demands, Muslim leaders know that many Americans are accepting the narrative that Islam is a religion of tolerance and peace.

To those evangelicals who would say that we should engage in interfaith dialogue and "build bridges" that will lead to evangelism, my response is twofold:

First, allowing false teachers to speak in our churches under any condition is forbidden by Scripture (see 2 John 1:6–11).

Second, evangelism is best accomplished by friendship, authentic discussions, and serving others, including our neighbors of different faiths. However, it is never right to give a representative of a false religion an unchallenged platform to win a hearing by carefully crafted deceptions, especially in a church setting.

If a church wants to learn what Islam believes, why not invite a convert out of Islam to come into a church and share his/her story? I've personally discovered that these testimonies are instructive and helpful to understand life in Muslim countries without the influence of Western values. We have much to learn, and there are many who can teach us.

As a means of evangelism, other opportunities exist for reaching Muslims with the love of Christ and the message of the gospel. Christians and Muslims can connect with each other in their homes, schools, neighborhoods, and workplaces. Jesus calls us to reach across the chasm and represent Him well wherever we find ourselves. This just might be the time for us to remember the words of Jesus to His disciples, "Behold, I am sending you out as sheep in the midst of wolves, so be wise as serpents and as innocent as doves" (Matt. 10:16).

Thankfully, we can count on the Good Shepherd to be among us each step of the way.

CHAPTER 9

TAKING THE CROSS INTO THE WORLD

Shamelessly Sharing the One Message That Can Save Us

Christianity is the only major religion to have as its central event the humiliation of its God." So writes Bruce Shelly in the opening line of his book on church history.[1]

The humiliation of God!

One indication we don't understand the cross today is in the difficulty of finding anyone who says anything against it. Crosses are worn as pendants by athletes and rock stars; it has become a symbol of general goodwill and acceptance. The cross is seen as an ancient symbol that can be easily combined with an undefined spirituality or, for that matter, with other religions.

Several years ago when Rebecca and I were flying to Cleveland, I was sitting in an aisle seat across from a woman wearing a necklace with a cross. I said, "Thank you for wearing that cross, we do have a great Savior, don't we?" She replied, "I guess I don't understand the cross like you do . . ." then she scooped the cross into her hand and showed me that behind it she also had a Jewish star and a pendant to the Hindu god Om. She said, "I believe that there are many ways to God." You can imagine the interesting discussion we had as I tried to explain why the cross, if properly understood, cannot be combined with other religious symbols and options.

Make no mistake. The early Christians saw the cross as a horrid reality reserved for the worst of criminals. Crucifixion was not simply designed to end one's life but also to inflict as much torture as possible. And, for good measure, crucifixions were always performed in the most public of places so that the victim would be dehumanized, both by the shouts of derision of passing crowds, and by being exposed naked to the delight of gawkers. The writer of Hebrews captures this when he says Jesus "endured the cross, despising the shame" (Heb. 12:2).

No wonder Paul writes that the cross is an offense (the Greek word is *skandalos*, a "scandal") to the Jews and the Greeks (1 Cor. 1:23 NLT). As for the Jews, they knew that the Old Testament affirmed that those who hung on the cross were cursed (Paul quotes this in Galatians 3:13–14). As for the Greeks and Romans, they thought of the cross as a defeat; no one would want to follow a loser.

Who, in his right mind, would want to stake his eternal destiny on the words and deeds of a leader who had been found worthy of death—especially death on a *cross*? The idea that the humiliating death of a self-proclaimed Messiah was God's most glorious saving event, simply didn't make sense to anyone, including the disciple Peter. He strongly rebuked Jesus for saying He was on His way to Jerusalem to be crucified (Matt. 16: 22–23). Even to Jesus' most faithful followers, the idea of a crucified Messiah was unthinkable.

A HEAVY CROSS, A POWERFUL WITNESS

There's a story about a man who dreamt he was carrying a heavy cross on his shoulder. He was exhausted; he wished that his cross was lighter. In the dream he saw a woodsman with an axe, so he asked that a good part of his cross be chopped off. After that, the man happily resumed his journey, thankful that his cross was so much lighter.

On his journey, he came to a chasm between two mountains. He wanted to continue but found that he couldn't bridge the gap; if only his cross had been longer, he could have laid it down and used it as a bridge. But the cross was short—by just the length that had been chopped off.

When the man awoke, he was glad this was only a dream. He now realized that only those who are willing to carry a heavy cross are able to scale the next mountain. Those who are constantly in search of a lighter cross will never go far in claiming territory for Christ. At some point, they will conclude that the price of obedience is too high. The obstacles too formidable.

Have we, as Christians, forgotten that we are asked to gladly bear the full weight of the offense of the cross? Sometimes we hear Christians say things like, "I have cancer. That is my cross." Is this what Jesus was referring to when He asked us to take up His cross?

I don't think so. To carry our cross means *to accept the trouble that comes along with believing and following Jesus.* This means the willing acceptance of ridicule, shame, and often the persecution that comes with being identified with our Savior. In short, it means we gladly identify with Jesus at the points of tension where we conflict with popular culture and even with our friends.

Often, the heavier our cross, the more powerful our witness. Unfortunately, we often prefer to make our cross lighter by bowing to cultural pressures.

LIVING IN AN OFFENDED GENERATION

Ours is an offended generation. Everybody is offended by something, and they believe that they have a right to *not* be offended. A law in New York City that details various offenses that can be penalized includes violating the wishes of the transgender community. If a woman identifies as a man, and you have been informed of this but you deliberately and intentionally continue to use female pronouns, you can be fined. These fines can reach up to $250,000.[2] As an example, if you referred to Bruce Jenner as a "he" and not as a "she" named Caitlyn, you could be fined for the offense. A Muslim said that singing the national anthem was offensive because it was a means of "mass assimilation."

This culture of offendedness is enfeebling our society. Yet it's promoted by the media, by our politicians, and by our government. It's promoted by various activist groups. It's as if a new "right" has been found in the constitution. "I never have to hear or see anything that offends me. In fact, my offense is so hurtful that whatever offends me should be illegal. Or at least the offensive person should be publicly shamed." Our culture tells us that "if you make me feel bad, you are a bad person."

A Christian man, getting his hair cut, told me that the barber asked him a lead question about his faith, but he replied only in generalities. He confided to me that he did not talk directly about salvation because he feared he would "offend" the man. Yet, no one gets saved unless, at least on some level, they are "offended." Peter, alluding to Psalm 118, writes, "'The stone that the builders rejected has become the cornerstone,' and 'A stone of stumbling, and a rock of offense'" (1 Peter 2:7–8).

Jesus is a Rock of offense!

To empty the cross of its offense is to empty it of its power.

Emptying the Cross of Its Offense

Let's consider how we might be doing what Paul feared he might do, namely to empty the cross of its offense.

We empty the cross of its offense by teaching that good works are necessary for salvation

Paul says that if he were to teach circumcision, he would no longer be persecuted, because "the offense of the cross has been removed" (Gal. 5:11). To put it briefly, we empty the cross of its offense when we teach that our works are meritorious in the act of salvation. If we say that circumcision, baptism, last rites, or any other ritual is necessary for salvation, then the gospel has been compromised and the "offense is removed."

Sometime ago, Hank Hanegraaff, a man known as the "Bible Answer Man," converted to Eastern Orthodoxy.[3] This shocked and confused many Christians who believe that salvation is by faith alone, in Christ alone, and in no way gained through a cooperative effort in which we do our part and God does His part. Space forbids a longer discussion of the differences between what evangelical Protestants believe and what Orthodox (and also Roman Catholics) believe, except to emphasize that the New Testament teaches that salvation is a free gift given to repentant sinners based solely on Christ's finished work, not on anything we do ourselves.

> The cross exposes our own sinfulness by showing the lengths to which God had to go in order to redeem us.

There is a danger here for us as evangelicals as well. We might be surprised at how many who worship in our churches believe that somehow they must make themselves worthy of God's grace, and hence, they look to their own goodness or spiritual rituals for assurance of salvation. Salvation by works in one form or another is our natural default inclination.

The apostle Paul says that if he were to teach that any work on our part is necessary, salvation is no more of grace. "For we hold that one is justified by faith apart from works of the law" (Rom. 3:28). Equally clear are these words, "For by grace you have been saved through faith. And this is not your own doing; it is the gift of God, not a result of works, so that no one may boast" (Eph. 2:8–9).

People are offended when told that they're too sinful to cooperate with God in salvation. They're offended when told that our only contribution in salvation is our sin; God supplies the faith and the gift of Christ's righteousness. The cross exposes our own sinfulness by showing the lengths to which God had to go in order to redeem us.

The cross humbles us. When God chose to save us, He took all of our works and, figuratively speaking, put them on a shelf and wrote across them, "unusable." He set aside our tainted efforts, and He Himself became our substitute. Every Sunday here in Chicago, thousands of people attend church and are told that Jesus is necessary for salvation. What they are not told is that Jesus is *enough*.

When we believe we have to *do* something to be saved rather than relying on what God has done for us, we give ourselves a bit of the credit. Blessed is the person who stands with the penitent publican and strikes his chest and says simply, "God be merciful to me the sinner!" Add works to the gospel, and the offense of the cross is removed. The hymn writer Augustus Toplady wrote: "Nothing in my hand I bring. Simply to Thy cross I cling."

The cross is God's final rejection of all human merit in salvation.

We empty the cross of its offense when we insist that Jesus did not bear God's righteous wrath on our behalf

Amazingly, there are some evangelicals who are seeking a substitute for the doctrine of substitution. Steve Chalke might not be known to many Americans, but he's a British evangelical broadcaster and an author of many books. In *The*

Lost Message of Jesus, he calls for a new understanding of the gospel. He says that since Christianity is seriously failing in the West, it needs a makeover.[4]

Sadly, he speaks for a growing number of evangelicals on this side of the ocean who are seeking for a more acceptable understanding of the atonement.

Chalke says that when Jesus died on the cross, He bore our pain and suffering, but that doesn't mean that He absorbed the wrath of God for our sin: "The fact is that the cross isn't a form of cosmic child abuse—a vengeful Father punishing his son for an offence he had not even committed. Understandably, both people inside and outside found this twisted version of events morally dubious and a huge barrier to faith."[5]

Of course, we should not view the Father as vengeful and the Son as the loving substitute. After all, "*God* so loved the world." Child abuse? No, for Christ voluntarily came to earth to save us from our sins. "For this reason the Father loves me, because I lay down my life that I might take it up again. No one takes it from me, but I lay it down of my own accord. I have authority to lay it down, and I have authority to take it up again" (John 10:17–18). Salvation is a plan agreed upon by all three members of the Trinity.

That being said, the Bible clearly speaks about God's anger against sin and that Jesus took our punishment.

There are dozens of Scriptures in both the Old and New Testaments that speak graphically of the wrath of God. "The LORD is a jealous and avenging God; the LORD is avenging and wrathful; the LORD takes vengeance on his adversaries. . . . Who can stand before his indignation? Who can endure the heat of his anger? His wrath is poured out like fire, and the rocks are broken into pieces by him" (Nah. 1:2, 6).

In the New Testament, Paul wrote that we are "to wait for his Son from heaven, whom he raised from the dead, Jesus who delivers us from the wrath to come" (1 Thess. 1:10). The book of Revelation vividly describes the anger of God against sinners (see Rev. 14:8–11). Yet, Chalke condemns Jonathan Edward's famous sermon, "Sinners in the Hands of an Angry God" and is grateful that such "ferocious rhetoric is a thing of the past."[6] But only the fact of Jesus bearing God's wrath can explain His excruciating cry, "My God, my God, why have you forsaken me?"

Many evangelicals do not deny God's anger against sin but simply ignore speaking or writing about it because that would not be "good news." So, they concentrate on the more positive aspects of the Christian faith, believing that the love of God is more appealing. But we empty the cross of its offense when we think that the message of the love of God can be understood independently of His wrath and justice.

John Stott said, "Before we can begin to see the cross as something done *for* us . . . we have to see it as something done *by* us."[7] Where is the greatest evidence of God's love seen? On the cross. Where is God's greatest judgment and wrath against sin most clearly seen? On the cross! So Jesus actually bears the wrath that is due us. God would have never put His Son through horrid suffering if there had been a cheaper way to do it. But Jesus absorbs what you and I should receive; in short, *He bore our hell.* And now that justice has been satisfied, Jesus is just and the justifier of those who believe on Him (see Rom. 3:26), which means now God is

We should not emphasize the love of God to the exclusion of the holiness and justice of God.

free to operate on the basis of grace and save even the vilest of sinners.

But if the heart of the gospel is denied, other doctrines also fall by the wayside: once you construct your theology on what you want to believe about God rather than on what He revealed, you are free to shape other doctrines according to your preference.

We do not get to choose the attributes that God has; if He reveals Himself as being wrathful against sinners, then we must accept this and be eternally grateful that He ordained a way by which we can be saved by the sacrifice of His Son.

I find it ironic that some Christians working among the poor, the despised, and the abused say that they don't refer to sin when they share the gospel because that would "not be good news." But the bad news prepares the way for the very good news!

Yes, we should emphasize the love of God because those who have been mistreated already know that sin exists. But we should not emphasize the love of God to the exclusion of the holiness and justice of God. We empty the cross of its offense when we think that the message of the love of God can be understood independently of His wrath and justice.

John Piper writes, "When Christ died for our sins, Satan was disarmed and defeated. The one eternally destructive weapon that he had was stripped from his hand, namely, his accusation before God that we are guilty and should perish with him. When Christ died, that accusation was nullified."[8]

Here's a question: Is it not true that the acknowledgment of sin in all of its hideous forms is exactly what makes the gospel such good news? Is it not the doctrine of hell that makes the grace and love of God and prospect of heaven all the more amazing?

My wife, Rebecca, and I know a woman who paid thousands of dollars to a vet to fix her lame dog, "Molly." Molly was severely crippled and needed special surgery. Now, as Molly scampers around the house, she has no understanding of the price paid on her behalf; all that she knows is that once she was lame and now she can walk! Just so, we simply cannot grasp the price paid for our salvation. All we know is "once we were blind and now we see!"

We empty the cross of its offense when we believe that other religions are able to bring us to God

Historically, the gospel has not only had to confront culture, but also other religions. And as the West becomes more diverse racially and ethnically, along with this comes the challenge of other religious options. Back in 1993, I attended the Parliament of World Religions in Chicago where 6,000 delegates from all over the world, representing more than a hundred different religions, met in order to explore ways in which the various religions can be united. Swami Chindanansa of the Divine Life Society summed up the premise of the conference by writing, "There are many effective, equally valid religions. They are, therefore, to be equally reverenced, equally recognized and equally loved and cherished—not merely tolerated ... [The Hindu Scriptures say] 'In whatever way men approach Me, even so do I go to them.'"[9]

What place did Christ have in the more than seven hundred workshops that were available during the eight-day conference? At times He was variously admired, quoted, and favorably compared to other religious teachers, ancient and modern. He was seen as one more stage in the evolutionary development of religion; indeed, He was a very necessary and important stage, but He was only one enlightened man among many.

What I saw and heard at the parliament is a microcosm of our schools, businesses, and communities. The people who live next door and our associates at work most likely believe that it doesn't matter what god one prays to because every deity is ultimately the same deity shrouded in a different name—each religion is but one more petal of a beautiful flower.

Which begs the question: Does Christ belong on the same shelf with Buddha, Krishna, Bahá'u'lláh, Zoroaster, or Muhammad? Like Christ, such leaders (and others) have taught some rather lofty ethical ideas. Even if we say Christ stands taller than the rest, have we given Him His due? Or is He to be placed on an entirely different shelf altogether?

Let me answer with an experience I had at the Parliament. I went into the display area where all the religions had their literature available; I went on a search for a sinless Savior who could take away my sins. (After all, I cannot have my sins taken away by a sinner, a man who is part of my predicament!) I began with the Hindus, then the Buddhists, then the Muslims, asking those in charge if they had a sinless Savior to recommend to me. Name the religion and they admitted they had only gurus and prophets, some of whom claimed enlightenment, but none claimed sinlessness; and none claimed to be a qualified Savior who could forgive sin and present us to God as holy. I quickly confirmed what I already knew: *among the religions leaders of the world, Jesus stands entirely alone.*

It is true, as some assert, that many other religions also demand a blood sacrifice for sins. But in Christianity, *God becomes the sacrifice* . . . "in Christ God was reconciling the world to himself" (2 Cor. 5:19). Only in Christianity is God alone the Redeemer. Other religions are man trying to seek God; only in Christianity has God come to seek man.

As Ravi Zacharias likes to say, "My premise is that the popular aphorism that 'all religions are fundamentally the same and only superficially different' simply is not true. It is more correct to say that all religions are, at best, superficially similar but fundamentally different."[10] Christianity, is indeed radically different: it has a Savior whose death and resurrection provides a solution for the greatest of sinners. The cross, and the redemption it wrought, exists only in Christianity.

When it comes to Jesus, all the good arguments are on our side. We must let our light shine in the hazy dusk of religious pluralism. This is not a time to hide the cross or neglect it; let us embrace the cross and resurrection and rejoice that we don't just have a prophet but a Savior who proved His qualifications. From our standpoint, the cross was God's finest hour.

As for unity with other religions, J. C. Ryle said it best: "Unity without the gospel is a worthless unity; it is the very unity of hell."[11]

Carrying the Cross into the World

How do we obey the invitation of Jesus to take up His cross and follow Him?

We carry our cross into the world by serving others

Jesus said that He came not to be served, but to serve. You may ask how the early church spread throughout North Africa; Tertullian wrote, "It is our care for the helpless, our practice of lovingkindness that brands us in the eyes of many of our opponents. 'Look!' they say, 'How they love one another! Look how they are prepared to die for one another.'"[12]

In Berlin, I've visited the Kaiser Wilhelm Church, which was bombed in World War II. When it was reconstructed after the war, the right arm of a statue of Christ was never found. Nevertheless, this statue is prominently displayed without the right arm; it stands as a reminder that we are the arms of Christ in a hurting and hopeless world.

I paraphrase the words of one theologian: "Tell me how much you have entered into the suffering of those around you, and I will tell you how much you love them."

We carry the cross into the world through our gospel-driven racial unity

I am writing at a time when racial issues dominate the headlines. In a nation addicted to rage, the church must keep its cool and be a calming voice of reason and broad political acceptance without being co-opted by one side or another in these escalating disputes. We must continue to stand united at the foot of the cross and invite other sinners to join us regardless of their backgrounds, race, political affiliation, or immigration status. The church is still America's best hope.

The cross makes us brothers and sisters with those with whom we have nothing in common, except that we have been purchased with the same blood and brought by the same Savior into the presence of the same heavenly Father.

Through the cross, Christ created one new temple, "a dwelling place for God by the Spirit" (see Eph. 2:14–22).

Churches must do more than intentionally cultivate multiethnic experiences and ministries, so that "racial reconciliation" is not just a slogan but a reality. Reconciliation and shared ministry must be seen, believed, and preached as exhibiting the heart of the gospel. Racial reconciliation is best seen in friendships, in seeking justice for the oppressed and equality for the marginalized.

During my time as pastor of The Moody Church, I told the congregation that racial diversity prepares us for heaven. We know that God's heart is such that in the heavenly realms we will have people from every tribe, tongue, and nation (see Rev. 5:9–11). I was so thankful to be able to say that at The Moody Church, on any given Sunday morning, we had people from more than seventy different countries of origin who worshiped with us. By no means had we achieved the integration we have sought, but we are on our way.

If you have not read Martin Luther King Jr.'s "Letter from Birmingham Jail," I urge you to do so. This should be a starting point for understanding unacknowledged racism and our need to seek justice for our brothers and sisters. We have only begun.

I am aware that my discussion of this important topic is all too brief, but others have written ably on the topic, so I point you to their writings. Becoming one in worship, work, and witness will never be finished. (Suggestions for further reading are found at the end of this chapter.)

We carry the cross into the world when we exalt it above political affiliations

This book is being written at a time of political wrangling and racial and ethnic tension. But—and this is my concern—our present toxic political, moral, and racial conflicts have stirred seething tensions that are tearing us apart. The idea of a nation held together by one language, one common core of values, and respected borders is passing us by.

I, for one, believe that politics is important; Christians should run for office at every level. Christians can also lead in recruiting support for their favorite candidate.

Also, I believe as Christians we should work toward just laws and support legal organizations that appeal to the law to maintain our freedoms. Paul the Apostle took advantage of his Roman citizenship, saying he should not be beaten but be tried in a Roman court (see Acts 22:22–29).

And yet, political change is best advanced under the banner of shared common grace, not the pulpit. Pastors should refrain from endorsing political parties or specific candidates, even if those parties or candidates are more closely aligned with Christian values. As Russell Moore wrote, "it would be a tragedy to get the right president, the right Congress, and the wrong Christ."[13]

I commend those pastors in Germany who preached against Hitler's political agenda; indeed, I agree with the German theologian Helmut Thielicke, who said that Germany was judged because it substituted the swastika for the cross. It is one thing to oppose the platform of a political party, but there are dangers in alignment with an alternative party, even if it appears to be more Christian. Neither in Germany nor in America is there a distinctly "Christian political party."

As pastors in the West, we should preach on biblical issues that are often associated with politics such as abortion, same-sex marriage, the infringement on religious freedom, etc. But that differs from direct alignment (endorsement) with one political party or another.

The unwise intertwining of evangelicalism and right-wing politics has resulted in a stumbling block to many who otherwise might be open to the message of Christianity. In addition, it has prompted some evangelicals to drift to the left or far left politically or to opt out of the political debate altogether.

To many people, the cross stands like a bulletin board with many different agendas nailed to it. My point is, let the cross stand above politicians and their own quest for influence. At all times, we must make clear that the cross of Christ stands in judgment on all parties, no matter their political leanings. To everyone we say, "Unless you humbly receive Jesus Christ as your Savior and accept the work of the cross on your behalf, you will find yourself in hell."

I like what Billy Graham said: "I'm not for the left wing or the right wing—I'm for the whole bird."[14]

We carry the cross into the world by witnessing to our faith

We carry our cross when we refuse to hide its message under the banner of "niceness." Some Christians are so anxious to not offend anyone that they never get around to explaining both the blessings of the cross and our need for it. We are often too nice, too timid, and too quick to be "inoffensive."

There are plenty of offensive Christians. They are offensive to me. They are offensive to you. They are judgmental. They don't know how to be kind. They are not winsome. They are looking for somebody to condemn, and they are "right" about everything. They love to "buttonhole" people with the truth.

The greatest advertisement for the gospel is Christians who listen well, who are welcoming, and who are eager to serve others. The greatest advertisement is those who have deep convictions, but act on them in redemptive ways. These Christians share their faith at great personal cost and "go to him outside the camp and bear the reproach he endured" (Heb. 13:13). And they do it with joy.

In his book *A Severe Mercy*, Sheldon Vanauken talks about his first encounter with Christians. That night he wrote these words:

> *The best argument for Christianity is Christians: their joy, their certainty, their completeness. But the strongest argument against Christianity is also Christians—when they are sombre and joyless, when they are self-righteous and smug in complacent consecration, when they are narrow and repressive, then Christianity dies a thousand deaths. . . . Indeed there are impressive indications that the positive quality of joy is in Christianity—and possibly nowhere else. If that were certain, it would be a proof of a very high order.*[15]

Many Christians are silent about their faith in Christ, because they don't want to be known as a "Bible thumper" or to be branded as part of the religious right. But the way to dispel such a stereotype is to share our faith with deep personal conviction along with a loving caring attitude of sacrifice and helpfulness.

Jesus had a word for those who were ashamed of being identified with Him: "For whoever is ashamed of me and of my words in this adulterous and sinful generation, of him will the Son of Man also be ashamed when he comes in the glory of his Father with the holy angels" (Mark 8:38).

If we don't delight in the privilege of being identified with Christ, we cannot expect to receive the favor of God. Jesus said, "We are blessed if our names are cast out as evil for His sake" (the literal Greek in Luke 6:22). The world's hatred of the gospel might be a positive sign, provided that it is offended by the message and not because we are obnoxious.

"Evangelism," someone has said, "is one beggar telling another we have found bread." Let us invite a hurting world to the table where we ourselves have found food for our weary souls. There we will find those whom God has already prepared for our witness.

We carry the cross into the world by accepting rejection without retaliation

I return briefly to the theme of opposition.

We carry our cross into the world when we suffer well. As Americans, we have to dispense with the notion that it is fundamentally unacceptable to be persecuted for what we believe and teach. We must not become wimps, unwilling to stand for truth and revealing our convictions. Like Martin Luther, we need Christians whose consciences are "captive to the Word of God."[16]

But as much as possible, we must hold these convictions

without rancor, threats, or retaliation, and without finger pointing. We must follow not only the model of Jesus but of the apostle Paul. "To the present hour we hunger and thirst, we are poorly dressed and buffeted and homeless, and we labor, working with our own hands. *When reviled, we bless; when persecuted, we endure; when slandered, we entreat. We have become, and are still, like the scum of the world, the refuse of all things*" (1 Cor. 4:11–13).

We forget that Jesus left us an example of how to suffer. "When he was reviled, he did not revile in return; when he suffered, he did not threaten, but continued entrusting himself to him who judges justly" (1 Peter 2:23).

It's not just what we say, but how we react when rebuffed that counts.

We carry the cross into the world by inviting the worst of sinners— yes, evil criminals—to believe the gospel

D. L. Moody, who founded both The Moody Church and the Moody Bible Institute, had an unquestionable faith in God's ability to save the worst of sinners. Let us listen to an excerpt of one of his sermons:

> *A young man told me last night that he was too great a sinner to be saved. Why they are the very men Christ came after!... The only charge they had against Christ is that He was receiving bad men. They are the very kind of men He is willing to receive. All that you have to do is to prove that you are a sinner and I will prove that you got a Savior. And the greater the sinner the greater the Savior. You say that your heart is hard. Well then of course you want Christ to soften it. You cannot do it yourself. The harder the heart,*

the more need you have of Christ. If your sin rises up before you like a dark mountain, bear in mind that the blood of Jesus Christ cleanses from all sin. There is no sin so big or so corrupt and vile but the blood of Christ can cover it.[17]

I read a fascinating book titled *Mission at Nuremberg*, the story of a Lutheran pastor who was the chaplain to the twenty-one Nazis who were hanged in Nuremburg.[18] (Hermann Goring cheated the executioners by swallowing a cyanide capsule the night before his scheduled execution.) The American government decided that there should be a chaplain for these criminals. Some people disagreed, but nonetheless, Henry Gerecke was chosen. He was from St. Louis but spoke German fluently, and so was asked to be the chaplain to these criminals.

People admonished him. "You should not shake hands with these men!" He replied, "If they are to believe my message, I have to be friendly to them," so he shook hands and interacted with them. Among the twenty-one prisoners were six Catholics and fifteen Protestants. In the chapel services, some of these Nazis participated in reciting the Lord's Prayer and knew the creed. According to Gerecke, five of these criminals, and possibly seven, came to saving faith in Jesus Christ before they died.

Ribbentrop, who was Hitler's foreign minister, before he was executed, said that he "put all his trust in the Blood of the Lamb that taketh away the sins of the world."[19]

The fact that some of Hitler's evil henchmen will be in heaven is offensive to us, especially when we realize that some of those whom they tormented might not join them in the heavenly city. But that is exactly a part of the scandal of the cross: grace pays no attention to the depths of our sin, it only asks that we believe the gospel.

God says in effect, "I think so much of what Jesus Christ did when He died on that cross, I can even forgive a criminal if he believes in Jesus. But I cannot forgive a sane, decent, taxpaying American who doesn't believe in Jesus."

I say it again: grace is so contrary to the way we think because it is bestowed without any reference to merit. In fact, grace is most clearly seen when there is absolutely no merit at all. Grace is unlimited to those who receive it.

JESUS IN WEAKNESS, CROWNED AS KING

The late Nabeel Qureshi who was raised Muslim but converted to Christianity, wrote an excellent book titled *Seeking Allah, Finding Jesus*. He testifies that as a Muslim, he saw the cross of Christ as weakness in the Christian conception of God; it was a defeat. But then, as he thought more about it, he began to realize that if God were only sovereign and all powerful—if that's all that God was, He might just be a dictator, a despot who demands obedience. We would have no basis to assume that He is also merciful.[20]

But now as a Christian, Qureshi understood the power of the cross. I recall hearing him explain how he now saw the cross as the strength of God. He began to realize that in Jesus, we have a God who is not only all-powerful but who is also loving and merciful. What at first appeared to be a weakness was actually a strength.

This is exactly the teaching of Paul in the New Testament, "For he was crucified in weakness, but lives by the power of

God. For we also are weak in him, but in dealing with you we will live with him by the power of God" (2 Cor. 13:4).

Here's a story that serves as a wonderful illustration:

In Africa, there was a fire, and a hut was burned very quickly. All but one of the family members died. An unknown stranger had run into the burning hut and rescued a small boy. The next day, the tribe was sitting around, trying to figure out what to do with this boy. One man said, "I am wise. I should have him." Somebody else said, "Yeah, but I've got the money." In the midst of that discussion, a stranger appeared and said that he had a prior claim. And then he showed them his hands, burned during the rescue of the previous evening.

Likewise, Jesus' wounds speak to His sacrifice and claim on us.

The other gods were strong; but Thou wast weak;
They rode, but Thou didst stumble to a throne;
But to our wounds only God's wounds can speak,
And not a god has wounds, but Thou alone.[21]

Jesus stumbled to His throne, was crucified in weakness, but yet, He was and is King. He even ruled from the cross. To the penitent thief He said, "Today you shall be with me in paradise." Thanks to the authority of a dying Savior, that thief had breakfast with his bad-to-the-bone friends in the morning and yet supped with Christ the King in the evening!

The cross of Jesus Christ divides the world into two groups—those who are saved and those who aren't.

The cross of Jesus Christ divides the world into two groups—not black and white, not by country,

245

nationality, or age, but by those who are saved and those who aren't. "For the word of the cross is folly to those who are perishing, but to us who are being saved it is the power of God" (1 Cor. 1:18).

No wonder Paul wrote, "But far be it from me to boast except in the cross of our Lord Jesus Christ, by which the world has been crucified to me, and I to the world" (Gal. 6:14). Obviously the world is not dead, but we are dead to it.

"When the drama of history is over," said Helmut Thielicke, "Jesus Christ will stand alone on the stage. All the great figures of history . . . will realize that they have been but actors in a drama produced by Another."[22]

Jesus alone on the stage! And all His redeemed at His side.

The following are but a few of the many excellent books and essays on race relations:

All Together Different by J. Brian Tucker and John Koessler

Divided by Faith: Evangelical Religion and the Problem of Race in America by Michael Emerson and Christian Smith

"Letter from a Birmingham Jail" by Martin Luther King Jr.

One Blood: Parting Words to the Church on Race and Love by John Perkins

Oneness Embraced: Reconciliation, the Kingdom, and How We Are Stronger Together by Tony Evans

CHAPTER 10

JESUS AT THE CHURCH DOOR

Prayerless Pulpits, Satisfied Saints, and Spiritual Blindness

The ministry *OneCry* is committed to unifying Christians around a central theme—prayer for the church, for our country, and for the world. Their preamble reads:

> *With heavy hearts, we recognize that the church in America is in a state of spiritual emergency. Like the churches warned in Revelation, we have become lukewarm and compromised, and the light of our witness has grown dim. We confess that despite access to more resources and biblical teaching than any other group of believers in history, we are not characterized by the supernatural power of the Holy Spirit. And we*

*acknowledge our lack of widespread impact for Christ
on our lost and disintegrating culture.*[1]

It's time for Christians to focus on the actual spiritual
health of the church; to see it through the eyes of Jesus and
His evaluation of an ancient church, which has direct relevance to us today. As it was then, so it is now.

We seek to answer three questions:

1. Why did Jesus find himself outside the church door at
   Laodicea, knocking, asking to be invited back in?

2. How do we invite Him back into our churches and individual lives?

3. What rewards does Jesus promise to those who take up
   His glorious invitation?

This chapter is one of rebuke, and also one of hope and encouragement. Remember, Jesus stands ready to supply everything we need to *be* all that we should be for His glory. Yes,
we have read these words many times, but let us reread them
with teachable minds and open ears. He is speaking to us.

> *"And to the angel of the church in Laodicea write: 'The
> words of the Amen, the faithful and true witness, the
> beginning of God's creation.*
> *"I know your works: you are neither cold nor hot.
> Would that you were either cold or hot! So, because you
> are lukewarm, and neither hot nor cold, I will spit you*

out of my mouth. For you say, I am rich, I have prospered, and I need nothing, not realizing that you are wretched, pitiable, poor, blind, and naked. I counsel you to buy from me gold refined by fire, so that you may be rich, and white garments so that you may clothe yourself and the shame of your nakedness may not be seen, and salve to anoint your eyes, so that you may see. Those whom I love, I reprove and discipline, so be zealous and repent. Behold, I stand at the door and knock. If anyone hears my voice and opens the door, I will come in to him and eat with him, and he with me. The one who conquers, I will grant him to sit with me on my throne, as I also conquered and sat down with my Father on his throne. He who has an ear, let him hear what the Spirit says to the churches.'

(REV. 3:14–22)

Let's simply take the text at face value and capture some of the scenes.

AN OPENING WORD FOR PASTORS

Jesus begins each of His letters with the words, "To the angel of the church . . ." Who are these angels? Most likely this is not a reference to an actual angel, but rather, the word *angel* means *messenger*. Evidently, each church had a messenger responsible for communication, for getting Jesus' letter to the congregation. As pastors, we should be the first to ponder this letter from Jesus to *our* churches. Rather than protecting the status quo, we pastors have a calling to help unleash the church's potential in joyful and sacrificial ministry. As the saying goes, the state of the pulpit is the state of the church.

I have a friend in Germany who said he attended a concert that included a piece played by a handbell choir. In the middle of their rendition, an intoxicated person walked up and yanked the cloth from the table, upsetting the handbells. But the music kept playing, uninterrupted! The embarrassed musicians were just going through the motions as the preprogrammed music played over the loud speakers! Just motions. Just another concert.

As a pastor, I have often asked myself, what if God wanted to do something in my church that was not listed in the bulletin? Are we as pastors open to the leading of the Spirit? Or are we just depending on the past without fresh wind for the present and the future? Are we making music or just acting as if we are?

For now, let us ask ourselves some hard questions: Why do so few of our churches see members delivered from addictions and failing marriages and wayward children brought back to the family of God? Jesus didn't mention prayerlessness in his letter, but as we shall see in a moment, prayer was implied by His emphasis on repentance.

> Every unanswered prayer should be a reminder to lean more directly into God.

I asked Jim Cymbala of the Brooklyn Tabernacle why people line up for blocks around their church before the doors open for their Tuesday night prayer meeting. He said, "Your people would pray too if they actually believed that God answers prayer!"

If we just believed that God answers prayer!

I was immediately convicted of the cynicism in my own heart. How many times have I not bothered to pray because I didn't believe it would make a difference? We've all had our share of disillusionment with unanswered prayer, and if we have enough of those experiences we're tempted to say, "What's the use?" We forget that every unanswered prayer should be a reminder to lean more directly into God. Desperation brings hope and repentance.

If sermons delivered people from their sins and addictions, we'd probably be a holy people. But sermons, Bible studies, and seminars, apart from the unction of the Holy Spirit and the impact of the body of Christ, have no lasting results. Consequently, believers go on for years with little emotional and spiritual development. They struggle with the same sins, the same behavioral patterns, and the same inner and outer conflicts.

We do well to listen carefully to the diagnosis Jesus gives to this church. He begins by saying, "The words of the Amen, the faithful and true witness" (Rev. 3:14). The word *amen* means *faithful*; it means *truthful*. Jesus is saying, "I am going to give you a true analysis of who you are. My diagnosis is 100 percent correct. I will tell you the truth about yourself— particularly the things you don't see, but things that mean a great deal to me."

Our Jehovah's Witness friends are wrong when they insist that the next phrase, "the beginning of God's creation" means that Jesus was created. Rather, the meaning is simply that Jesus is the *originator* of God's creation. "For by him all things were created, in heaven and on earth, visible and invisible" (Col. 1:16).

A. W. Tozer wrote, "The man who preaches truth and applies it to the lives of his hearers will feel the nails and the thorns. He will lead a hard life, but a glorious one. May God raise up many such prophets. The church needs them badly."[2]

Let us say, Amen! Now let's listen to our Creator and Redeemer and Head.

JESUS OUTSIDE THE CHURCH

Why would Jesus, the one who loves the church and created her for His own glory feel unwelcomed in this church? Why is He knocking, from the outside looking in?

Unacknowledged Lukewarmness

Jesus points to the spiritual temperature of the church. "I know your works: you are neither cold nor hot. Would that you were either cold or hot! So, because you are lukewarm, and neither hot nor cold, I will spit you out of my mouth" (Rev. 3:15–16). Strong words. Imagine being spit out of the mouth of our Savior!

This passage has often been misinterpreted. I've heard it said that Jesus meant, "I would prefer that you were really hot; but if you are not hot, I would prefer that you were stone cold, *dead*; but what I dislike most is for you to be lukewarm." But I think that is a wrong interpretation.

Years ago Rebecca and I visited the seven cities of the churches of Revelation. We walked through the ruins of ancient Laodicea. We discovered that just miles away on a plateau is Hierapolis, with a large lake of hot, practically boiling,

252

water that was brought down to Laodicea through an aqueduct whose ruins were yet visible. But on the opposite side of the city, there was a stream of cold water that also flowed into the city from the direction of Colossae.

Jesus was saying that both hot and cold water are acceptable. Hot water heals you; cold water refreshes you; both are needed, and both are a blessing. Be hot so that you can bring healing to those who are helpless and hopeless; but also be cold so that you can refresh the weary. "Be one or the other, but don't be lukewarm, or I will spit you out of my mouth."

Many of our churches are awash with lukewarmness, which could be defined as indifference, a feeling of self-satisfaction, a lack of passion for Christ, and a lack of desperation. Many no longer have prayer meetings. Few members witness. Like one church member told me, "In our church, as long as our city's football team is winning, not much else matters."

Think back to the church in the book of Acts. They had no representation in the Roman senate; they had no clout among the rulers of Jerusalem. Politically, they were powerless, but they could not be ignored. Sometimes they were like a hot stream of water that brought life to those who were spiritually dead; other times they were like a cold fountain where people could be revived and find the courage to continue in their witness for Christ.

Today, we as evangelicals are intimidated by our culture. As already emphasized, we don't want to offend anybody, we do not want to take a stand that will put us at odds with onerous court decisions or cultural streams that carry us along like an aimless log of wood. We are silent when we should speak; we are passive when we should act.

Jesus asked us to be both salt and light, but too often we are neither. When the salt loses its saltiness, it is to be "thrown out and trampled under people's feet" (Matt. 5:13), and when the light flickers and fades away, darkness reigns. Have we forgotten that the church of Jesus Christ is the best hope for the world? But rather than seeing our predicament as a test of faithfulness, we are weak, seething with anger or perhaps even collapsing into hopelessness.

Ancient Laodicea lies in ruins today. As we walked among those stones, I thought, "So this is what it looks like when Jesus spits a church out of His mouth." Of course, I realize that historically that may not be totally accurate, because the church to whom Jesus dictated this letter might have repented. But if we take the long view, we can say that the light of Laodicea has been out for centuries. You can see traces of the viaducts that brought the hot and cold water into the city; today, they are powder dry. The streams that blessed the city have long since vanished.

Jesus judged them for lukewarmness, indifference, and earthly agendas. They were lukewarm within the church but quite alive when it came to accepting the values of their culture.

Satisfied with Riches

Jesus continues, "For you say, I am rich, I have prospered, and I need nothing" (Rev. 3:17). This was the church in town to attend. They were a magnet for the "well-to-do" crowd. They were quite self-sufficient. Laodicea was at the crossroads of important trade routes. So the city prospered more than other cities in the immediate vicinity. In fact, nearby was the healing center of the world. They had baths and salve to keep eyes from degeneration. These medicinal remedies made them famous and wealthy.

Let's talk about textiles! They had clothes, rugs, and special Laodicean garments that were the Neiman Marcus of the region. They were well dressed, and why not? Why not enjoy the blessings of God and His promises of prosperity? But Jesus—the one who promised He'd always tell them the truth about themselves—said, "you are . . . poor . . . and naked" (Rev. 3:17)!

It seems as if evangelicals have not distinguished between the American way of life and the Christian way of life.

It seems as if evangelicals have not distinguished between the American way of life and the Christian way of life. Prosperity, apparently, is considered to be the right of every respectable evangelical Christian. I am the first to affirm that my family and I have been prosperous, living a middle-class lifestyle, and we have no special attraction to poverty. But I am haunted by these words of Jesus and ask myself: to what extent has my rather comfortable lifestyle blinded me to the true condition of my heart and affections?

Recently, we visited the Czech Republic and were told that before the fall of communism, the church was vibrant. Believers were few and determined that they wouldn't compromise their faith, but be true to Christ. Their commitment was strengthened by their prayers and their Christian community. Sadly, since the collapse of communism, the focus of the church has dissipated and the prospering younger generation has little interest in Christianity, the Bible, or the gospel itself. They are busy making money, enjoying the world, and in short, becoming a part of a prosperous culture. They want to live like Americans.

Years of prosperity here in America have produced a younger generation that is not as loyal as their parents to their church and Christian ministries. Many are less likely to object to degrading movies, alternate sexual lifestyles, and various doctrinal compromises. Such people have bought into the self-absorbed culture in which we live. Take a good look at American culture, and you are essentially looking at our "church culture."

Jesus taught that physical poverty doesn't necessarily translate into a more spiritually vibrant relationship with God. But He did warn that it's almost impossible to raise up true worshipers in a prosperous culture; it was difficult—though not impossible—for a rich man to enter into the kingdom of heaven. Today, the Christian way of life is the American way of life. To put it more clearly, *we are the culture.*

Wilbur Rees, author of *$3.00 Worth of God*, described risk-free faith when he wrote:

> *I would like to buy $3 worth of God, please. Not enough to explode my soul or disturb my sleep, but just enough of Him to equal a cup of warm milk or a snooze in the sunshine. I don't want enough of Him to make me love a black man or pick beets with a migrant. I want ecstasy, not transformation. I want the warmth of the womb, not a new birth. I want a pound of the eternal in a paper sack, please. I would like to buy $3 worth of God, please.*[3]

Three dollars' worth of God! We are more like a country club than a hospital. We have said, in effect, you can have the best of both worlds. You can enjoy earth over here and heaven over there. While you are here on earth, your only responsibilities are to attend church on Sunday, give as little or as much as you "feel led" to give, then have your children go to Sunday school and camp. Expect Jesus to say, "Well done! You are a good and faithful servant, for you have listened to 3,345 sermons!"

Yet, Jesus says to us, "You are rich [and we are] and prosperous and self-satisfied, but I see you as poor and naked." Perhaps it's not too strong to say that the so-called gospel of prosperity, as taught by many TV preachers, is a devilish scheme to divert the church from its mission. This teaching lures believers to worldly desires while giving them the illusion that they're serving the Lord. What does such teaching say about the Christians who are being martyred in Iran, Iraq, and Egypt? Where is their theology of persecution, martyrdom, and unanswered prayers for healing?

Laodicea was rebuked by Jesus because wealth gave the people a false view of how well they were doing spiritually. Such illusions die hard.

But the worst diagnosis is yet to come.

Gratifying Self-Deception

And now we get to the heart of the matter. We've already introduced the concept of self-deception, but Jesus makes it explicit. The church was seeing itself as "increased with goods and of need of nothing." In contrast, Jesus said, "*not realizing* that you are wretched, pitiable, poor, blind, and naked."

These Christians honestly saw themselves quite differently than Jesus did. He said they were lukewarm when they thought they were quite hot, thank you very much! He said they were poor when in point of fact they thought they were wealthy. They couldn't think of any reason to repent. Their scorecard told them they were doing well. "We have enough money, we have enough friends, the church is stable. Three dollars' worth of God, please!"

Jesus calls them "wretched, pitiable, poor, blind, and naked" (Rev. 3:17). Let's translate the words of Jesus and apply them to ourselves. We might say, "What do you mean wretched and beggarly? Don't we have retirement funds? Don't we use up-to-date technology? Aren't we growing? Are we not respected in the city? What do you mean, wretched and beggarly?"

Jesus is not finished. "And you are also blind and naked." Blind? The Laodiceans would push back reminding Jesus that just across the way there was a healing center, with salve that helped those with degenerative eyesight to see better (see Rev. 3:18). And Jesus says, "Yes, blind."

And also, "You are naked."

Can't we just hear the response? "Naked? We're all dressed in our Laodicean best. We wear the clothes other cities are willing to fight to have. Our coats have labels that others can only covet."

Jesus said, "Sorry, but you are naked."

Their problem? They had one opinion of themselves, and Jesus had another. They gave themselves a B+ in their success as a church and Jesus gave them an F. It was their spiritual blindness that prevented them from seeing things as they were; they could only see things the way they wanted them to be.

At a Moody Bible Institute pastors' conference, a pastor from Uganda talked about the great devastation that took place in his country, saying, "Our churches didn't pray until we had these terrible massacres." Then he asked us in the audience, "Are you Americans going to seek God because of *desperation*, or will it have to be *devastation?*" I'm sure you join me in hoping that it's desperation and not devastation.

Jesus reminds us that we judge from the outer aspects; He judges from the heart. He judges us by our love for Him. He looks beneath the surface and seems to say, "Your self-deception runs deep. I feel as if my space in the church is being co-opted by other interests, so I've stepped outside the door. I've not left you, I'm knocking to return. *Invite me back in!*"

INVITING JESUS BACK INTO THE CHURCH

Jesus doesn't leave us there; He tells us how we can invite Him back into our church.

For their poverty, He offers special gold. "Buy from me gold refined by fire" (Rev. 3:18). Jesus is using the language of the marketplace. "Do business with me!" Salvation cannot be purchased; His refined gold is freely offered to the repentant. He is speaking about us coming to Him to experience those spiritual resources that add up to true riches. And when we do business with Jesus, we'll be surprised at how many of His "wares" are actually free!

Of the Scriptures David said, "More to be desired are they than gold, even much fine gold" (Ps. 19:10). The gold "refined by fire" refers to Jesus Himself. Jesus is saying, "You put more value on your gold (money) than you do Me. If you treat Me as of lesser importance than the things of this world, I will spit you out of My mouth."

"With My gold you are truly rich."

For their blindness, He offers them salve, "to anoint your eyes, so that you may see" (Rev 3:18). See what? See ourselves as we are, not as we perceive ourselves to be. At last we admit to our hitherto unacknowledged self-absorption and pride. We acknowledge that we have allowed rot to grow largely uncontested in our lives.

For their nakedness, He offers them special garments, "white garments so that you may clothe yourself and the shame of your nakedness may not be seen" (Rev. 3:18). Garments of righteousness, to be sure, but also the cleansing of repentance. Jesus sees us as we appear to Him, not as we appear to ourselves. Could you imagine if all the hidden shame of our lives and of our churches would be revealed? Thankfully, we do not have to expose all our ignominy to others, but repentance means exposing all our defilement to Jesus who can give us the assurance of forgiveness and cleansing. What beautiful imagery!

Please don't miss the fact that Jesus has a complete answer to this church's spiritual need—and ours. To repeat: For their poverty He has gold, for their blindness He has salve, and for their nakedness He has garments.

Zealous Repentance

Jesus is not yet finished, "Those whom I love, I reprove and discipline, so be zealous and repent" (Rev. 3:19).

Of what should we repent? There is a cost to repentance, a cost to seeing beyond ourselves to our neighborhood, our colleagues, our friends and relatives. There may be a cost to loving our LGBT neighbor or the Muslim family down the street.

Here are some suggestions that are not taken directly from this text, but I believe can be justified from other priorities of Scripture. Please understand this is not just another "to-do" list. Without heartfelt repentance, new resolutions go nowhere. I list these only so that we might be stimulated to search our hearts.

1. We have too much noise and not enough quietness. Too many videos and emails, and too much television. Let us regularly turn off the noise to contemplate God in private worship and scriptural meditation.
2. We have too much self-promotion and narcissism, as well as unrebuked covetousness, pride, and individualism. Let us intentionally become involved in the lives of those who hurt, the poor, and the lonely.
3. We have too much self-righteousness, a feeling of superiority toward people who are different than we are racially, sexually, or religiously. Let us ask God to see people as He does, for all are created in God's image. And then let us befriend them.
4. We have too little prayer, too little weeping for both the saved and the unsaved. Too little passion for God, but much passion for our own schedules and interests. Let us witness to others through friendships and by helping them on their spiritual journey.
5. We're too selfish with our money and time; the little that we give to the kingdom might give us a deep sense of personal satisfaction, but it does not reflect the generosity of God toward us. Let us prove the words of Jesus, "It is more blessed to give than to receive."

6. We have too many marriages in crisis with seemingly no resolution of their conflicts, though both spouses claim to be Christians. Let us give priority to our own marriages and befriend those who are hurting, the divorced, the single parent, and the lonely child.

7. We have too little effort in preserving the unity of the body: racially, economically, and ethnically. Let us intentionally build friendships within and outside our churches with those who are different than we are, learning and listening.

Jesus said we should be zealous about our repentance. Repentance is not just an event but a way of life; it is a daily acknowledgment of our total dependence on God. It is receiving grace to live for Christ day by day. We need prayer meetings that focus on repentance and faith. Repentance is remembering that our light is as borrowed as is the light of the moon.

Repentance before God leads to sensitivity for people. Indifference for God leads to indifference for others. We speak about winning America for Christ, but we are self-satisfied and resentful that the America we once knew is gone. We don't take kindly to those who are different from us.

George Sweeting, a former president of Moody Bible Institute, once told about a woman who said to her pastor, "I know something is wrong with my life, but I don't know what it is." To this her pastor replied, "Just get on your knees and guess at it!" Down deep, we probably know exactly what we should repent of.

Bishop Samuel, who died in a hail of gunfire when Anwar Sadat was assassinated in Egypt in the early 1980s, told a friend of mine how Christianity conquered North Africa. Christians were marginalized, and, at best, were given the hardest jobs, such as working in the fields or collecting garbage. When the plagues came, dead bodies were stacked up and burned. Whenever possible, the Christians washed the bodies and buried them, arguing that in light of the resurrection, even the wicked have a right to a decent burial.

They didn't have abortion like we do, but unwanted babies were left out on the streets or in alleys to starve, unless someone wanted them. The church organized "baby runs" to find these abandoned babies. Of course, there were no baby bottles in those days, so the babies were brought to nursing mothers who nursed them as if they were their own.

And the pagans asked, "Where is all of that love coming from?"

Cyprian said that the church would not have expanded in North Africa were it not for the plagues because it gave the Christians an opportunity to risk their own lives for others and showed their willingness to sacrifice for others. Another thing the pagans saw: Christians died with hope, and that made the pagans wonder where all that hope was coming from. Pagans attending a Christian funeral said, "They carried their dead as if in triumph."

It's true that the world can outnumber us, out-entertain us, and out-finance us, but let it never be said that they can out-love us, because the love of God is shed abroad in our hearts by the Holy Spirit, who was given unto us.

Jesus will not feel comfortable in our churches without our repentance—humility on our part and the exaltation of Him in all we do. Our love for Him welcomes Him back.

THE REWARD FOR THOSE WHO RESPOND

Jesus dictated this letter to the entire church, but His actual appeal is to individuals. "If anyone hears my voice and opens the door, I will come in to him and eat with him, and he with me" (Rev. 3:20). "If *anyone* hears my voice and opens the door ..." Your church may not be open to the idea of seriously inviting Jesus back, but you can invite Him for full fellowship within your own heart. "I will eat with him and he with me."

In the Middle East, that kind of fellowship at a table was reserved for intimate friends. I can understand that I want fellowship with Christ, but that He wants fellowship with me is staggering. As John Stott put it, "We are not worthy that He should come under our roof, and will He sit at our table?"[4] The picture is one of shared joy.

And Jesus isn't finished.

In each of the seven letters, He speaks about "the one who conquers." Is every Christian a conqueror? Many theologians say "yes" based on this promise, "For everyone who has been born of God overcomes the world. And this is the victory that has overcome the world—our faith" (1 John 5:4). So, on one level, yes, it is true that every Christian is a conqueror (overcomer) in the sense that they will arrive in heaven. But I cannot imagine that a Christian who lived for self and sin is a conqueror as described in this verse.

All Christians will not be equally rewarded. Speaking to Christians, Paul warned, "For we must all appear before the judgment seat of Christ, so that each one may receive what is due for what he has done in the body, whether good or evil" (2 Cor. 5:10). Elsewhere Paul speaks about Christians who build their lives on wood, hay, and stubble, and such will be saved in the end: "he will suffer loss, though he himself will be saved, but only as through fire" (1 Cor. 3:15).

Please understand, I believe that everyone in heaven will be filled with joy and bring glory to God. But like a chandelier in which some bulbs give more light than others, so in heaven, some will receive greater rewards for greater faithfulness. Good theologians disagree with me, but I don't think every Christian will inherit the promise Jesus now makes to the conquerors—a promise beyond our imagination. "The one who conquers, I will grant him to sit with me on my throne, as I also conquered and sat down with my Father on his throne" (Rev. 3:21). A throne is a symbol of conquest, of authority, and responsibility. And that throne is shared with the faithful who have been redeemed!

Is Jesus really saying that if we conquer, we will sit with Him on His throne? That is exactly what He's saying. He rescues us from the pit and raises us to His palace; He cleans off our mud and invites us to walk on marble. This has nothing to do with New Age notions about us becoming God; it has everything to do with undeserved, incomprehensible grace.

HEARING WHAT THE SPIRIT SAYS

Let us look at the conclusion of this letter carefully. Jesus wrote to only one early church, the church at Laodicea. But now He addresses us all, "He who has an ear, let him hear what the Spirit says to the churches" (Rev. 3:22). Don't miss the plural, churches.

This is a word from Christ for all churches in all eras. This is His letter to us.

I read an account about when the plane hit the Pentagon on 9/11. One of the large rooms was so filled with smoke and approaching fire that people were disoriented, unable to find the exit. But one person who did find the door, kept shouting, "Follow my voice! Follow my voice!" So even though the people were blinded by thick soot and smoke, they followed the voice that led them to safety.

Will we hear the one voice that leads us at a time of national confusion and need? "Blessed are those who hear what the Spirit says to the churches!"

Jesus, we invite You back into our churches!

CHAPTER 11

THE CHURCH THAT WILL SURVIVE IN BABYLON

Prevailing in a Hostile Culture

"It just didn't happen as expected!"

Thousands of people gathered in Pontiac, Michigan, on Sunday, December 3, 2017, to witness the demolition of the Detroit Silverdome, a massive stadium that opened in 1975. Now, no longer used because of its aging infrastructure, the building was to be demolished so that the valuable land could be reclaimed. Explosives were put near each of its steel pillars and at precisely 8:30 a.m., the crowd gathered to witness the spectacle of the collapsing stadium. The moment the dynamite was detonated, dust and debris shot out from around the base of the stadium, but to everyone's surprise, the structure remained standing. The steel beams were damaged but still able to keep the stadium upright. "It was just built too well," one observer commented.

The church of Jesus Christ is built "too well" to be demolished. Its pillars are stronger than some people want us to believe. Perhaps the demise of the evangelical church in America is overstated. Although some prognosticators are huffing and puffing about our weakness and lack of influence, the pillars of evangelicalism might be stronger than expected. We are not collapsing or walking away without a fight. The church's foundation cannot be demolished by attacks that come from pop culture or our critics and the elites who believe they have the right to tell us how we should live.

Our worst enemy might be ourselves.

In his book *The Great Evangelical Recession*, John S. Dickerson writes, "The tree of evangelicalism in the United States is centuries old. She is a mighty oak with deep roots. So many saplings have grown up under her shade—trees of education, reform, freedom, invention, work ethic, resourcefulness, wealth and science."[1] But he reminds us that two forces kill old, strong trees: the rot within that is caused by many diseases; and then, of course, there are the storms and forest fires.

There are plenty of diseases that create rot: the hollowing out of Bible doctrine, the strife between members, and the lack of urgency and failure to feel the weight of the momentous task we have been given. All of this is evidenced by the casualness of many Christians; their stinginess in giving; and their lack of vision beyond themselves. Add to that our self-righteousness and lack of transparency, and no wonder we are not having the impact we should.

Then there is the unwillingness of churches to discipline members who have drifted from the faith and live in open rebellion. In short, we are vulnerable to causing our own tree to rot. A pastor once said that the church reminded him of Noah's Ark in that "you couldn't take the stench within if it wasn't for the storm without."

Let's talk about the storm without. Many believe that we are witnessing the most rapid transformation of a culture in history. Dickerson writes: "the culture is changing faster than it typically has in world history. Ten years from now it will be changing even faster, due to accelerating technology advancements. As a result, it is impossible to anticipate just how quickly United States culture will quake and reshape during our lifetime."[2]

Barna agrees. "The historic foundations on which our society was developed are facing some severe challenges. It's not easy to be the kind of Christian that Jesus longs to have as His ambassadors in this place, at this time."[3]

What kind of a church will be able to face the unrelenting storms, the floods, and fires? What are those pillars that will remain standing when the serious hardship comes . . . when at last the church is left on its own to withstand political, social, and religious opposition?

PILLARS THAT REMAIN STANDING WHEN THE FINAL BLOWS COME

People, not Just Buildings

A surviving church must invest in people, not buildings. When Muslim armies swept across North Africa in the seventh century, effectively wiping out Christianity, the church was so identified by its edifices, its priestly rituals, and leadership hierarchy that when the armies destroyed these symbols of Christianity, those few Christians who were left found themselves unable to survive. The church disappeared without a trace.

The church can survive without buildings, but not without dedicated saints. Helmut Thielicke once told the story of watching while his home and his church were reduced to rubble during World War II. In his hand, he was holding a key for a building that did not exist. The buildings were gone, but members of his congregation who survived constituted the true church; that is, the people, called by God as a witness to His name. The true church was not destroyed, even by bombs that decimated its buildings.

I am not saying that we should sell our church buildings or that we should not build new ones, if warranted. What I am saying is that we had better think beyond the building and ask: what will happen if churches lose their tax exempt status? What will happen if giving for the various ministries decreases and we can no longer pay our bills? What will happen if churches have to pay hefty fines if they don't use their facilities to wed same-sex couples? What will happen when more Christians are marginalized, lose their jobs, and support to the church plunges? We need to think outside the box and ask: how will the remnant survive when the larger majority of members judge that the price of living for Christ is just too high? And risky?

Community, not Just Crowds

Years ago when I was speaking in California, friends took me to see the redwood trees that grow so tall and straight up to the sky. I learned something about these impressive trees: their roots are relatively shallow, but they are all interconnected. I was told that if you could see beneath the ground, it would look like a giant spider web that would span the entire forest area.

This has a great advantage: each redwood is somewhat dependent on the other for its support and even its nourishment. Suppose one tree is far from moisture and other trees are closer to a stream. Those stuck in the desert area will actually receive their nourishment from those that have an excess of moisture. The redwoods would not do well if individually planted; they need each other for their stability and strength.

Church crowds come and go, depending on the likes and dislikes of the music, the preaching, the programs, and the location of the building; but community binds people who are united in heart and mind, not just because they like a similar worship style or church program.

The church that survives hard times is the church that is bound together in community, not in social media likes, but in genuine friendships and unselfish caring for others. Members stand with each other in good times and in hard times; they are together for accountability, for ministry, and for prayer. The "one anothers" of the New Testament are proof that God never expects us to navigate our way through Babylon solo. Such a commitment goes beyond attending church once a week and then going home believing that one's duty has been done.

Today, there is so much talk about how to make our church services more culturally relevant, especially to the unconverted. However effective this might be in drawing "seekers," it was not so in the early church. Their services equipped the saints to be witnesses wherever they found themselves. The church meeting collectively on Sunday will not win the world, nor will more seminars on church growth; rather, what we need are more equipped individuals who share their faith in hospitals, banks, factories, warehouses, office buildings, and neighborhoods. In his letters from prison, Bonhoeffer spoke of Jesus as "the man for others." And we as His followers should carry the same attitude into the world.

Training, not Just Telling

We have to change our church philosophy from *telling* to *training*. This fact is illustrated in a letter a pastor wrote to me recently:

> *I am coming to the conclusion that my sermons are not having as lasting an effect I thought they did. I work hard during the week, pray much, and even when I deliver my soul, people walk out of church, and within minutes their attention is diverted. I wish I could look*

deeply into the minds of people to see if they were in any way changed or affected by the sermon. I have heard that the average church member goes to church out of a sense of duty or pride and not necessarily to worship and be changed by God. After many years of preaching, I have ruefully come to the conclusion that although God has promised to bless the preaching of the Gospel, we cannot make disciples en masse. Jesus had twelve men with whom he traveled and lived for three years, and even they did not understand nor act on all He taught them. Jesus knew that disciples are best made by life on life interaction, living transparently, watching and observing, along with extensive times of question and answer. And we must do the same. His last words were to "Go therefore and make disciples of all nations." We have to stop emphasizing an "attractional" model and adopt a training and sending model of church philosophy.

We can structure our services to make them more appealing with every part of the service timed to the minute (or second). We can make sure that the music fits the tastes of all who attend (as if that is possible!). And we can prepare interesting sermons that speak to real life matters. Yet, the core of people's hearts and values may remain essentially unchanged.

In his book *A Better Story*, Glynn Harrison writes:

Even where Christians maintain an intellectual allegiance to orthodox teaching, years of watching TV and movies have captured hearts and emptied minds. . . . What chance does an awkwardly structured thirty-minute sermon delivered once a week by an averagely gifted preacher have against such cultural power? What chance a fumbling talk about sex given by a red-faced father to a squirming eleven-year-old, set against the images and stories that have been tumbling across his screens for years?[4]

The bottom line: churches that rely on a thirty-minute sermon every Sunday morning will be powerless against a torrent of media-driven content that is antithetical to Christian values and extols the pleasures of a sensually driven lifestyle. We have work to do.

There are many resources available to help us do training, but even these fall short if we do not share life-on-life and heart-to-heart. As the old adage goes, "Some things are better caught than taught." Discipleship is not just what you know; it is a lifestyle lived. As suggested earlier in this book, our problem is that we are trying to give swimming lessons on dry ground.

Prayer, not Just Programs

Programs don't work on a congregation whose hearts have been stolen by the world.

Perhaps the most telling missing ingredients in our churches today are a godly vision, the burden for prayer, and a lifestyle of daily repentance. Partly, this is because of how prayer meetings have been conducted; namely, praying the same thing in the same old way, time after time. But praying as a united body for the things on God's heart, as the Concert of Prayer movement has done globally, exemplifies how corporate prayer that uses Scripture and emphasizes spiritual needs along with different modes of intercession, can make our time meaningful and joyful.[5]

I've learned that programs—which at times may be good and necessary—simply do not bring about the anticipated results when imposed upon a congregation whose hearts and values have been stolen by the world. Running to the next seminar on church growth, church management, discipleship, or any other relevant topic, is helpful only to those churches that are spiritually alive. These seminars cannot bring the dead to life or create a passion that can only be generated by the Holy Spirit. Programs can direct energy but they cannot give life.

Only brokenness over our sin and constant dependence on God can raise the spiritually dead to life.

Hard Truths, not Just Positive Suggestions

The surviving church is one that has a holistic view of the Scriptures and doesn't simply cherry-pick themes and teachings that are more to individual likings and aptitudes. It is a church that preaches to felt needs, to be sure, but emphasizes that when we stand in the presence of a holy God, our greatest felt need will be for the righteousness of Christ. It is a church that teaches us how to live on earth but with the greater purpose of preparing for the life to come. It is a church that is not afraid of talking about hell.

Such a church understands that persecution of various kinds does not mean that God is against us; it actually might mean that God is for us. Testing us.

There is a persuasive assumption that if the church in America were all that it should be, if we all were Spirit-filled and in a state of revival, then we would have favor with our politicians, our judges, the media, and our neighbors. But this assumption cannot be proven by church history, nor by the Scriptures. In fact, the opposite is often true: the more we are living lives that are a credit to Christ, the more opposition we can expect. As Paul put it, "Indeed, all who desire to live a godly life in Christ Jesus will be persecuted" (2 Tim. 3:12).

We forget that we are called to suffer, a doctrine that is often neglected in the Western church. When Paul was converted, God called him not merely to preach, but also to suffer. When Ananias was understandably wary of believing that Saul (Paul) had actually been converted, the Lord said to him, "Go, for he is a chosen instrument of mine to carry my name before the Gentiles and kings and the children of Israel. *For I will show him how much he must suffer for the sake of my name*" (Acts 9:15–16).

Suffering strategically positions us for blessing. After Paul spoke about the glory of the church, he wrote, "So I ask you not to lose heart over what I am suffering for you, which is your glory" (Eph. 3:13). Peter told us that we should not be surprised at the fiery trial that comes upon us, and then continues, "if you are insulted for the name of Christ, you are blessed, because *the Spirit of glory and of God rests upon you*" (1 Peter 4:14).

Today in the Middle East, Christians are routinely driven from their homes, and many are killed as Islam continues its relentless war for total supremacy. Just being a Christian, and thus believing in the Trinity and Jesus as the Son of God is the highest blasphemy worthy of death. I personally am glad that I probably will not have to endure such affliction, but I want to remind you that in the day of judgment, these believers will be rewarded in ways we can only imagine. Among the dozens of passages of Scripture that speak about how to respond to persecution, I find this one the most incredible.

> *But recall the former days when, after you were enlightened, you endured a hard struggle with sufferings, sometimes being publicly exposed to reproach and affliction, and sometimes being partners with those so treated. For you had compassion on those in prison, and you joyfully accepted the plundering of your property, since you knew that you yourselves had a better possession and an abiding one. Therefore do not throw away your confidence, which has a great reward. For you have need of endurance, so that when you have done the will of God you may receive what is promised.*
>
> (HEB. 10:32-36)

Let's take this more slowly. These believers, upon receiving the gospel, were, (1) "publicly exposed to reproach and affliction," and yet they (2) identified themselves with other believers who were imprisoned, which added to their persecution, and (3) they *joyfully accepted the plunder of their property*! They were convinced that if this was happening because of their love for Jesus, it would be worth it, and their reward would be great!

Alan Hirsch, director of Forge Mission Training Network, writes:

> *Persecution drove both the early Christian movement and Chinese church to discover their truest nature as an apostolic people. Persecution forced them away from any possible reliance on any form of centralized religious in-*

*stitution and caused them to live closer to, and more con-
sistently with their primal message—namely, the gospel.
. . . it purified them from the dross and any unnecessary
churchly paraphernalia.*[6]

It also forced them to become dependent on relational
networks rather than an institutional structure. Life is short;
eternity is long.

Looking Without, not Just Within

The church that survives in Babylon is one whose members
accept their lot with both sorrow but also a joy that is inex-
plicable. It is a church that attempts to silence its
critics by its authenticity and commitment to
others. It is a church that is willing to follow Jesus all the way to the cross.

A church that is content with itself is a church that is on its way to its demise.

It is not possible to have a heart for
God without having a heart for people and their deep and abiding needs.
Earlier, I emphasized that Christianity
is at its best when even its critics have
to admit that we are selfless, serving, and
sacrificing. A church that is content with
itself is a church that is on its way to its demise. A church that does not welcome the diversity
of its neighborhood will soon wither and eventually die.

Someone has well said that farmers plant seed in a field,
not a barn.

Christ, not Just the Pastor

Finally, the church that survives in Babylon is one that continually sees Christ as the head of the church, and is totally committed to His sovereignty over all things. It is a church that is radically committed to the words of Jesus: "All authority in heaven and on earth has been given to me" (Matt. 28:18). He not only has authority over His church but over the entire world. A church like that will accept setbacks and discouragement as part of God's eternal plan.

A church that follows Jesus will be known for its humility, its brokenness, and its desperation to see God glorified in its community and the world. It is a church that is willing to take reasonable risks (and at times even *un*reasonable risks!) to advance the gospel. J. Oswald Sanders said, "More failure comes from an excess of caution than from bold experimentation with new ideas. . . . The wife of Archbishop Mowll said, 'The frontiers of the kingdom of God were never advanced by men and women of caution.'"7

Nothing else matters, except the glory of God. A church that looks for ways to sacrifice for the sake of Christ; a church that lives for others, not itself—there will always be room for a church like that in the world.

And what was God doing during the early days of the church when persecution was the norm? The same chapter that tells us that James was killed with the sword is the one that ends, "But the word of God increased and multiplied" (Acts 12:24).

> We might not win in this life, but we will win in the life to come.

We began this book by affirming that Jesus does not lead us into a future that He has not already prepared for us. The path may be one of suffering, disappointment, and loss. But it is a sure path that enables us to honor God. We might not win in this life, but we will win in the life to come.

Think back to Daniel and his three friends. They stand with a host of men and women and children who throughout history have battled against cultural currents at great sacrifice. God's people have always been an island of righteousness in a sea of paganism.

The question is: Do we love Christ enough to risk everything to follow Him?

Among my heroes of the faith is Dietrich Bonhoeffer who stood against Hitler's Nazi Germany. Bonhoeffer is famous for saying, "When Christ calls a man, he bids him come and die."[8]

Jesus confirms that with a promise in Revelation 2:10:

Do not fear what you are about to suffer. Behold, the devil is about to throw some of you into prison, that you may be tested, and for ten days you will have tribulation. Be faithful unto death, and I will give you the crown of life.

We end with this final admonishment: "He who has an ear let him hear what the Spirit says to the churches."

ACKNOWLEDGMENTS

I want to thank the entire team at Moody Publishers for shepherding this book from its early beginnings through to its finished product.

Duane Sherman, God bless you for encouraging me to continue even though I was far behind in my writing schedule and knew I could not make the initial deadline; nor the second, nor the third! Thanks to you, I did not give up despite a busy schedule and unexpected delays.

Amanda Cleary Eastep, you, as my editor, refused to accept my manuscript as it was but helped me shape the chapters to reflect more accurately what I wanted to communicate. You painstakingly worked on endnotes and insisted that we track down obscure references. Because of your expertise, it is a better book! Thank you!

Erik Peterson, you eagerly embraced this project and used your skill to make the book presentable to a wide audience.

You were "on board" from the earliest inception of the idea of this book.

To all others at Moody Publishers, the sales force, the advertisers, and the proofreaders, thank you! This was a community project.

I also want to thank my lovely wife, Rebecca, who often wondered what I was writing that took so long! Without your patience, encouragement, and prayers this book would never have seen the light of day.

To all who in one way or another contributed to this project, I remind you of this promise: "For God is not unjust so as to overlook your work and the love that you have shown for his name in serving the saints, as you still do" (Heb. 6:10).

Finally, and most importantly, I want to thank my Lord and Savior Jesus Christ for helping me write these pages. I dedicate this book to Him, and I pray that it will make at least a small contribution to the revitalization of the church for which He died.

Sola Deo Gloria

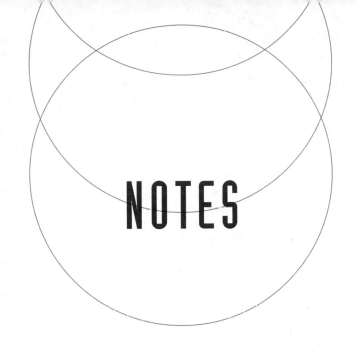

NOTES

Heeding the Call

1. Michael Lipka, "Why America's 'nones' left religion behind," Pew Research Center, August 24, 2016, http://www.pewresearch.org/fact-tank/2016/08/24/why-americas-nones-left-religion-behind/.

2. David Kinnaman and Gabe Lyons, *UnChristian—What a New Generation Really Thinks About Christianity . . . and Why It Matters* (Grand Rapids: Baker, 2007), 35.

3. Ronald J. Sider, *The Scandal of the Evangelical Conscience: Why Are Christians Living Just Like the Rest of the World?* (Grand Rapids: Baker, 2005), 12–13.

4. Ibid., 50–51.

5. Emily James, "'I've gone back to being a child': Husband and father-of-seven, 52, leaves his wife and kids to live as a transgender SIX-YEAR-OLD girl named Stefonknee," *Daily Mail*, December 11, 2015, http://www.dailymail.co.uk/femail/article-3356084/I-ve-gone-child-Husband-father-seven-52-leaves-wife-kids-live-transgender-SIX-YEAR-OLD-girl-named-Stefonknee.html.

6. "Trans Conference Celebrates Getting People Fired for Not Calling Men Women," *The Federalist*, March 20, 2017, http://thefederalist.com/2017/03/20/trans-conference-celebrates-getting-people-fired-not-calling-men-women/.

7. Biola University, "Haddon Robinson: Preaching Into the Wind—National Ministry Conference," YouTube Video, 1:50, July 9, 2012, https://www.youtube.com/watch?v=ToAIWQNedMA.

8. Rod Dreher, "The Benedict Option's Vision for a Christian Village," *Christianity Today*, February 17, 2017, http://www.christianitytoday.com/ct/2017/march/benedict-options-vision-for-christian-village.html.

9. Winston A. Reynolds, "The Burning Ships of Hernán Cortés." *Hispania* 42, no. 3 (September 1959): 317–24.

Chapter 1: Welcome to Babylon

1. Francis Schaeffer, *No Little People* (Wheaton, IL: Crossway, 2003), 25.

2. Leonard Ravenhill, quoted in Bryon Paulus and Bill Elliff, *OneCry: A Nationwide Call for Spiritual Awakening* (Chicago: Moody, 2014), 34.

Chapter 2: A Light to the City, a Heart for God

1. John Newton, *The Works of John Newton: Volume 1* (Edinburgh: Banner of Truth Publications, 2015), 75.

2. Ed Stetzer, *Subversive Kingdom—Living as Agents of Gospel Transformation* (Nashville: B&H, 2012), 220.

3. Ibid., 12.

4. Lee Beach, *The Church in Exile—Living in Hope After Christendom* (Downers Grove, IL: InverVarsity, 2015), 53.

5. Robert P. Jones, *The End of White Christian America* (New York: Simon and Schuster, 2016), 1–2.

6. Ibid., 1.

7. Ibid., 3.

8. John S. Dickerson, *The Great Evangelical Recession* (Grand Rapids: Baker, 2013), 22ff.

9. Russell Moore, *Onward: Engaging the Culture without Losing the Gospel* (Nashville: B&H, 2015), 8.

10. Al Mohler Jr., *Culture Shift—The Battle for the Moral Heart of America* (Colorado Springs: Multnomah, 2008), 53.

11. Jim Daly, "Education Options for Christian Families," *DalyFocus* (blog), April 13, 2016, http:/jimdaly.focusonthefamily.com/educational-options-christian-families/.

12. Rod Dreher, "The Idea of a Christian Village," *Christianity Today* March 2017, 36.

13. Daniel Henderson, "Don't Feel Like Praying?," Strategic Renewal, 2014, http://www.strategicrenewal.com/2014/11/10/dont-feel-like-praying/.

14. Paul Dwight Moody and Arthur Percy Fitt, *The Shorter Life of D. L. Moody* (Chicago: The Bible Institute Colportage Association, 1900), 79.

15. D. L. Moody, http://www.azquotes.com/quote/523866.

16. By The Hand Club For Kids, bythehand.org.

17. The Legacy, legacychristianfellowship.org.

18. Ron Ferguson, *George MacLeod: Founder of the Iona Community* (Glasgow: Wild Goose Publications, 1990), 265.

Chapter 3: Conflicts of Conscience

1. Russell Moore, *Onward: Engaging the Culture without Losing the Gospel* (Nashville: B&H, 2015),8.

2. Larry Osborne, *Thriving in Babylon—Why Hope, Humility, and Wisdom Matter in a Godless Culture* (Colorado Springs: David C. Cook, 2015), 39.

3. Ibid., 41.

4. Michael F. Haverluck, "Ministries tackle 70% rate of college students leaving faith," One News Now, August 13, 2017, https://www.onenewsnow.com/church/2017/08/13/ministries-tackle-70-rate-of-college-students-leaving-faith.

5. Ashley Null, "The Power of Unconditional Love in the Anglican Reformation" in *Reformation Anglicanism. A Vision for Today's Global Communion*, Ashley Null and John W. Yates III, eds. (Wheaton, IL: Crossway, 2017), 55.

6. Joshua J. Mark, "Nebuchadnezzar II," *Ancient History Encyclopedia*, July 20, 2010, https://www.ancient.eu/Nebuchadnezzar_II/.

7. Ed Stetzer, *Subversive Kingdom—Living as Agents of Gospel Transformation* (Nashville: B&H Publishing, 2012), 5.

8. *Spiegel Online*, "Only the Old Embrace God in Former East Germany," April 19, 2012, http://www.spiegel.de/international/zeitgeist/report-shows-highest-percentage-of-atheists-in-former-east-germany-a 828526.html.

9. Tim Keller, "Exiles in a Foreign Land," from *Living in a Pluralistic Society* (Bible study), (New York: Redeemer Presbyterian Church, 2006) http://s3.amazonaws.com/churchplantmedia-cms/chatham_community_church_pittsboro_nc/engage-series-discussion-guide.pdf.

Chapter 4: When the State Becomes God

1. Jacob Poushter, "40% of Millennials OK with limiting speech offensive to minorities," Pew Research Center, November 20, 2015, http://www.pewresearch.org/fact-tank/2015/11/20/40-of-millennials-ok-with-limiting-speech-offensive-to-minorities/.
2. John Villasenor, "Views among college students regarding the First Amendment: Results from a new survey," *Brookings* (blog), September 18, 2017, https://www.brookings.edu/blog/fixgov/2017/09/18/views-among-college-students-regarding-the-first-amendment-results-from-a-new-survey/.
3. "Vote No. 237," Parliament of Canada, March 23, 2017, http://www.ourcommons.ca/Parliamentarians/en/votes/42/1/237/.
4. Art Moore, "Punishment Includes Islam Indoctrination: Canadian to resume hate-crimes sentence under Muslim direction," *WND*, October 31, 2002, http://www.wnd.com/2002/10/15738/.
5. Christian Legal Soc. Chapter of Univ. of Cal., *Hastings College of Law v. Martinez* (No. 08-1371), Cornell University of Law School, https://www.law.cornell.edu/supct/html/08-1371.ZS.html.
6. "Protecting Conscience & Privacy Against the Heavy Hand of Government," Alliance Defending Freedom.
7. "Robert George, Timothy George, and Chuck Colson, Manhattan Declaration: A Call of Christian Conscience," Manhattan Declaration, November 20, 2009, http://manhattandeclaration.org/man_dec_resources/Manhattan_Declaration_full_text.pdf.
8. Jonathan Edwards's first two resolutions are often summed up as quoted in the text; however the original versions can be found here: *The Works of Jonathan Edwards* vols. 1-26 (New Haven, CT: Yale Univ. Press, 1957-2008).
9. Michael Rydelnik, "Daniel," in *The Moody Bible Commentary*, Michael Rydelnik and Michael VanLaningham, gen. eds., (Chicago: Moody, 2014), 1293.
10. "John Chrysostom, Early church's greatest preacher," Christian History, *Christianity Today*, https://www.christianitytoday.com/history/people/pastorsandpreachers/john-chrysostom.html.
11. Saint John Chrysostom, quoted in Stefano Tardani, *Whose Children Are We? The Future That Awaits Us* (Bloomington, IN: WestBow, 2016), 126.

Chapter 5: The Church, Technology, and Purity

1. Neil Postman, *Amusing Ourselves to Death* (New York: Penguin, 2005), 84.

2. Brad J. Bushman, PhD and L. Rowell Huesmann, PhD, "Short-term and Long-term Effects of Violent Media on Aggression in Children and Adults" (abstract), JAMA Network, https://jamanetwork.com/journals/jamapediatrics/fullarticle/204790.

3. Thomas Kersting, *Disconnected: How to Reconnect Our Digitally Distracted Young People* (CreateSpace, 2016).

4. Kenneth A. Myers, *All God's Children and Blue Suede Shoes* (Wheaton, IL: Crossway, 1989), xiii.

5. Ravi Zacharias, "Think Again—The Gentle Goldsmith," RZIM, December 14, 2012, http://rzim.org/just-thinking/think-again-the-gentle-goldsmith/.

6. Mark I. Bubeck, *Raising Lambs Among Wolves* (Chicago: Moody, 1997).

7. Jesus Live Network, "Josh McDowell: Relationships—Rules without Relationships Lead to Rebellion," Vimeo video, 2:27, July 19, 2014, https://vimeo.com/101157052.

8. Rusty Benson, "Vile Passions, Part 3," American Family Association, August 12, 2014, https://www.afa.net/the-stand/culture/2014/08/vile-passions-part-3/.

9. Tammy Bruce, *The Death of Right and Wrong* (Roseville, CA: Forum, and Imprint of Prima Publishing, 2003), 87

10. Ibid., 88.

11. Ibid., 195.

12. Ibid., 94.

13. C. Everett Koop and Francis Schaeffer, *Whatever Happened to the Human Race?*, rev. ed. (Wheaton, IL: Crossway, 1983), 2.

14. Ibid, 3. Emphasis added.

Chapter 6: Transgenderism, Sexuality, and the Church

1. Lawrence S. Mayer, MB, MS, PhD and Paul R. McHugh, MD, "Sexuality and Gender: Findings from the Biological, Psychological, and Social Sciences," *The New Atlantis: A Journal of Technology & Society*, Number 50, Fall 2016, https://www.thenewatlantis.com/docLib/20160819_TNA50SexualityandGender.pdf, 87.

2. Eliza Gray, "Meet the New Generation of Gender-Creative Kids," *Time*, March 19, 2015, http://time.com/3743987/gender-creative-kids/.

3. Tara Culp-Ressler, "Forcing Kids to Stick to Gender Roles Can Actually Be Harmful to Their Health," ThinkProgress, August 7, 2014, https://thinkprogress.org/forcing-kids-to-stick-to-gender-roles-can-actually-be-harmful-to-their-health-34aef42199f2#.aqjbvr2i8.

4. "Girls feel they must 'play dumb' to please boys," Warwick, August 5, 2014, http://www2.warwick.ac.uk/newsandevents/pressreleases/girls_feel_they/.

5. Elly Fishman, "The Change Agent," *Chicago Politics & City Life*, May 18, 2015, http://www.chicagomag.com/Chicago-Magazine/June-2015/Doctor-Rob-Garofalo/.

6. Ibid.

7. Christin Scarlett Milloy, "Don't Let the Doctor Do This to Your Newborn," *Slate*, June 26, 2014, http://www.slate.com/blogs/outward/2014/06/26/infant_gender_assignment_unnecessary_and_potentially_harmful.html.

8. "KU libraries' gender pronoun pins part of inclusion push," *Associated Press*, December 28, 2016, https://apnews.com/8a34880ee68f4f2ab23756e32a429196/Kansas-school's-libraries-offer-students-pronoun-pins.

9. Jamie Dean, "Suffer the children," *World Magazine*, April 15, 2017, https://world.wng.org/2017/03/suffer_the_children.

10. Ibid.

11. "Trans Conference Celebrates Getting People Fired for Not Calling Men Women," *The Federalist*, March 20, 2017, http://thefederalist.com/2017/03/20/trans-conference-celebrates-getting-people-fired-not-calling-men-women/.

12. Transgender Law Center, "State-by-State Overview: Changing Gender Markers on Birth Certificates," PDF, https://transgenderlawcenter.org/resources/id/state-by-state-overview-changing-gender-markers-on-birth-certificates.

13. Mayer and McHugh, "Sexuality and Gender," 7–9.

14. Dean, "Suffer the children."

15. Buzz Bissinger, "Caitlyn Jenner: The Full Story," *Vanity Fair*, June 25, 2015, https://www.vanityfair.com/hollywood/2015/06/caitlyn-jenner-bruce-cover-annie-leibovitz.

16. John Wooden, quoted in Bob Stouffer, *Light of Darkness: Reclaiming the Light in Sports* (Urbandale, IA: Three Circles Press, 2011), 97.

17. Michael W. Chapman, "Johns Hopkins Psychiatrist: Support of Transgenderism and Sex-Change Surgery Is 'Collaborating with Madness,'" CNSNews.com, June 2, 2016, http://www.cnsnews.com/blog/michael-w-chapman/johns-hopkins-psychiatrist-support-transgenderism-and-sex-change-surgery.

18. Sarah Boesveld, "Becoming disabled by choice, not chance: 'Transabled' people feel like impostors in their fully working bodies," *National Post*, June 3, 2015, http://nationalpost.com/news/canada/

becoming-disabled-by-choice-not-chance-transabled-people-feel-like-impostors-in-their-fully-working-bodies.

19. Rianne M. Blom, Raoul C. Hennekam, and Damiaan Denys, "Body Integrity Identity Disorder," *PLoS ONE* 7, no. 4 (2012), https://www.ncbi.nlm.nih.gov/pmc/articles/PMC3326051/.

20. Emily James, "'I've gone back to being a child': Husband and father-of-seven, 52, leaves his wife and kids to live as a transgender SIX-YEAR-OLD girl named Stefonknee," *Daily Mail*, December 11, 2015, http://www.dailymail.co.uk/femail/article-3356084/I-ve-gone-child-Husband-father-seven-52-leaves-wife-kids-live-transgender-SIX-YEAR-OLD-girl-named-Stefonknee.html.

21. Joe Carter, "The Diabolic Logic of Transableism," *The Gospel Coalition*, June 5, 2015, https://www.thegospelcoalition.org/article/the-diabolic-logic-of-transabelism/.

22. Ibid.

23. Andrew T. Walker and Denny Burk, "National Geographic's 'Gender Revolution': Bad Argument and Biased Ideology," *The Witherspoon Institute*, January 6, 2017, http://www.thepublicdiscourse.com/2017/01/18491/.

24. Glenn T. Stanton, *Loving My LGBT Neighbor* (Chicago: Moody, 2014), 103.

25. Kaeley Triller, "Bathroom Rules Must Protect, Not Enable," *Decision*, January 16, 2017, 12–13.

26. Janet Parshall interview "Peace in the Storm," Moody Radio, March 6, 2018, https://www.moodyradio.org/programs/in-the-market-with-janet-parshall/2018/03-2018/3.6.18-i-cant-remember---peace-in-the-storm/.

27. Dean, "Suffer the children."

28. Ibid.

29. Walt Heyer, "I Was a Transgender Woman," *The Witherspoon Institute*, April 1, 2015, http://www.thepublicdiscourse.com/2015/04/14688/.

30. Ibid.

Chapter 7: Islam, Immigration, and the Church

1. "Global Trends Forced Displacement in 2016," *UNHCR*, http://www.unhcr.org/globaltrends2016/.

2. "Most U.S. Muslims say there is more than one true way to interpret Islam," *Pew Research Center*, July 24, 2017, http://www.pewforum.org/2017/07/26/religious-beliefs-and-practices/pf_2017-06-26_muslimamericans-06-05/.

3. *The Qur'an*, Surah 8:74, trans. Abdullah Yusuf Ali.

4. Hadith Collection: Jami at-Tirmidi, Volume 5: Book #42, Hadith 2863.
5. Andrew C. McCarthy, *The Grand Jihad: How Islam and the Left Sabotage America* (New York: Encounter Books, 2011), 59.
6. "What is the Muslim Brotherhood?", Al Jazeera, June 18, 2017, http://www.aljazeera.com/indepth/features/2017/06/muslim-brotherhood-explained-170608091709865.html.
7. William James, "UK criticizes Muslim Brotherhood, defends Western policy," *Reuters*, December 7, 2017, https://www.reuters.com/article/us-mideast-crisis-britain/uk-criticizes-muslim-brotherhood-defends-western-policy-idUSKBN1E11JI.
8. William J Boykin and, et. al, *Shariah: The Threat to America: An Exercise in Competitive Analysis (Report of Team B II)*, (Washington, D.C.: The Center for Security Policy, 2010), 47.
9. Ibid., 125–26.
10. Jonathan Stearns, "How Europe's Refugees Are Testing Its Open Borders: QuickTake", *Washington Post*, November 20, 2017, https://www.washingtonpost.com/business/how-europes-refugees-are-testing-its-open-borders-quicktake/2017/11/20/c2e7d6e4-ce05-11e7-a87b-47f14b73162a_story.html?utm_term=.6c08e56f969f.
11. "Abul Ala Maududi," *Counter Extremism Project*, https://www.counterextremism.com/extremists/abul-ala-maududi.
12. Abu Ala Maududi, as cited in S. Solomon and E. Alamaqdisi, *The Mosque Exposed* (Charlottesville, VA: ANM Press, 2006), 48–50.
13. McCarthy, *The Grand Jihad: How Islam and the Left Sabotage America*, 162.
14. Ibid., 127–28.
15. Ibid., 51.
16. Ibid., 28.
17. Boykin, *Shariah: The Threat to America*, 47.
18. Dore Gold, "Embracing the Muslim Brotherhood," *The Algemeiner*, June 22, 2012, https://www.algemeiner.com/2012/06/22/embracing-the-muslim-brotherhood/.
19. Quran 5:47.
20. Boykin, *Shariah: The Threat to America*, 43.
21. Hannah Roberts, "ISIS threatens to send 500,000 migrants to Europe as a 'psychological weapon' in chilling echo of Gaddafi's prophecy that the Mediterranean 'will become a sea of chaos,'" *Daily Mail*, February 18, 2015, http://www.dailymail.co.uk/news/article-2958517/The-Mediterranean-sea-chaos-Gaddafi-s-chilling-prophecy-interview-ISIS-threatens-send-500-000-migrants-Europe-psychological-weapon-bombed.html.

22. Maggie Sullivan and Timothy S. Rich, "Many refugees are women and children. That changes whether Americans want to admit them," *Washington Post* Online, November 29, 2017, https://www.washingtonpost.com/news/monkey-cage/wp/2017/11/29/americans-like-refugees-better-when-theyre-women-and-children-especially-republicans/?utm_term=.29914d923fe4.
23. *The Qur'an*, Surah 4:100, Saheeh International.
24. "Ellis Island," *Wikipedia*, last edited on April 5, 2018, https://en.wikipedia.org/wiki/Ellis_Island#Immigrant_inspection_station.
25. Kamran Ahmed, "Why do some young people become jihadis? Psychiatry offers answers," *The Guardian*, May 26, 2017, https://www.theguardian.com/commentisfree/2017/may/26/jihadis-muslims-radicalisation-manchester.
26. "Repairing Evangelical Political Theology: Getting the State Right," *Capstone Report*, January 21, 2018, http://capstonereport.com/2018/01/21/repairing-evangelical-political-theology-getting-the-state-right/31843/.
27. Alexander Hamilton (Lucius Crassus), "Examination of Jefferson's Message to Congress of December 7, 1801," viii, January 7, 1802, in Henry Cabot Lodge, ed., *The Works of Alexander Hamilton*, vol. 8 (New York: Putnam's, 1904).
28. Stephen Bauman, Matthew Soerens, and Dr. Issam Smeir, *Seeking Refuge—On the Shores of the Global Refugee Crisis* (Chicago: Moody, 2016), 22.
29. Ibid., 75.

Chapter 8: Five False Gospels within the Evangelical Church

1. Peter Marshall, "Keepers of the Springs," in *Mr. Jones, Meet the Master: Sermons and Prayers of Peter Marshall* (n.p.: Pickle Partners Publishing, 2016), 142.
2. H. Richard Niebuhr, *The Kingdom of God in America* (Middletown, CT: Wesleyan University Press, 1988), 193.
3. Wm. Paul Young, *Lies We Believe About God* (New York: Atria Books, 2017).
4. Michael Brown, *Hyper-Grace: Exposing the Dangers of the Modern Grace Message* (Lake Mary, FL: Charisma, 2014).
5. Ibid., 153.
6. Ibid.
7. R.C. Sproul, "Does God Hate the Sin but Love the Sinner?", R. C. Sproul and John MacArthur Q&A [Psalm 11:5], YouTube Video, May 5, 2017, https://www.youtube.com/watch?v=DXX0r8enBdY.

8. Joseph Prince, *Destined to Reign: The Secret to Effortless Success, Wholeness and Victorious Living* (Tulsa: Harrison House Publishers, 2007), 49–50.
9. Brown, *Hyper Grace*, 13.
10. Ibid., 25.
11. Ibid., 20.
12. Ibid., 30.
13. Thomas Watson, "The Doctrine of Repentance," 1668, http://www.gracegems.org/Watson/repentance3.htm.
14. Trevin Wax, *Counterfeit Gospels: Rediscovering the Good News in a World of False Hope* (Chicago: Moody, 2011), 68.
15. Joel James and Brian Biedebach, "Regaining Our Focus: A Response to the Social Action Trend in Evangelical Missions," *The Master's Seminary Journal*, Spring 2014, 29.
16. Wax, *Counterfeit Gospels*, 184.
17. Quoted by Michael Horton in *Christless Christianity* (Grand Rapids: Baker, 2008), 15.
18. Barbara Brown Taylor, *An Altar in the World—A Geography of Faith* (New York: HarperCollins, 2009), 13.
19. Hezekiah Butterworth, *The Story of the Notable Prayers of Christian History* (Boston: D. Lothrop and Company, 1880), 92–97.
20. "Competing Worldviews Influence Today's Christians," Barna, May 9, 2017, https://www.barna.com/research/competing-worldviews-influence-todays-christians/.
21. Anthony Bright Atwam, *Building Your Life on the Principles of God: The Solid Foundation* (Bloomington, IN: AuthorHouse, 2014), 86.
22. Henri Nouwen, *Pray to Live* (Notre Dame, IN: Fides Publishers, 1972), 19–28.
23. Thomas Merton, *Conjectures of a Guilty Bystander* (New York: Doubleday, 1989), 157–58.
24. Ibid.
25. Richard Rohr, dedication in *The Divine Dance, The Trinity and Your Transformation* (United Kingdom: SPCK Publishing, 2016).
26. Ibid., 67.
27. Ibid., 68.
28. Ibid., 58.
29. Ibid., 140.
30. "Windy City Times: LGBT Protest at Apostolic Church of God, 7-30-2017," YouTube.com playlist (video 9, 7:06, and video 10, 0:36), posted by Tracy Baim, Windy City Times Media Group, last updated July 30,

2017, https://www.youtube.com/playlist?list=PLO7LP6UYPfqyfATlG
7IktA7hcwgsRNWwx.

31. "The Table Briefing: Engaging the LGBT community with Truth
and Love," *Bibliotheca Sacra* 73, no. 692 (October–December 2016):
478

32. "Nashville Statement," https://cbmw.org/nashville-statement/.

33. John S. Dickerson, The Great Evangelical Recession (Grand Rapids: Baker, 2013), 53.

34. Al Mohler, "The Agonizing Ordeal of Eugene Peterson," *Albert Mohler*
(blog), July 17, 2017, https://albertmohler.com/2017/07/17/eugene-peterson/.

35. Ibid.

36. Chuck Colson, *Kingdoms in Conflict* (Grand Rapids: Zondervan,
1989), 146.

37. Stephen Coughlin, *"Bridge-Building" to Nowhere: The Catholic
Church's Case Study in Interfaith Delusion* (Washington, D.C.: The
Center for Security Policy, 2015), 9.

38. Ibid., 19.

39. Ibid., 8.

40. "C.A.I.R. IS HAMAS: How the Federal Government proved that
the Council on American-Islamic Relations is a front for terrorism,"
Center for Security Policy, n.d., https://www.centerforsecuritypolicy
.org/wp-content/uploads/2016/12/CAIR_is_HAMAS.pdf.

41. Muhammad Shafiq and Mohammed Abu-Nimer, *Interfaith Dialogue, A Guide for Muslims* (Herndon, VA: The International Institute of Islamic Thought, 2011).

42. Ibid., 59.

43. Ibid., 31.

44. Ibid., 108.

45. Ibid., 42.

46. Ibid.

47. Ibid., 45.

48. Ibid., 70.

49. Ibid., 78.

50. Ibid., 103.

51. Ibid., 100–101.

52. Coughlin, *"Bridge-Building,"* 7.

Chapter 9: Taking the Cross into the World

1. Bruce L. Shelly, *Church History in Plain Language* (Waco, TX: Word
Books, 1982), 15.

2. "NYC Commission on Human Rights Announces Strong Protections for City's Transgender and Gender Non-Conforming Communities in Housing, Employment and Public Spaces," *Official Website of the City of New York*, December 21, 2015, http://www1.nyc.gov/office-of-the-mayor/news/961-15/nyc-commission-human-rights-strong-protections-city-s-transgender-gender.

3. Sarah Eekhoff Zylstra, "'Bible Answer Man' Converts to Orthodoxy," *Christianity Today* online, April 12, 2017, http://www.christianitytoday.com/news/2017/april/bible-answer-man-hank-hanegraaff-orthodoxy-cri-watchman-nee.html.

4. Steve Chalke and Alan Mann, *The Lost Message of Jesus* (Grand Rapids: Zondervan, 2003).

5. Harry Farley, "Steve Chalke: Heaven is not just for Christians," April 11, 2018, https://www.christiantoday.com/article/steve-chalke-heaven-is-not-just-for-christiansexecute1/128317.htm.

6. Ibid., 56.

7. John Stott, *The Cross of Christ* (Downers Grove, IL: InterVarsity, 2006), 63.

8. John Piper, "The Fall of Satan and the Victory of Christ," *Decision Magazine*, January 2018, 16.

9. Swami Chindanansa, "Authentic Religion," The Divine Life Society, last updated May 29, 2017, http://www.dlshq.org/religions/authrel.htm.

10. Interview with Ravi Zacharias, "Ravi Zacharias: Jesus Talks with Krishna," *CBN*, n.d. http://www.cbn.com/entertainment/books/raviz-qa.aspx?mobile=false&u=1.

11. J. C. Ryle, *Warnings to the Churches* (Edinburgh: Banner of Truth, 1967).

12. George Sweeting, *Who Said That? More Than 2,500 Usable Quotes and Illustrations* (Chicago: Moody, 1995), 78.

13. Russell Moore, *Onward: Engaging the Culture without Losing the Gospel* (Nashville: B&H, 2015), 31.

14. Billy Graham as quoted in Larry Ross, "The Preacher and the Press," *Christianity Today*, April 2018, 112.

15. Sheldon Vanauken, *A Severe Mercy* (New York: Harper & Row, 1977), 85.

16. John MacArthur, "A Conscience Captive to God's Word," *Grace to You*, April 3, 2014, https://www.gty.org/library/blog/B140403.

17. Timothy George, ed., *Mr. Moody and the Evangelical Tradition* (New York: T&T Clark International, 2004), 5.

18. Tim Townsend, *Mission at Nuremberg: An American Army Chaplain and the Trial of the Nazis* (New York: HarperCollins, 2014).
19. Ibid., 271.
20. Nabeel Qureshi, *Seeking Allah, Finding Jesus: A Devout Muslim Encounters Christianity* (Grand Rapids: Zondervan, 2014).
21. Edward Shillito, "Jesus of the Scars," *The Jesus Question*, posted October 28, 2013, https://thejesusquestion.org/2013/10/28/jesus-of-the-scars-by-edward-shillito/.
22. Helmut Thielicke, *The Waiting Father*, quoted in Paul E. Little, *Know What You Believe* (Downers Grove, IL: InterVarsity, 2003), 184.

Chapter 10: Jesus at the Church Door

1. "A Declaration of Spiritual Emergency," OneCry, https://onecry.com/join/.
2. A. W. Tozer, *Of God and Men* (Chicago: Moody, 2015), 25–28.
3. Wilbur E. Rees, *$3.00 Worth of God* (Valley Forge, PA: Judson Press, 1971).
4. John Stott, "What Christ Thinks of the Church," in *Preaching for Today* (Grand Rapids: Eerdmans, 1959), 124.

Chapter 11: The Church That Will Survive in Babylon

1. John S. Dickerson, *The Great Evangelical Recession* (Grand Rapids: Baker, 2013).
2. Ibid., 42.
3. George Barna, *Futurecast: What Today's Trends Mean for Tomorrow's World* (Carol Stream, IL: Tyndale, 2012), x.
4. Glynn Harrison, *A Better Story: God, Sex and Human Flourishing* (Downers Grove, IL: InterVarsity, 2017), 56.
5. David Smithers, "World Christian Living Concert of Prayer," *The Traveling Team*, http://www.thetravelingteam.org/articles/concert-of-prayer.
6. Alan Hirsch, *The Forgotten Ways—Reactivating the Missional Church* (Grand Rapids: Brazos Press, 2006), 20–21.
7. J. Oswald Sanders, *Spiritual Leadership, Principles of Excellence for Every Believer* (Chicago: Moody, 2007), 155.
8. Dietrich Bonhoeffer, *The Cost of Discipleship*, (New York: Touchstone, 1959), 89.

HOW DO WE LIVE FAITHFULLY IN A CULTURE THAT PERCEIVES OUR LIGHT AS DARKNESS?

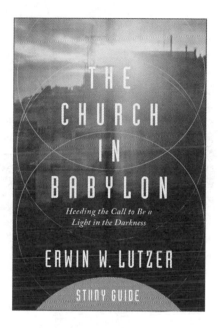

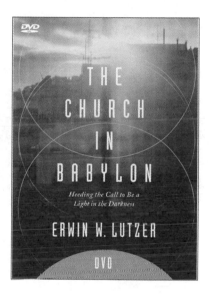

Dr. Lutzer shows us what we can learn from the Israelites about maintaining our faith in the midst of a pagan culture. This study guide will help you to engage the material via study questions, discussion points, and personal reflection.

978-0-8024-1356-7
also available as an eBook

In this DVD, Dr. Lutzer will walk you through the many parallels between the church in America and Israel in Babylon. Then he'll explain what we can learn from the Israelites about maintaining our faith in the midst of a pagan culture.

978-0-8024-1355-0

MOODY Publishers®

From the Word to Life

More books by Erwin W. Lutzer

CRIES FROM THE CROSS
A Journey into the Heart of Jesus
ERWIN W. LUTZER
978-0-8024-1311-6

GOD'S DEVIL
The Incredible Story of How Satan's Rebellion Serves God's Purposes
ERWIN W. LUTZER
978-0-8024-1313-0

More than 100,000 in print!
How You Can Be Sure You Will Spend
ETERNITY WITH GOD
ERWIN W. LUTZER
978-0-8024-1310-9

More than 700,000 in print!
ONE MINUTE AFTER YOU DIE
ERWIN W. LUTZER
978-0 8024-1411-3

More than 100,000 in print!
YOUR ETERNAL REWARD
Triumph and Tears at the Judgment Seat of Christ
ERWIN W. LUTZER
978-0-8024-1317-8

also available as eBooks

MOODY Publishers®
From the Word to Life®

STUDY THE BIBLE WITH PROFESSORS FROM MOODY BIBLE INSTITUTE

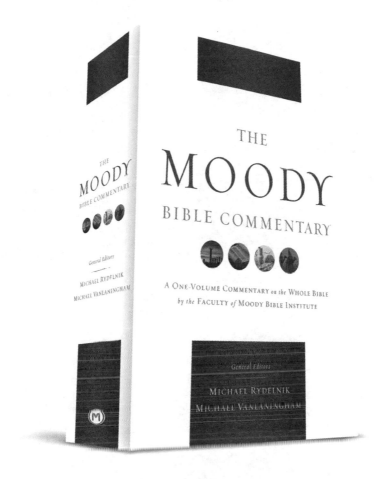

BECOMING A PERSON OF GODLY COURAGE IN A SINFUL WORLD